D0904244

Credit Scoring, Response Modelling and Insurance Rating

Credit Scoring, Response Modelling and Insurance Rating

A Practical Guide to Forecasting Consumer Behaviour

Steven Finlay

palgrave
macmillan

First published 2010 by
PALGRAVE MACMILLAN

Palgrave Macmillan in the UK is an imprint of Macmillan Publishers Limited, registered in England, company number 785998, of Houndmills, Basingstoke, Hampshire RG21 6XS.

Palgrave Macmillan in the US is a division of St Martin's Press LLC, 175 Fifth Avenue, New York, NY 10010.

Palgrave Macmillan is the global academic imprint of the above companies and has companies and representatives throughout the world.

Palgrave® and Macmillan® are registered trademarks in the United States, the United Kingdom, Europe and other countries

ISBN 978-0-230-57704-6   hardback

This book is printed on paper suitable for recycling and made from fully managed and sustained forest sources. Logging, pulping and manufacturing processes are expected to conform to the environmental regulations of the country of origin.

A catalogue record for this book is available from the British Library.

Library of Congress Cataloging-in-Publication Data

Finlay, Steven, 1969–
    Credit scoring, response modelling and insurance rating : a practical guide to forecasting consumer behaviour / Steven Finlay.
        p. cm.
    Includes bibliographical references.
    ISBN 978-0-230-57704-6 (alk. paper)
        1. Credit analysis. 2. Consumer behavior–Forecasting. 3. Consumer credit.
    I. Title.
    HG3701.F55 2010
    658.8'342–dc22   2010033960

10   9   8   7   6   5   4   3   2   1
19 18 17 16 15 14 13 12 11 10

Printed and bound in Great Britain by
CPI Antony Rowe, Chippenham and Eastbourne

To Ruby & Sam

Contents

List of Tables

List of Figures

Acknowledgements

I am indebted to my wife Sam and my parents Ann and Paul for their support. I would also like to thank Dr Sven Crone, of the Management Science Department at Lancaster University, for his input to some of the research discussed in the book. Also my thanks to Professor David Hand of Imperial College London for bringing to my attention a number of papers that helped form my opinion on a number of matters. I'm also grateful to the Decision Analytics Division of Experian UK (Simon Harben, Dr Ian Glover and Dr John Oxley in particular) for their support for my research over a number of years, as well as Dr Geoff Ellis for providing information about SPSS during a number of interesting discussions about the merits/drawbacks of different statistical packages.

1
Introduction

As IT systems have evolved, the amount of information financial services organizations maintain about individuals and the speed at which they can process information has increased dramatically. One consequence of this development is a paradigm shift in the way organizations manage their relationships with consumers. At one time, when dealing with large populations, standard practice was to segment people into relatively few homogenous groups, and then apply an identical relationship management strategy to everyone in each group. Take the case of a provider of home insurance wanting to launch a promotional campaign to recruit new customers. The marketing department may have decided, somewhat arbitrarily, that its target audience were white collar families with children. Its promotional strategy would be to send identical mail shots to all households in middle class suburbs where it was believed the majority of its target audience resided. Some mailings would be received by the intended audience, but many would be wasted because they would be sent to singles, the unemployed or those on low incomes who just happened to live in middle class suburbs. Similarly, white collar families living in inner cities or rural communities represented a missed opportunity because they lived outside the target areas.

At the other end of the spectrum, where customer relationships needed to be managed on a case by case basis, deciding how to deal with someone was a laborious, time consuming and expensive process. A classic example is when someone wanted a loan from their bank. The process would begin with them making an appointment to see the manager of their local branch, and they may have had to wait several weeks before an appointment was available. The customer would arrive at the meeting in their best clothes, in order to make a good impression, and the bank manager would question them about their personal and financial circumstances in order to form an opinion about their creditworthiness. If the bank manager felt they were likely to repay what they borrowed and represented a good investment, then they would be granted a loan. However, if the bank manager didn't want to grant the loan then they were under no obligation to do so. Many people had their loan requests declined due to their gender, because they belonged to a minority group, or simply because the bank manager was in a bad mood and didn't fancy granting any loans that day. Even if the loan was granted, the time taken between the initial enquiry and receipt of funds could be considerable.

Within the financial services industry today, most decisions about how to deal with people are taken automatically by computerized decision making systems. These assess each person on a case by case basis using geo-demographic information that is known about them. Human involvement in such decisions is very much the exception rather than the rule. At the heart of these decision making systems lie mathematically derived forecasting models that use information about people and their past behaviour to predict how they are likely to behave in future. Decisions about how to treat people are made on the basis of the predictions generated by the forecasting model(s). These days, the insurer would use a response model to predict the likelihood of someone on their mailing list responding to a promotional mail shot. If the model predicted that the person was likely to respond by requesting an insurance quotation, then they would automatically be mailed with an individually tailored communication – regardless of where they lived or which socio-economic group they belonged to. Likewise, a loan provider will use a credit scoring model (a model of creditworthiness) to predict how likely an applicant is to repay the loan they are applying for. Loans will only be offered to those the model predicts are creditworthy and likely to make a positive contribution towards profits. Those that the credit scoring model predicts are uncreditworthy will be declined.

The application of automated decision making systems brings many benefits. One is that they make better decisions, more quickly and more cheaply than their human counterparts. This allows decisions to be made in real time while the customer is in store, on the phone or on the internet. A second benefit is they allow tailored decisions to be made, based on an individual's propensity to behave in a certain way, instead of vague estimates about the general behaviour of large populations. Another advantage is that they are consistent in their decision making. Given the same information twice, they will always arrive at the same decision. This is something that cannot be guaranteed with human decision makers. Developed correctly, these systems also display no unfair bias in terms of gender, race or any other characteristic deemed undesirable by society. Automated decision making systems also facilitate centralized decision making. This means that changes to an organization's strategy for dealing with customers can be made quickly and easily at the site where the decision making system is controlled. This removes the need to coordinate changes in decision strategy across many different branches/offices/regions.

Not surprisingly, the value of automated decision making systems to the organizations that employ them is substantial. A large financial services organization will make billions of dollars worth of decisions each year, based solely on predictions made by their forecasting models. There is therefore, considerable effort expended to ensure that the forecasting models an organization employs perform in an optimal capacity.

1.1   Scope and content

The goal of this book is to convey an understanding of how forecasting models of consumer behaviour are developed and deployed by major financial services organizations such as banks, building societies (saving and loan companies) and insurers. However, before going any further, I want to make two things clear. First, this is a book about the development and application of forecasting models of consumer behaviour within business environments. It is not a book about forecasting techniques. What's the difference? In the classroom it's not unusual to spend 80–90 percent of the time learning about the mathematical/statistical processes underpinning methods such as logistic regression and discriminant analysis that are used to construct models of consumer behaviour. Rarely is more than 10–20 percent of teaching time (and sometimes none at all) spent discussing wider issues that drive model development and usage in real world environments. Within the commercial sector the opposite is true. On average, well over 80 percent of the effort involved in the successful delivery of a modelling project is concerned with business issues. This includes spending time doing things such as: drawing up a project plan to determine how long the project will take and what resources are required, working out how much the project will cost, deciding what behaviour the model should predict, agreeing where the data to construct the model will come from, complying with audit and legal requirements, producing documentation, deploying the model within the business and determining how the performance of the model, once deployed, will be monitored to ensure it continues to work as intended. Only a few percent of a project's resources will actually be spent working with the statistical techniques that are used to construct the model. A typical bank, for example, will take anywhere between four and 12 months to develop and implement a new suite of credit scoring models to estimate the creditworthiness of people applying for a product such as a credit card. Yet, no more than a few days or weeks will be required for the modelling part.

The second point I want to make is that this is a book about practice. It is not a theoretical text, nor is the intention to provide a comprehensive literature review of the subject. References are made to theory and relevant academic material, but the primary objective is to explain, in simple terms, the steps required to deliver usable, high quality forecasting models within realistic timeframes, based on my personal experience of working in this area of financial services. There are very many complex data analysis/modelling/forecasting techniques and practices (and more are being developed all the time), that in some situations may achieve marginally better results than the methods discussed here, or which are more appropriate from a theoretical perspective. However, the effort required to develop, implement and maintain such solutions means that in practice few organizations employ them – the cost/benefit case just doesn't add up. Where such methods are employed the justification for doing so is often questionable. In some cases the decision to use a given modelling technique is driven by political pressures, originating from people who want to say that they and the organization that employs them are working at the cutting edge, not because there is a good business case for doing so. I have also come across many examples where one method of model construction appears to work much better than another, but on closer inspection the difference is found to be due to errors in the way models have been constructed and/or poor methodology when validating results. When the errors are corrected the differences, more often than not, disappear or are so small as to have no practical significance. Remember – Occam's razor applies – all other things being equal, simple solutions are best.

Given the aforementioned points, there are two groups I have written this book for. The first are those who are not model builders themselves, but who would like to know more about how models of consumer behaviour are constructed and used. Perhaps you work with model builders, or manage them, and feel you should understand more about what they do. For this audience I would like to emphasize that a degree in statistics or mathematics is not a requirement for understanding the material in this book. There are some formulas and equations, but the maths is kept to a minimum, and where it appears I have attempted to explain it in simple terms without assuming that the reader has much prior knowledge. If you can get through this introductory chapter, then you should not have any trouble with any material in subsequent chapters. The second group are those with a more technical background who may be, or about to be, involved in model construction, but who have little practical experience of how models are constructed within business environments. Maybe you are a graduate working in your first job or an experienced academic who wants to know more about the development and application of models within the financial services sector. For readers in this group, I don't claim to offer much that is new in terms of theory, but I do hope to provide some useful guidance about the practical aspects of model development and usage.

With regard to the structure of the book, in the remainder of this chapter the idea of a forecasting model is introduced, which going forward I shall simply refer to as "a model". This covers the type of behaviour that models are used to predict, the different forms of model that can be developed and the main stages that comprise a typical modelling project. Chapters 2 through 8 look at the key processes involved in developing a model, starting with project planning, then moving on to consider sampling, preparing data, data analysis, data pre-processing and modelling. Chapter 9 looks at the problem of sample bias. Sample bias is when behavioural information is missing for some cases, due to previous decisions made about them. This can lead to sub-optimal (biased) models, unless appropriate corrective action is taken. Chapter 10 discusses implementation and how models are monitored, post implementation, to see how well they are performing. The final chapter discusses a number of topics, in particular, small sample validation methodologies and multi-model 'fusion' systems, which generate a forecast of behaviour by combining several different forecasts together.

1.2   Model applications

There are many different behaviours that financial services organizations are interested in forecasting. Table 1.1 summarizes the most common behaviours that models are used to predict.

I do not claim that Table 1.1 provides an exhaustive list of every type of model used within the financial services industry, but it probably covers over 95 percent of the models in use today.

Table 1.1   Model applications

Model	Behaviour the model predicts
Classification models	
Response	The likelihood someone responds to direct marketing activity such as a mail shot. Marketing activity is only targeted at people the model predicts have a high likelihood of responding.
Conversion	The likelihood someone becomes a customer. For example, the likelihood that someone who responded to a mail shot by asking for an insurance quote, subsequently accepts the quote they are given.
Creditworthiness (Credit scoring/ Probability of default)	The likelihood someone will repay money that they owe. Models of this type are used to decide whether to offer credit in the form of personal loans, credit cards, mortgages and motor finance.
Fraud	The likelihood a credit application or an insurance claim is fraudulent. Fraud models are also widely used to predict if a credit card transaction is fraudulent.
Attrition (Retention/ Churn)	The likelihood that a customer defects to a rival or fails to renew a relationship.
Revolver	The likelihood a credit card customer revolves the balance (does not pay the balance in full) on their account each statement period.
Recovery (Collections)	The likelihood someone pays the arrears owing on a credit agreement when they have already missed one or more scheduled repayments.
Insurance risk	The likelihood someone will make a claim against their insurance policy.
Regression models	
Response time	The time it takes someone to respond to a marketing communication.
Affordability	Someone's disposable income after bills, rent, mortgage and so on have been taken into account. This type of model is used to check that people who are applying for a new line of credit have sufficient income to be able to meet their repayments.
Revenue	The income generated from a customer over a given time horizon.

Table 1.1   Model applications – *continued*

Model	Behaviour the model predicts
Customer lifetime value	The financial contribution a customer makes over the lifetime of the relationship.
Exposure at default	The amount someone owes when they default on a credit agreement. For a product such as a credit card, this takes into account any further advances that are made prior to default occurring.
Loss given default	The loss incurred from a customer who defaults on a credit agreement, taking into account the exposure at the time of default and any recoveries that are made after default has occurred.
Loss given claim	The loss incurred from a customer who makes a claim against their insurance policy.

You will note from Table 1.1 that the models have been segmented into two types: classification models and regression models. Classification models are used to predict how likely a customer behaviour is to occur. A response model, for example, predicts how likely someone who is targeted with a marketing communication, encouraging them to buy a product or service, will respond to it. A credit scoring model predicts whether or not someone will make their loan repayments, and a fraud model predicts the likelihood that someone acts fraudulently. In each case the output generated by the model – the model score – can be interpreted as a probability that someone will or will not exhibit the behaviour in question.

Regression models are used to predict quantities; that is, the magnitude of something. Typically, this will be a financial measure such as how much the customer is likely to spend (a revenue model), how much you expect to make from a customer over the lifetime of the relationship you have with them (a customer lifetime value model) or the loss you can expect to incur when someone defaults on a credit agreement (a loss given default model).

With regard to the split between classification and regression, the most popular usage is classification. Credit scoring models were the first classification models to be widely used in a commercial setting, with their origins dating back to the 1940s (Durand 1941; Wonderlic 1952). As better technology became available, so there was a corresponding growth in the application of classification and regression models to direct marketing and insurance. Today, credit assessment, direct marketing and insurance rating are the areas where models of consumer behaviour are most widely applied within the financial services community.

1.3   The nature and form of consumer behaviour models

The Compact Oxford English Dictionary provides seven definitions of the word "model". The one that applies here is: "A simplified mathematical description of a system or process, used to assist calculations and predictions." In other words, a model is an equation (a function), or set of equations, that estimates how something or someone is likely to behave under a given set of circumstances. There are many different forms that a model can take, so it is probably best to start with an example. Model 1 is a classification model that estimates how likely someone is to make an insurance claim:

$$
\begin{aligned}
\text{Score} = &\; + 0.350 \\
&- 0.005 * \text{Age of driver (in years)} \\
&+ 0.003 * \text{Age of vehicle (in months)} \\
&+ 0.098 * \text{Previous claims in last five years}
\end{aligned}
\qquad \text{(Model 1)}
$$

The model score is calculated as a function of a constant (+0.350) three predictor variables and three weights. The predictor variables are: the age of the driver, the age of vehicle to be insured and the number of previous claims in the last five years made by the driver. The corresponding weights are –0.005, +0.003 and +0.098 respectively. The output of the model (the score) provides an estimate of how likely someone is to make one or more claims against their car insurance in the next 12 months. So for someone aged 40, with a car that's three years (36 months) old and with one previous claim in the last five years, the score is calculated as:

$$
\begin{aligned}
\text{Score} = &\; + 0.350 \\
&- 0.005 * 40 \\
&+ 0.003 * 36 - \\
&+ 0.098 * 1 \\
= &\; 0.356
\end{aligned}
$$

For someone with other characteristics, the score will be different. A good question to ask at this point is what does a score of 0.356 actually mean? A classification model provides a measure of how likely a specific customer behaviour, such as an insurance claim, is to occur. For Model 1 the event of interest is someone making an insurance claim. In this example, a score of 0.356 means that the estimated probability[1] of someone making a claim in the next 12 months is 0.356. To put it another way, the odds of them making a claim are slightly more than 1 in 3.

Let's look at another example. Model 2 is a regression model that predicts the value of insurance claims, should a claim be made:

Score = +$3,780.00
+   67.34 * Age of driver (in years)
−   37.65 * Age of vehicle (in months)   (Model 2)
−$1,088.90 * Previous claims in last five years

The score is calculated in the same way as before, with a constant, the same three predictor variables and three weights. However, this time the model provides an estimate of how much the claim is likely to be, rather than a probability of the claim occurring. So, for our 40 year old, driving a 36 month old car and with one previous claim in the last five years, the score is $4,029.30. To put it another way, the model predicts that for someone with this set of characteristics, the value of any claim will be $4,029.30.

Model 1 is a classification model that predicts the likelihood someone will make a claim in the next 12 months, and Model 2 is a regression model that estimates the value of an insurance claim, should a claim be made. Each model can be used on its own for various purposes, but together they can be used to estimate how much someone should pay for their insurance premiums. The total expected cost incurred from granting someone insurance is calculated by multiplying the two model scores together; that is, the likelihood of a claim occurring generated by Model 1, by the expected cost of the claim generated by Model 2. Continuing with the previous example, the probability of a claim was estimated to be 0.356 and the value of a claim, should one be made, was estimated to be $4,029.30. Therefore, the expected value of claims in the next 12 months will be 0.356 * $4,029.30 = $1,434.43. What this means is that if the insurance company wants to make a profit, it needs to charge customers like this insurance premiums of at least $1,434.43 plus administrative costs.

1.3.1 Linear models

One way of thinking about a model is as a representation of the relationships that exist between different items of data. In particular, the relationship between the value of the predictor variables that describe an individual's current state such as their age, occupation and residential status, and the dependent variable; that is, the behaviour they subsequently exhibit such as making an insurance claim.

Models 1 and 2, introduced in the previous section, are examples of linear models. To qualify as a linear model, the relationships captured by the model must satisfy two requirements. First, the effect of a change in the value of each predictor variable in the model must result in a change of constant proportion to the model score. Consider the following two functions:

$$\text{Profit} = \$0.30 * \text{Price} \tag{A}$$
$$\text{Profit} = \$0.80 * \sqrt{\text{Price}} \tag{B}$$

Figure 1.1 provides a graphical representation of the two functions.

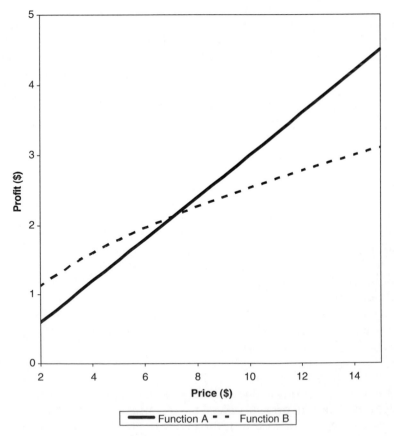

Figure 1.1   Linear and non-linear relationships

As illustrated in Figure 1.1, for Function A, a unit increase in price always results in the same increase in profit. If the price changes from $3.00 to $4.00, the increase in profit is $0.30. Likewise, if the price changes from $4.00 to $5.00, profit also increases by $0.30. Graphically, this relationship is represented by a straight line, and there is said to be a linear relationship between price and profit. For function B the relationship can't be represented by a straight line. A unit increase in price will result in a different increase in profit, dependent upon the current price. If the price changes from $3.00 to $4.00 the profit will change from $1.39 to $1.60 – an increase of $0.21. If the price changes from $4.00 to $5.00 the profit will change from $1.60 to $1.79 – an increase of $0.19. For Function B there is said to be a non-linear relationship between price and profit.

The second requirement of a linear model is that the function that combines the effects of multiple predictor variables to generate the model score must be additive. Consider the following two functions:

Profit = ($0.30 * Price) + ($0.50 * Advertising Spend) (C)

Profit = ($0.30 * Price) * ($0.50 * Advertising Spend) (D)

For function (C) the effects of price and advertising spend on profit are additive. However, for function (D) the effects are multiplicative. For Function C profit is a linear function of price and advertising spend. However, for Function D, the relationship between price and advertising, and profit is non-linear. More generally, a linear model can be written in the form:

$$S = a + b_1x_1 + b_2x_2 + ,..., + b_kx_k$$

where:

- S is the output generated by the model; that is, a measure of the value you are trying to predict, based on the values of the predictor variables. S is calculated by taking a and adding the other terms of the equation to it. Common industry practice is to refer to S as the model "Score" and this naming convention is adopted going forward.[2]
- a is a constant, and can take any positive or negative value.
- $x_1 ... x_k$ are a set of k predictor (independent) variables. Examples of typical predictor variables are someone's age, how long they have lived at their address or how much they earn.
- $b_1 ... b_k$ are the *weights*, also known as *parameter coefficients*[3] assigned to each predictor variable. These are measures of how much each

predictor variable contributes, positively or negatively to the model score (*S*).

A linear model can be used for classification or regression, and is the most popular form of model used to predict consumer behaviour. Linear models have two main strengths. The first is that many of the techniques that can be used to construct them are very quick and easy to apply. The second is that their operation is transparent. By this, I mean it is very easy to understand what relationships the model has captured and the contribution each predictor variable makes to the final score, by considering the size and magnitude of the parameter coefficients (the *bs*).

The main downside of linear models is they can only represent relationships in data in a linear way. If the relationships in the data are linear then that's fine. Alternatively, it may be possible to apply transformations to generate a set of new predictor variables that display approximately linear relationships with the behaviour of interest. However, if the underlying relationships are highly non-linear and this non-linearity can't be dealt with by transforming the data, then it will not be possible to fully capture the relationships with a linear model. As a result, the predictions made by the model will be poor.

1.3.2   Classification and regression trees (CART)

Another popular model form is the classification and regression tree (CART). Like a linear model, a CART model can be used for classification or regression. A CART model is created by splitting a population into smaller and smaller segments, using splitting rules based on the value of the predictor variables. Individuals in different segments display different behaviour, and decisions about how to treat someone are based on the properties of the final segment into which they fall after all splitting rules have been applied. An example of a CART model that predicts the likelihood of someone making an insurance claim is shown in Figure 1.2.

In Figure 1.2 the properties of the model are illustrated using a sample of 6,000 individuals who took out an insurance policy and whose claim performance was observed for 12 months. Node 1 shows claim performance for the full sample of 6,000 cases, before any splitting rules have been applied. Five thousand had not made a claim and 1,000 had made a claim. The average claim rate – the proportion of the population who made a claim – is 0.167 (1,000 / 6,000). The tree "grows" from the top down. Each split in the tree is defined using predictor variables that were available at the time when the application for insurance was

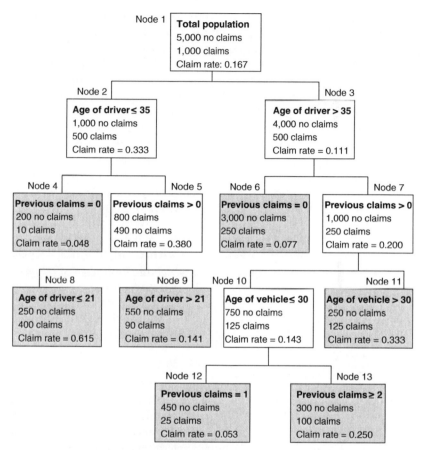

Figure 1.2   A classification and regression tree model

made, such as the age of driver, age of vehicle and number of previous claims. In this example, the population is initially split into two groups (those in nodes 2 and 3), based on the age of the driver. Those aged 35 or less fall into node 2 and those older than 35 into node 3. As Figure 1.2 shows, younger drivers in node 2 are three times more likely to make a claim than older drivers in node 3.

The splitting process is repeated, with nodes 2 and 3 (termed parent nodes) each segmented into two subsidiary (child) nodes. The process stops when there are too few individuals in a parent node for it to make sense to split it further, or when no further differentiation between groups can be found; that is, the claim rate in all potential child nodes is the same as the parent node. Common terminology is to describe each segment in the tree as a "Node" and each of the end nodes without any children as "leaf nodes".[4] Decisions about how to treat someone are based on the properties of the leaf node into which they fall. Although the tree does not generate a score as such, the score for an individual is usually taken to be the average claim rate (or other value that the tree is used to predict) of the leaf node into which they fall. In Figure 1.2 the leaf nodes are shaded in grey. So the 40 year old, whose car is 36 months old and with one previous claim, will fall through the tree, ending up at node 11. The score associated with this node is 0.333.

Like linear models, CART models are easy to understand and explain. CART is also a non-linear form of model. This means CART models are able to represent non-linear relationships that exist.

1.3.3   Artificial neural networks

A third form of model is the artificial neural network. In the early days of research into artificial neural networks, many analogies were made with the operation of the human brain, and therefore, some of the terminology used to describe artificial neural networks is taken from the biological analogy.

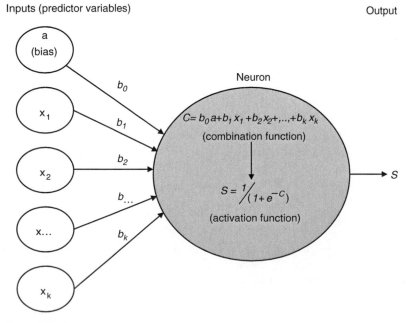

Figure 1.3   A neuron

An artificial neural network is made up from a number of component units, referred to as "neurons". The operation of a neuron is illustrated in Figure 1.3.

There are two stages to the operation of the neuron. In the first stage a function is used to combine the predictor variables (the inputs in Figure 1.3) and the weights. In network terminology this is called a combination function. In nearly all practical applications the combination function is a linear model of the form $C = b_0 a + b_1 x_1 + b_2 x_2 +, ..., + b_k x_k$ – very similar to the linear model introduced in section 1.3.1.[5] The only difference is that there is now a weight, b_0, assigned to the constant.[6] In the second stage the value produced by the combination function, C, is subject to a transformation by the activation function.[7] The purpose of the activation function is to transform the value generated by the combination function so that it lies within a fixed range, often 0–1 or –1, +1. There are many different activation functions that exist, but in Figure 1.3 the logistic activation function is used which is popular.[8] The value produced by the activation function (S) is the score output by the neuron.

Apart from the standardization resulting from applying the activation function, the score produced by the neuron is, to all intents and purposes, the same as the score generated by a linear model. The real benefits come when several neurons are combined together to form an artificial neural network. An example of an artificial neural network to predict the likelihood of insurance claims is shown in Figure 1.4.

Figure 1.4 provides an example of the most common form of artificial neural network used within the financial services industry. It contains three layers: an input layer, a hidden layer and an output layer. The input layer does not contain any neurons as such, but represents the predictor variables that are presented to the network, with one input for each predictor variable. The number of neurons in the hidden layer depends on the problem at hand, but usually ranges from somewhere between 2 (as in this example) to $2k$, where k is the number of predictor variables in the input layer. The output layer contains a single neuron. The inputs to the neuron in the output layer are the outputs from the neurons in the hidden layer. The output from the neuron in the output layer is the final score generated by the model.

One way to think about the operation of the network in Figure 1.4 is as a function of three separate linear models. The two neurons in the hidden layer each produce a linear model via the combination function. The outputs are then transformed via the activation function,

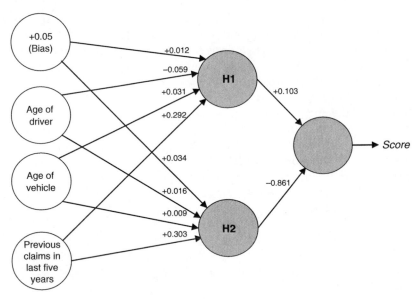

Figure 1.4   A neural network

and these form the components of the third linear model, represented by the combination function in the output layer neuron. So for the 40 year old driver discussed previously, the estimated likelihood of them making a claim is calculated as:

For the hidden neuron H1:

Combination function = 0.05 * 0.012 – 0.059 * 40 + 0.031 * 36 + 0.292 * 1 = **–0.951**
Activation function = $1/(1 + e^{-0.951})$ = **0.279**

For the hidden neuron H2:

Combination function = 0.05 * 0.034 + 0.016 * 40 + 0.009 * 36 + 0.303 * 1 = **1.269**
Activation function = $1/(1 + e^{-1.269})$ = **0.781**

For the output layer neuron:

Combination function = 0.103 * 0.279 − 0.861 * 0.781 = −0.643
Activation function = $1/(1 + e^{-0.643})$ = **0.344**

So the estimated likelihood of a claim generated by the model is 0.344. The big selling point of artificial neural networks is their ability to model problems that are highly non-linear in nature, and therefore, cannot be well represented by simple linear models such as those discussed in section 1.3.1. Since the mid-1980s there has been much excitement, a huge amount of academic research and lots of publicity, about how these "brain like" structures can solve complex problems and predict different types of behaviour with a high degree of accuracy. In some problem domains the promise of improved prediction has been well founded and artificial neural networks have been demonstrated to deliver marked benefits in comparison to many other forms of model. However, when it comes to predicting consumer behaviour within financial services, the evidence is less supportive. There is some evidence that neural networks can make better predictions than linear models and decision trees by a small, albeit statistically significant, margin (West et al. 1997; Baesens et al. 2002; Kim et al. 2005). However, many empirical studies covering direct marketing, credit scoring and insurance risk have found the performance of neural networks to be about the same, or even marginally worse, than linear models (King et al. 1995; Arminger et al. 1997; Zahavi and Levin 1997; West 2000; Viaene et al. 2002; Baesens et al. 2003a; Linder, et al. 2004).[9] The general conclusion from these different research studies is that no one model form is universally better than any other in terms of its ability to predict consumer behaviour, and many different approaches to modelling consumer behaviour yield very similar results for many problems. Therefore, the choice of model form is often dependent upon factors such as the simplicity and explicability of the model, rather than its predictive ability or theoretical appropriateness. Compared to linear models and CART models, artificial neural networks are complex. This leads to greater costs in terms of the effort required to develop and implement them within operational environments. Understanding how an artificial neural network model makes its decisions is also difficult, due to the interdependent nature of the neurons and weights within the network.[10] This means they tend not to be used for decision making in areas where explicable models are required. For example, in the US lenders must give explicit reasons why an individual has been declined for credit. If a decision to grant a loan has been made using a credit score generated from a linear model that predicts the likelihood of repayment, then one can simply look at the sign and magnitude of the weights in the model to see how each predictor variable contributed towards the applicant's credit score. Likewise, one can look at the splits within a CART model and come to a similar understanding. This intuitive understanding is not present with artificial neural networks. The overall result is that artificial neural networks are used in only a small minority of "back-end" decision making systems within the financial services industry, such as fraud detection (Hand 2001; Crook et al. 2007).

1.4   Model construction

For linear models and artificial neural networks the relationship between the predictor variables and the dependent variable are represented by the weights in the model, and for CART models by the splits within the tree. Model one, introduced in section 1.3 describes the relationships between three predictor variables (the age of the driver, the age of vehicle to be insured, and the number of previous claims made by the driver) and the likelihood of insurance claims. The relationship between the age of the driver and the driver's likelihood of making an insurance claim, for example, is represented by the weight of –0.005. This means that the likelihood of a claim decreases by 0.005 for each year of the driver's age. Similar relationships are described by the weights associated with the other two predictor variables.

A central task for all modelling projects is to determine which predictor variables are important, and what the weights associated with each variable should be (or the splits for a CART model) – a process commonly referred to as "parameter estimation" or "model construction". Typically, model construction is undertaken by applying "Data mining" to a representative sample of data. Data mining is a widely used term to describe the methods used to examine large and complex data sets in order to identity the important relationships that exist within the data. Data mining is a very broad area of study that draws from many other disciplines including mathematics, statistics and artificial intelligence. Creating predictive models of consumer behaviour represents just one application area of data mining – there are many others.

Usually, what one is interested in is predicting how a consumer will behave in the future based on what we know about them today.[11] Therefore, the data used to construct models needs to come from the past to allow inferences to be drawn over time. The insurance claim model predicts the likelihood that someone applying for insurance today makes a claim any time within the next 12 months. This means that to obtain a sample of data that is suitable for model construction it is necessary to gather information about people who took out insurance 12 months ago or more so that 12 months of claim behaviour is available for analysis.

The need for historical data has two important implications. First, if an organization wants to develop predictive models of consumer behaviour, they need to maintain enough data, over a sufficient period of time, to allow good quality models to be built. Historically, a lack of data has been one of the biggest obstacles to building better models, and although the IT systems of the major financial institutions have improved markedly within the last few years, many organizations still don't have access to as much data as they would like. As a consequence, their models are not as good as they could be. Second, a fundamental assumption of this type of forecasting is that the future is like the past; that is, the relationships that are found to exist within the historic sample used for model development are stable over time and are still valid when the model is deployed. If the relationships in the data have changed significantly since the sample was taken, then the predictive power of the model will be substantially reduced.

At one time it would have been necessary to have a detailed understanding of the mathematical theory underpinning a model building technique in order to be confident that you were applying it correctly, and you may have needed to write computer code using a programming language such as Fortran or C. These days such knowledge is only necessary if one is undertaking research or studying for a degree in statistics or applied mathematics. Most statistical software, such as SAS and SPSS, provide Windows-based point and click interfaces, will produce models automatically and take care of all required calculation. What is important is that the model developer has an appreciation of the sensitivities and limitations of each modelling technique. They also need to know how to interpret the model diagnostics that the software generates, and what remedial action to take if the diagnostics indicate that the model is flawed in some way.

A suitable analogy is driving a car. In the early part of the twentieth century cars were unsophisticated and unreliable. If you owned one it made sense to understand something about what went on under the bonnet so that you could keep it running and get to where you wanted to go. Without that knowledge you would invariably break down, and if you couldn't fix the problem yourself you were stranded. In the twenty first century cars are much more reliable. Today, most people know nothing about engine mechanics, and how much someone knows about the workings of their car bears little relation to how well they drive it. If a warning light appears on the dashboard, then you know something is wrong and you need to do something about it. If you break down then you call your recovery service or the local garage. Another, sometimes controversial, perspective is that at the end of the day it really doesn't matter how a model is created. The key question is, how well does the model perform? If it performs to expectation then the process used to derive it, is arguably, irrelevant.

1.5   Measures of performance

An absolutely crucial part of building a model is evaluating how good the model is; that is, how well the model satisfies the business objectives of the organization that commissioned it.

For most modelling projects there will be several different performance criteria, but the criteria that receive most attention, by a considerable margin, relate to predictive accuracy, based on the difference between what the model predicted and what actually happened. At this point it is important to make it clear that the score produced by a model is only an estimate about what will happen. I have never yet come across a model of consumer behaviour that comes anywhere close to generating perfect predictions every time. There will always be some error; that is, a degree of discrepancy, between prediction and reality. In general, the smaller the error the better the model.

Imagine that the 40 year old driver takes out an insurance policy and subsequently makes a claim. The probability of the driver making a claim is now a certainty – a probability of 1.0. For the linear model (model 1), introduced in section 1.3, the estimate of a claim occurring was only 0.356. The error between prediction and reality is $1 - 0.356 = 0.644$. For the CART model of Figure 1.2, the estimate was 0.333, an error of $1 - 0.333 = 0.667$ and for the artificial neural network $1 - 0.344 = 0.656$. The linear model would seem to be best because the error is smaller than that for the CART and artificial neural network models. In practice however, it is impossible to draw conclusions about the predictive accuracy of a model from just one or two examples. Instead, many hundreds of test cases are required to allow statistically significant conclusions to be drawn about how well a model performs, or which model is best when several competing models are under consideration.

Measures of error, based on the difference between actual and predicted values are popular, but there are others. For example, measures of rank, where the size of the errors is not important. What is important is that the model score places someone correctly, relative to others in the population (Thomas et al. 2001). For example, retailers will often enter into an agreement with a third party credit provider to provide the credit that customers use to buy items such as TVs, sofas and washing machines. The retailer does not provide credit itself. As part of the agreement the retailer will require that a minimum percentage of its customers are granted credit – say at least 80 percent.[12] Therefore, what the credit provider is interested in is ranking customers in order of creditworthiness so that the best 80 percent can be identified. These have their credit applications accepted and the remaining 20 percent of applications are declined. The accuracy of individual predictions is irrelevant as long as the model allows the best 80 percent of customers to be identified. Ranking and other performance measures are discussed in more detail in Chapter 8.

From a wider business perspective, there are other measures that ultimately determine how well a model meets its objectives. The time and cost to develop and deploy a model is one factor. It is very rare for a business to choose to undertake a modelling project where the only objective is to maximize the model's predictive ability, without regard for the cost or time involved. Instead, the project will usually have a budget assigned to it and be expected to be delivered for a fixed date in the diary. If this means developing a simple solution that is technically sub-optimal and cuts a few corners, but which is delivered on time and to cost, then this will be deemed a greater success than a more technically sophisticated and theoretically correct solution that misses its target implementation date and/or overruns its budget.

In some environments there is a requirement for models to be simple and explicable. It must be possible to provide a clear and objective explanation as to why a model generates a given score in terms of the predictor variables. Simple models also aid understanding with a wider audience. Complex modelling solutions mean that understanding is restricted to a few specialist individuals. This makes it almost impossible for senior managers to make informed decisions about the validity or appropriateness of the models that have been constructed by the people who work for them. It is interesting to note that one of the conclusions of the Turner Report into the causes of the worldwide banking crisis of 2007–8 was that:

> The very complexity of the mathematics used to measure and manage risk, moreover, made it increasingly difficult for top management and boards to assess and exercise judgement over the risks being

taken. Mathematical sophistication ended up not containing risk, but providing false assurance... (Financial Services Authority 2009, p. 22)

The move to using more sophisticated forecasting models to predict the risks within the banking system didn't work because the right people didn't understand them.

In some environments the parameter coefficients of the predictor variables in the model must conform to what senior management judge to be common sense. A widely held view in the consumer credit industry is that the longer someone has been in their job the more creditworthy they will be. A credit manager would expect to see this relationship represented by a positive parameter coefficient within a linear credit scoring model. All other things being equal, the longer someone has been in their job the higher the score they receive. If the opposite relationship was seen; that is, the parameter coefficient for Time in Employment was negative, then the model would probably be rejected out of hand. This is regardless of any statistical evidence that the observed relationship was true. The model developer would be forced to go away and redevelop the model with a different set of parameter coefficients, even if this led to a model that was sub-optimal in terms of its predictive ability.

1.6   The stages of a model development project

A project to develop a model involves a number of stages, as shown in Figure 1.5.

A modelling project will be initiated when someone in authority decides that a new model is required and authorizes the development to proceed. For small scale "one-off" projects such as the production of a mailing list containing a few thousand names, this may be the analyst who is going to develop the model or their immediate line manager. For larger projects involving models that will be used to make millions of dollars worth of decisions each day, such as those used to assess creditworthiness or claim propensity, the decision to develop a model will invariably be taken at senior management level.

Once a project is up and running the next step is to undertake a project planning exercise to establish precisely what needs to be done, how long its going to take/cost and who needs to be involved. Amongst other things, this will include: identifying stakeholders, defining project objectives, producing a project plan, documenting risks and issues, identifying sources of data, agreeing the statistical process that will be applied to

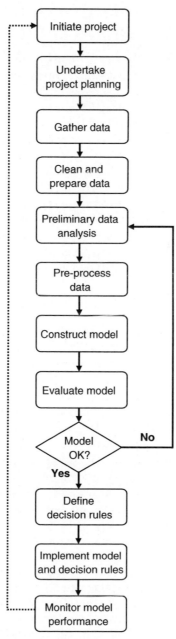

Figure 1.5 Stages of a model development project

construct the model and setting the criteria by which the success of the project will be judged. The amount of effort that goes into the project planning phases depends on the nature of the project and the approach to project management adopted by the organization developing the model. In many large organizations a formal project management process will be required such as PRINCE II. This is particularly likely to be the case if the project is identified as one where substantial financial risk exists should the project be incorrectly executed. In these situations project planning may take several weeks or even months to complete, with all requirements captured within a formal business requirements document that requires sign-off by the project stakeholders before further work can commence. In other situations, where the model is less business critical or the development is relatively small, an ad-hoc or Rapid Application Development (RAD) project management style may be more appropriate. Bureaucracy and associated paper work are kept to a minimum, and it is not unusual for the project requirements to consist of nothing more than a set of e-mails detailing what people think needs to be done, that evolves over time as the project progresses.

When the planning phase has been completed, the next task is to gather the data that will be used for model construction. Data can come from many different internal and external sources, and these need to be matched together to produce a single database for modelling purposes. If data sets are large, then sampling may be required to produce a manageable data set which can be processed in realistic time. Data will then need to be prepared; that is, formatted and cleaned to deal with missing, erroneous and inconsistent data items. Following this, preliminary data analysis is undertaken to identify the important patterns and relationships, and to enable the data to be interpreted from a business perspective. It is at this point where many errors and spurious relationships in the data are identified and dealt with. Data can then be pre-processed (transformed) so that it is in a suitable format to be presented to the software used to construct the model.

Once a model has been constructed its ability to predict behaviour needs to be evaluated. This will include statistical measures of how well the model predicts the behaviour of interest, but other features of the model will also be important, such as the structure of the model and how stable it is over time. Model construction and evaluation are iterative processes. On the basis of the results of the model evaluation, changes may be made to the data pre-processing and/or the methodology used to derive the model. A revised model will then be created. The process will be repeated, perhaps many times, until the model developer is satisfied that the model is as good as possible and meets the requirements of the business.

Once the final model has been arrived at, consideration can be given to the decision rules that determine how the model will be used. Principally, this means defining the cut-off scores that will be applied; that is, the different actions that are taken when someone scores above or below a given score. These will then be combined with business (policy) rules that are used to override score based rules in certain circumstances. Consider a model that predicts response to a mailing, where the higher the score the more likely someone is to respond. The relationship between the model score and the likelihood of response is illustrated in Figure 1.6.

If the business requirement is that it is only cost effective to mail people where the likelihood of response is more than 2 percent, then from Figure 1.6 it can be determined that the decision rule will be to mail people with a score of 720 or more. Anyone with a score of less than 720 won't be mailed. The organization also has a policy of not mailing people who are under 18 (the legal age of consent in many countries). Therefore, a policy override rule is also defined, not to mail anyone under 18, regardless of the score they receive.

Once the decision rules have been established, the model and the decision rules can be put to use. Sometimes standalone models are developed for one-off or ad-hoc purposes, and in the classroom models

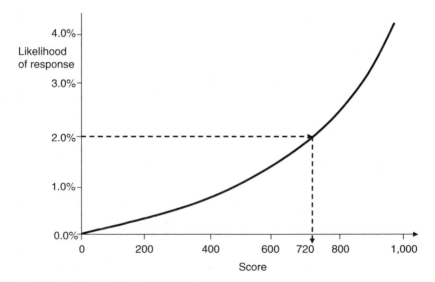

Figure 1.6   Likelihood of response by score

are often presented in this context. In practice, the most important models financial services organizations employ are used in support of their day-to-day decision making processes, as part of an automated decision making system. This means that in order for a model to be deployed, it needs to be integrated into an organization's business infrastructure. Consider an application processing system that a bank might use to process new credit applications, as shown in Figure 1.7.

In Figure 1.7, the process begins when a customer submits a credit application, via the customer interface. The customer interface encompasses all of the people and systems involved in communication with the applicant, acting as an intermediary between the applicant and the application processing system. The primary role of the customer interface is to gather information from the applicant and to provide information back to them about the status of their application. The customer interface may be a data processing centre that receives paper application forms, where staff type the details provided on the form into the application processing system. Alternatively, for applications made by phone, the customer interface will involve an operator capturing the applicant's details via their computer terminal. A similar process will occur if someone goes into their local branch, with a customer services representative providing the interface. If an application is made via the internet, then the website provides an interface that feeds data directly to the application processing system.

Within the application processing system there are two main subsystems. The data management unit is responsible for collating data from different internal and external sources, such as an organization's database of existing customers and credit reports obtained from credit reference agencies. The data is then provided in an efficient and timely manner to the business functions that need it. The scoring and strategy sub-system uses data passed to it by the data management unit to calculate scores and make decisions about how applications should be treated. These decisions are then passed back to the data management unit where they are acted upon. For applications that are accepted, the data management unit will pass the applicant's details to the account management system so that an account can be created. Information about the terms of the credit agreement will also be passed back to the customer interface to be communicated to the customer.

Implementing a model within a system such as that in Figure 1.7 is often a non-trivial task. This is particularly true if the model includes new items of data that were not previously captured via the customer interface, requiring changes to systems and interfaces, and training for

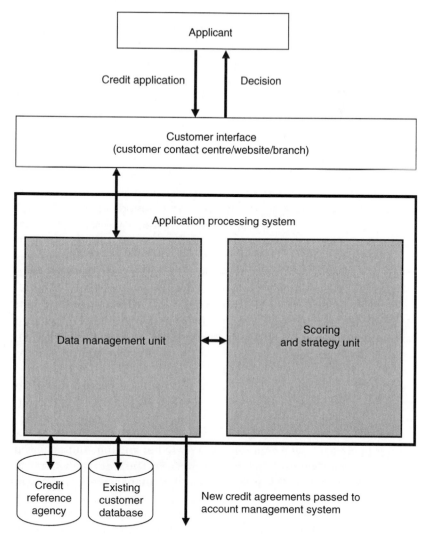

Figure 1.7 Application processing system for credit assessment

customer facing staff who use the systems. Often the person or team responsible for implementing the model will be someone other than the model developer. This means that suitable documentation needs to be produced to explain to the implementer the structure of the model, along with the decision rules that will be applied. An application processing system for new credit applications or insurance quotations is a business critical system, responsible for making millions, or even billions, of dollars worth of decisions each year. It is therefore, very important that the model is implemented correctly. Consequently, extensive testing is required prior to the model going live. For many banks, the testing and audit processes associated with credit scoring models can often take longer to undertake than all of the other stages of a project put together.

Once a model is in use the process is not yet over. All models of consumer behaviour deteriorate over time, meaning that at some point a decision will be taken to discard the current model and develop a new one. Therefore, model performance needs to be monitored on an ongoing basis to establish the point at which the development of a new model is justified. The only exception to this is if the model is developed for a "one-off" purpose that is not business critical. Even so, it is important that the performance of the model is evaluated to determine if it performed as expected, and what, if any, lessons can be learned and incorporated into the next modelling project that is undertaken.

It is important to note that Figure 1.5 represents a somewhat idealized view of the model development process. In practice, each stage may be revisited several times as further analysis is undertaken and new information comes to light. Even with a well planned project, changes to business requirements can be made fairly late in the day, requiring the processes that follow to be reworked accordingly.

1.7   Chapter summary

All major financial institutions use mathematically derived forecasting models to predict how consumers are likely to behave in the future, based on information that is known about them today. Decisions about how to treat someone are then taken on the basis of the forecasts that have been made.

Models of consumer behaviour can be classified into two types: Classification and Regression. Classification models predict which behaviour someone is likely to exhibit. Examples include, response models that predict the likelihood someone responds to a mailing and credit scoring models that predict the likelihood that someone repays a loan. Regression models estimate the magnitude of behaviour. Examples include models of customer lifetime value that estimate the financial worth of someone should they become a customer and loss given default models that estimate the loss incurred from an individual in the event that they default on a loan.

There are many different model forms that can be employed to generate forecasts of behaviour. For example, classification and regression trees, artificial neural networks and linear models. Of these, linear models are the most popular by a considerable margin. This can be attributed to the fact that they generate accurate forecasts, are easy to develop and implement, and it is relatively easy to determine how each of the predictor variables contribute towards the model score by simple examination of the model's parameters.

The parameter coefficients (weights) in a model represent the strength of the relationships between individual predictor variables and the behaviour of interest. There are many different model construction techniques that can be used to decide what the parameter coefficients of a model should be (or how the splits in a CART model should be defined), using a wide variety of mathematical techniques.

All model construction techniques are based on the analysis of historic data, to establish what the important relationships are. Having good quality data from a recent period of history, is therefore, one of the most important requirements for building models that will accurately predict how individuals are likely to behave in the future.

In business environments the technical aspects of a model building project, associated with estimating the parameter coefficients of the model form only a small, albeit very important, part of the project as a whole. For many projects, and particularly those that are of strategic importance, most of the time and resources required to deliver the project will be spent on other things. For example, scoping and definition of project requirements, collating and understanding data, deciding what decision rules to apply on the basis of the model score, documentation for internal/external audit purposes and implementing the model within the organization's operational systems.

2
Project Planning

Project planning is the process of deciding what the project's objectives are, agreeing who needs to be involved, determining what needs to be done to deliver the objectives and what the time and costs will be of doing so. Sometimes there can be pressure to just "get on with it" and start gathering and analysing data as soon as possible. Project planning is viewed as a form of procrastination, delaying the start of the real work that needs to be done. This may be the case, but the old adage "more haste, less speed" generally holds true. As a rule, making changes towards the end of a project is much more time consuming (and hence more costly) than making the same change near the start. This is because of the knock on effects each change has on subsequent activities. Spending even a little bit of time and effort project planning at the beginning of a project will result in a lot less time reworking things to correct errors and misunderstandings as the project progresses. This isn't to say that good project planning will prevent all need for reworking, but it will help minimize the changes that are required.

The requirements for a modelling project can be classified into two types: business requirements and technical requirements. Business requirements are things that must be considered to ensure the model supports organizational goals and is integrated smoothly into to the organization's infrastructure. Typical business requirements include:

- Roles and responsibilities. It should be clear who will be required to do what during the course of the project.
- Objectives and scope. This covers what the project is trying to achieve and the benefits that it will bring to the organization.
- Legal issues. There is a host of legislation and regulation the financial services industry must comply with. It is important that the model and associated decision rules comply with these.

- Implementation. This covers how the model is going to be integrated into the organization's business systems so that it can be used on a day-to-day basis. Consideration also need to be given to how the implementation of the model will affect other areas of the business such as IT, call centres and so on.
- Resource planning. There should be a project plan showing how long the project will take, what it will cost and what resources will be required.
- Risks and issues. These are things that could potentially get in the way of the project being completed successfully. Action will need to be taken to resolve issues and mitigate risks.
- Documentation and reporting. This is about how information about the project is recorded and disseminated to stakeholders. Considerable documentation may also be required to comply with internal/external audit procedures.

Technical requirements deal with analytical issues. These include:

- The modelling objective. This is the behaviour the model will predict, and should be aligned with the business objectives that have been defined. In statistics/data mining the modelling objective is often called the "dependent variable", the "target variable" or the "objective function".
- The outcome period (forecast horizon). This is the length of time in the future over which the model will predict behaviour.
- Data sources and predictor variables. This covers where the data for the model will be sourced and which predictor variables are available for model construction.
- Sample selection. There is often lots of data that could potentially be used for model building. Sample selection is the process of deciding which sub-set of the available data should be used to construct the model.
- Model form and method of construction. In some situations any form of model may be acceptable, and a wide variety of methods are suitable for determining the model's parameters. For other situations, there may be a requirement for a model of a particular form constructed using a particular method.

There can be overlap between technical and business requirements, and sometimes it can be difficult to say into which category a particular requirement falls. However, technical requirements are generally concerned with those things that influence the predictive properties of the model, such as the modelling objective and the time horizon over which the model predicts. Business requirements on the other hand are primarily concerned with ensuring that the objectives of the project stakeholders are achieved. It doesn't matter how good a model is from a technical perspective. If it fails to receive approval from key figures within the organization then the organization will view it as a failure. This means that in many situations the final model will be sub-optimal from a statistical perspective because of the business requirements that are imposed upon it. Over the years I've worked with many model developers who have been frustrated with the organizations they work for because they find themselves, as they see it, making compromises in terms of model quality in order to deliver something that is acceptable to the wider business. My view is that this is the wrong way to look at the problem. Instead, a model developer should embrace business requirements. They should think of business requirements as a set of constraints that form an integral part of the project's objectives, that need due consideration within the technical solution they deliver.

Each section in the remainder of this chapter focuses on a different technical or business requirement that needs consideration during the project planning phase. Note that sample selection is covered as a separate topic in Chapter 3.

2.1   Roles and responsibilities

A typical modelling project involves several people, and it is prudent for everyone to know who is involved and in what capacity. The typical roles associated with modelling projects are:

- Project sponsor. This is the person who is championing the project. The project sponsor is usually a member of senior management or the head of the department responsible for building the model.
- Project manager. The project manager is the central point of contact for the project. The project manager has a number of responsibilities. These include: obtaining and managing the resources the project requires, ensuring relevant company procedures are followed, facilitating communication between team members, production of a project plan, monitoring progress against the plan and dealing with risks and issues as they arise.
- Decision makers. These are the people in authority who will make the key decisions. For example, providing budget approval and signing off

the finished model prior to implementation. The project sponsor often takes on the role of the primary decision maker, but it could equally be a more senior member of staff – such as the sponsor's line manager.

- Analysts. Analysts are the people who undertake the bulk of the work associated with construction of the model(s). Analysts will also be heavily involved in testing, implementation and the production of documentation. The analyst role in a modelling project is analogous to that of a tradesman working on a construction project or a computer programmer on an IT project.
- Stakeholders. A stakeholder is anyone who has an interest in the project. This will obviously include the analyst(s), the project manager and so on, but will also include anyone who is going to be affected by the deployment of the model. If a new credit scoring model results in fewer referrals to underwriters, then the person responsible for the underwriting team is a stakeholder and they should be informed about relevant issues that affect them.

It is important to realize this list refers to roles not people. It is not uncommon for someone to take on two (or more) roles within a project. For small projects in particular, the project manager may also be the project sponsor, or a senior analyst who is given project management responsibility in addition to their other duties. A second point is that although the project manager role is central to the success of a project, project management is about the means not the ends. By this, I mean that it's not the project manager's role to decide what the objectives are, how much the company can spend or the deadline for the project,[1] but rather to make sure that what has been decided is delivered on time and to budget.

It is vital that project roles are identified at an early stage so that everyone can have their input into the project requirements sooner rather than later, and it is clear who is responsible for what. A common project management failing is to exclude someone important or forget to have representation (a stakeholder) covering a particular business function that will be affected by the project. Usually, the result of such an omission is trouble further down the line when some additional project requirement is put forward that was not covered originally.

Compared to some IT and construction projects that may involve hundreds or thousands of people and cost tens of millions of dollars, most modelling projects are relatively small scale affairs. In my experience the project team for a modelling project will contain somewhere between two and 20 people, and maybe half of these will be stakeholders with little day-to-day involvement. Most projects involve only one or two analysts in a full-time capacity, and even for a large programme of work, involving considerable data gathering, data preparation, analysis and the construction of several models, it is unusual for more than four or five analysts to be required at any one time.

Ultimately, a project is successful because the people in authority believe their objectives have been achieved. This is typically the project sponsor and/or the decision makers. It is therefore important, that everyone knows who is ultimately in charge, and everyone is attuned to what these people perceive the project's objectives to be.

2.2   Business objectives and project scope

From an analytical perspective it's easy to think about objectives purely in terms of generating the most predictive model possible, but from a business perspective this is not how senior management see objectives. Business objectives vary from organization to organization and from project to project, but they usually fall within one (or more) of the following categories:

1. Financial. There is a desire to improve the financial performance of the business. This might be to increase net revenues by underwriting more insurance policies, or to reduce costs by granting fewer loans to people who default and have their debt written-off.
2. Volume. The objective is to increase the volume of customers. This may be by increasing response rates, increasing conversion rates, reducing attrition rates, increasing policy renewals and so on, ideally without detrimental effect to the organization's financial position.
3. Operational. Often a model will be introduced to reduce the level of human involvement in decision making, to facilitate faster decision making or to make better use of the resources that are currently available.
4. Legal/regulatory. A new model may be required to make the business compliant with new legislation. Typically, this will mean replacing or upgrading the existing decision making infrastructure so that it becomes compliant.
5. Political. Sometimes an organization undertakes a project to bolster its image, by being able to say that they are using the latest techniques, or to give the impression that they are employing cutting edge technology.

One perspective is that the model is just a tool that can be used to help an organization meet its business objectives. The model has no intrinsic value in itself, unless it can be used in this capacity.

If the business objectives are financial and/or volume based, if the new model generates better predictions of customer behaviour than the existing system, then the business objectives and the modelling objectives are likely to be well aligned (Finlay 2009). However, it's important not to confuse financial objectives with volume based ones. More customers does not necessarily mean more profit. A bank may set the marketing team an objective of recruiting 75,000 new credit card customers this quarter. Therefore, the marketing team will, if necessary, recruit uncreditworthy customers to ensure its target is met. This strategy is common in the early stage of a product's life. The goal is to build up the customer base as fast as possible, even if this means sacrificing profitability in the short term. Sometimes this can be a good strategy, but it was just this type of behaviour that lead to the US sub-prime mortgage crisis in the mid-2000s and the worldwide credit crunch that followed. In a saturated mortgage market, US mortgage providers continued trying to expand their customer bases. They did this by moving into the sub-prime market, granting mortgages to people who clearly couldn't keep up their repayments in the long term. For a short period of time the strategy appeared to work well because of the resulting increase in business volumes. However, within a few months many banks were incurring huge losses as uncreditworthy customers defaulted on their mortgages in large numbers.

If a model is to be used for the first time, as an operational tool replacing human decision makers, then a key objective may be to develop a very simple (linear or CART) model, containing just a few predictor variables. This is so that everyone can understand the model and so facilitate the acceptance of such models within the organization. In a similar vein, another operational reason for a modelling project may be to simplify the existing decision making system. Decision making systems have a tendency to evolve over time as additional models are developed and more complex sets of decision rules are applied. The end result is a complex and unstable system that no one really understands. As complexity increases, there comes a point where the time and cost involved in making further enhancements becomes prohibitive. Therefore, the only practical option is a complete redevelopment to deliver a more manageable system.

Sometimes models are replaced because new data becomes available, creating the possibility that more predictive models can be built than those currently in place. In these cases a project may be tackled in two phases. The first phase is a "proof of concept" exercise to establish how much benefit, if any, a model incorporating the new data provides over and above the incumbent model. As a "proof of concept" model that will not be used operationally, it may be possible to adopt a Rapid Application Development (RAD) approach, and bypass many standard control/audit/ documentation procedures in order to deliver some initial results very quickly. The project only moves into a more formal and controlled second phase if there is clear evidence that a new model will provide enough uplift in performance to justify its cost of development and implementation.

New consumer legislation is appearing all the time. This can mean that it is no longer permissible to continue using certain data items in decision making processes. In the early 2000s in the UK, the use of all data about other individuals, such as other family members, was deemed illegal under data protection legislation.[2] In this type of scenario the goal is not to build a more predictive model (although this is an added benefit if it proves to be the case) but rather to construct a model that complies with the new law. Alternatively, new legislation may result in changes in the relationships between certain items of data and how people behave. Again, taking a UK example, the introduction of Individual Voluntary Agreements (IVAs) in 2004 (a formalized debt management procedure used instead of bankruptcy) resulted in customer's exhibiting a new type of behaviour (applying for an IVA). Many existing credit scoring models could not predict IVAs very well, and therefore, required redevelopment.

2.2.1   Project scope

Project scope refers to the tasks and deliverables that fall within the project's remit. Things that will be undertaken or delivered as part of the project are described as "in scope". Things that are someone else's responsibility and will not be considered by the project are "out of scope".

It seems obvious that delivery of a model will be within the scope of a modelling project, but there are a lot of other tasks that occur around the construction of a model that may, or may not, form part of the project. Therefore, a clear view of what is in and out of scope should be established at an early stage. Some typical scoping issues to consider are:

- Who has responsibility for gathering the data that will be used to build the model?
- Who is going to sample, clean and prepare the data?
- Who is going to build the model?
- Who is going to determine the decision rules that determine how the model will be used?
- Where does responsibility for implementation of the model lie?

- If the implementation of the model has knock on effects to other systems across the business – who is responsible for dealing with these effects?
- If the model is to be deployed operationally, how will the performance of the model be monitored to ensure it continues to make accurate forecasts? Who is going to do this, the model developer or someone else?

If responsibility for model implementation is within scope, then due consideration must be given to the resources required to do this. If the model sits within a business critical system, such as an insurance quotation system or a credit card application processing system, then this will include a comprehensive test plan that needs to be completed satisfactorily before the implementation goes live. A detailed risk assessment may also be required. Likewise, consideration needs to be given to other systems and processes that may be affected by implementation of the model. If new items of data need capturing from credit or insurance customers, customer service staff will need educating about the changes they will see in the information their computer screens prompt them to ask. To educate staff about changes to their screens may only require a short time, but if staff are not informed about the changes before the amended system goes live, chaos will ensue when staff arrive at work to find that the system they work with has changed. Another thing to think about is how call centre staff are assessed and incentivized. If staff performance is based on the average number of applications they process each day, then lengthening customer contact time by adding additional questions to operators' scripts will cause problems and impact staff moral, unless the metrics used to assess performance are revised appropriately.

If the decision rules associated with a new model result in more or less cases being referred for review by human assessors, then appropriate thought needs to be given to the staffing levels required to meet the change in workload.

Sometimes modelling projects are contracted out to external model developers. In this case there will in effect be two modelling projects running concurrently and each project will have its own scope. From the external developer's perspective, their project may begin only when their client provides them with a sample of data. They undertake analysis of the data, pre-process it and construct a model that they deliver to their client. From the client's perspective, their project begins much earlier with gathering and cleaning the data that is then handed over to the external developer to do their bit. The project only ends when the model delivered by the developer has been implemented within their operational systems and regular monitoring of the model is underway. So although both organizations would describe themselves as undertaking a modelling project, the scope of the external developer's project is much narrower than that of its client.

2.2.2   Cheap, quick or optimal?

The performance of any project can be measured by the following three criteria:

1. Delivery. Has the project delivered what was intended to the required quality standard?
2. Time. Has the project been completed by the planned date?
3. Cost. Has the project been delivered to the agreed budget?

Organizations often want to deliver a lot, but are always constrained by time and cost. This means there has to be compromise between what is delivered, the time the project takes and what it costs. Consider an insurer that has seen the number of new policies it underwrites falling by 2–3 percent year on year. At the start of the financial year it has been agreed that to reverse the declining trend the company's response and conversion models will be redeveloped – the goal being to generate more responders from the same marketing spend, and of these responders convert a greater proportion of them into policy holders. There are two proposals on the table.

- Proposal 1. Construct a suite of new models, and at the same time upgrade the organizations systems to provide access to a range of new data sources that will mean far more predictive models can be constructed. The project manager believes this will take a minimum of 12 months to complete. It is estimated that this approach will yield a 30 percent increase in the number of new policies underwritten.
- Proposal 2. Construct a simple set of models and limit the project to consider only existing data sources so that no changes are required to the existing IT infrastructure. This option could be delivered in only three months, if some of the work was contracted out to a specialist modelling consultancy. However, the expected benefit from this solution is estimated to be only a 10 percent increase in the number of policies underwritten.

Overall, the estimated cost of the two proposals is about the same. The project sponsor (and primary decision maker) is the newly appointed marketing director, who has been tasked with reversing the declining trend in new policies by the end of the year. Therefore, she logically goes for the second option because this will help her achieve her objectives, even though the long term benefits to the company are likely to be greater if the first option was pursued.

What this example illustrates is a situation where the quality of the deliverable has been compromised to obtain benefit quickly. These types of trade-offs can also occur once a project is up and running. All projects are subject to a degree of uncertainty and things don't always go to plan. The main way in which the project manager deals with unforeseen events is to trade-off objectives against each other (Mantel et al. 2007, pp. 6–7). If the project slips behind schedule because data analysis is more complex than originally envisaged, then the project could be brought back on track by obtaining more analyst resource (at more cost). If this is not possible then a decision may be made to reduce the number of things that are delivered, or settle for something that works, but is sub-optimal.

If the quality of the deliverables has been deliberately sacrificed to obtain a quick win, then it is very important that this decision is approved by senior management and documented for prosperity. Otherwise, it can leave the project team exposed to accusations of cutting corners and shoddy work at a later date. On more than one occasion I have witnessed very capable and highly skilled people being accused of incompetence and blamed for delivering sub-standard solutions by people who only became involved in the project towards its conclusion, and were unaware of the quality/time/cost trade-off decisions that were made or the reasons for them.

2.3   Modelling objectives

One of the most important questions the project team must answer is: given the project's business objectives and scope, what behaviour should the model predict? Sometimes the answer is relatively unambiguous and flows naturally from the business objectives that have been set. Consider an insurance firm that has set itself an objective of increasing the number of quotations being converted into policies. The firm has decided that to achieve their business objective they want to lower the premiums quoted on some policies, while at the same time maintaining the overall losses that arise due to insurance claims that are made. One way this objective can be achieved is by upgrading the incumbent claim forecasting model so that more accurate forecasts of claim propensity are made. This results in some people receiving a revised estimate of claim propensity that is lower than under the old system. These people can therefore, be offered a lower premium than they would have received previously, which will increase conversion rates without increasing costs. Consequently, the modelling objective is to develop a classification model to predict the likelihood that someone makes a claim, which generates better forecasts of claim propensity than the incumbent forecasting system.

For many problems the choice of modelling objective is not so clear cut. There may be many possible alternatives that could be chosen, and it is important that the right choice is made. Otherwise, the resulting model will predict something other than the behaviour of interest. Credit scoring, for example, is usually treated as a classification problem. The objective is to predict the likelihood that someone who applies for a loan will be a "good" or "bad" payer. However, as we shall discuss in more detail later, what one means by "good payer" and "bad payer" is open to debate. One extreme is to consider someone a good payer only if they have never missed a payment over the entire term of the credit agreement. At the other end of the scale everyone may be considered a good payer *unless* they have missed so many payments that their loan has had to be written off. In practice there are many graduations between these two extremes, and the actual definition of what constitutes a good payer varies between lenders, and sometimes alternative definitions may even be adopted by different departments within the same organization.

It doesn't matter how good the rest of the model development process is, if the modelling objective is not well aligned with the business objectives then the project is unlikely to be a success.

2.3.1   Modelling objectives for classification models

As discussed in Chapter 1, the most popular customer forecasting problems are binary (two class) classification ones. The objective is to predict whether a behaviour will or will not occur. In order to discuss binary classification models in general terms, throughout the rest of the book common credit scoring terminology is adopted. Behavioural events are described in terms of "Good" and "Bad" behaviour. Good is used to describe when someone exhibits desired behaviour(s) and bad when they do not. Common parlance is to refer to the modelling objective as the "good/bad definition". From a direct marketing perspective, good would be where a response to direct marketing activity is received, whereas bad would be when there was no response. Likewise, for insurance, not making a claim would be classified as good behaviour and making a claim would be classified as bad behaviour.[3] Note that good and bad are taken to be mutually exclusive events. One or the other can occur, but not both.

Sometimes, there are more than two classes of behaviour a customer can exhibit. It is possible to construct multi-class models that predict the probability of each behaviour occurring. However, this is not a popular approach and does not necessarily give good results (Reichert, et al. 1983). Standard practice is to reduce the problem to just two classes; that is, good and bad. There is therefore, a requirement to decide which behaviours should be classified as good and which as bad. In credit scoring, those with a perfect repayment record are best (good) and those where the full loan amount ends up being written-off are worst (bad). However, many loan customers will miss odd payments now and again. Some customers will enter a state of serious delinquency for a considerable period of time and be subject to extensive debt recovery action, but eventually repay what they owe. There are also situations where a small proportion of the debt is written-off, but overall the lender has made a

Table 2.1   Good/bad definition

		Good/Bad definition for a personal loan			
Group	Current delinquency status (months past due)	Worst delinquency status (months past due) in the last six months	Good/bad definition	Number of cases	% of cases
1	0	0	Good	198,932	79.57
2	0	1	Good	19,953	7.98
3	1	0	Good	8,500	3.40
4	1	1	Good	4,650	1.86
5	0	2	Good	2,268	0.91
6	1	2	Indeterminate	2,775	1.11
7	0	3	Indeterminate	1,328	0.53
8	0	4+	Bad	374	0.15
9	1	3+	Bad	443	0.18
10	2	3+	Bad	727	0.29
11	3+	0+	Bad	10,051	4.02

	Totals	
Goods		234,303
Indeterminates		4,103
Bads		11,595

Odds =	20.21	
Bad Rate =	4.72%	

Note: Worst delinquency status in the last six months excludes the current delinquency status.

profit from the relationship. With a credit card, many customers will receive a card, but never use it. So while the customer has always maintained an up-to-date repayment record, the account is loss making due to the cost of running the account. Which of these behaviours should be classified as good and which as bad? Typically, behaviours will be ranked from best to worst. A decision is then taken as to which group each behaviour should be assigned. An example of such an exercise undertaken for a personal loan product is shown in Table 2.1.

In Table 2.1 the good/bad definition is based on two measures of repayment behaviour. These are the current delinquency status of someone's account and the historic delinquency status of their account over the previous six months. Groups 1–5, where there has only ever been a history of mild delinquency, are classified as good. Those currently 3+ months past due and/or with a history of serious delinquency within the last six months are classified as bad (groups 8–11).

At this point it is worthwhile introducing the two measures at the bottom of Table 2.1. The first is the bad rate and the other is the good:bad odds (or just odds). These are the two most widely used statistics in consumer behavioural modelling and are defined as:

$$Odds = G/B$$
$$Bad\ Rate = B/(G + B)$$

Where G is the number of goods in the population and B is the number of bads.[4] The odds and bad rate are different ways of expressing the proportion of goods and bads within the population and each can be expressed in terms of the other:

$$Bad\ Rate = 1/(1+Odds)$$
$$Odds = 1/(Bad\ Rate) - 1$$

In Table 2.1 you will notice that those in groups 6 and 7 have been assigned to a third category of behaviour: "indeterminate". In theory it should be possible to classify any account as good or bad, but in practice there are nearly always some cases where it is difficult to be certain which classification should apply. This may be because there is insufficient information within an organization's IT systems to determine if a given behaviour is good or bad, or it may be due to internal political issues. It is not unusual for different parts of an organization to have slightly different views as to what constitutes good and bad behaviour, reflecting the somewhat different (and sometimes conflicting) business objectives that business functions are tasked with achieving. Therefore, the good/bad definition may be somewhat ambiguous and/or subjective in nature.

If indeterminates exist, then they are usually excluded from the process used to construct the model, although a sample of indeterminates is usually taken so that the scores generated by the model can be examined for the indeterminate population. Removing indeterminates means that the problem remains binary in nature, with the objective of creating a model that predicts good/bad behaviour. From a theoretical perspective this raises questions about the appropriateness of the model that is developed, because by excluding indeterminates the model will be biased towards the goods and bads, and it won't necessarily provide good estimates for indeterminates. In practice, if the number of indeterminates is relatively small (which in my experience is less than about 5 percent of the population) then the effects on model performance will not be very significant. There is also an argument that defining some marginal behaviours as indeterminate leads to better models. This is because by removing cases around the margin there is a clear divide between good and bad behaviour, and this makes it easier to develop models that can distinguish between each behaviour. However, if the proportion of indeterminates within the population is very high (which in my experience is where they constitute more than about 25 percent of the population) then the model risks being significantly sub-optimal because it will only be good at identifying the very best and worst cases (although it might be very good at doing this). High quality predictions will not be made for those in the middle – which is precisely the region where organizations typically want to make decisions.[5]

2.3.2   Roll rate analysis

A good question is: how is the mapping between individual behaviours and the good/bad definition, such as the one shown in Table 2.1, determined? In many organizations a standard good/bad definition exists. Therefore, the decision may be simply to continue applying this definition to all modelling projects going forward, and no additional work is required to establish what the good/bad definition should be. If the good/bad definition is up for debate, then the decision about how to define it is usually based on a mixture of expert opinion and statistical analysis. Experienced credit professionals will express their opinions about what they believe constitutes good/bad behaviour, and these opinions will be tested by examination of the available data. One tool that is widely used to assist in this process is roll rate analysis, as illustrated in Table 2.2.

Table 2.2   Roll rate analysis

Number of months delinquent in May	Number of months delinquent in June (one statement period later)							
	0	1	2	3	4	5	6+ Write-off)	Total
0	92%	8%	0%	0%	0%	0%	0%	100%
1	79%	11%	10%	0%	0%	0%	0%	100%
2	55%	0%	22%	23%	0%	0%	0%	100%
3	11%	0%	0%	17%	72%	0%	0%	100%
4	3%	0%	0%	0%	10%	87%	0%	100%
5	1%	0%	0%	0%	0%	4%	95%	100%

Note: Sometimes an account may partially recover. If an account is four months delinquent and two full payments are made, then the account will roll from four to two months delinquent.

Table 2.2 shows how the arrears positions (delinquency status) of personal loan customers changes from one month to the next. In the first row 92 percent of customers who were up-to-date with their repayments in May remained up-to-date in June, one month later. The remaining 8 percent missed a payment and became one cycle delinquent. The roll rate between up-to-date and one cycle delinquent is said to be 8 percent. Likewise, of those accounts that were already one cycle delinquent in May, 79 percent rolled back to an up-to-date status, meaning that they made their next payment and cleared the arrears owning on the account. Eleven percent remained one cycle delinquent. This indicates they resumed repayments but did not make up the arrears owing. The remaining 10 percent missed another payment, rolling to two cycles delinquent.

The way Table 2.2 is used is to begin with the assumption that the worst possible behaviour is bad and the best possible behaviour is good. For this example, the worst behaviour is when an account is six cycles delinquent and is written-off. Therefore, these accounts are classified as bad. Likewise, those that are up-to-date are classified as good. The next stage is to consider where accounts in other states are likely to end up, based on the movement between delinquency states over time. If the roll rates to good or bad are very high, then these cases are also classified as good or bad respectively. In Table 2.2, of those that are five cycles delinquent in May, 95 percent roll to write-off one month later. Only 1 percent pay the arrears owing, with the remaining 4 percent making a single payment, and therefore, remaining five cycles delinquent. So there is a good case for saying that accounts that are currently five cycles delinquent should be classified as bad because they are very likely to end up being written-off eventually. If we continue with this logic, then there is also a strong case for classifying those that are three or four cycles delinquent as bad, because the roll rate from four to five delinquent is 87 percent, and the roll rate from three to four is 72 percent. However, the roll rates from two cycles delinquent to three cycles delinquent is only 23 percent – the majority recover. Therefore, there is a much weaker case for classifying them as bad. There is no specific rule to say what roll rates should lead to accounts being classified as good or bad, but in general if more than 50 percent of cases roll to a worse status it is probably sensible to classify these cases as bad.

There is no industry standard good/bad definition for consumer credit products, and every lender has their own definition of what constitutes good or bad loan repayment behaviour. However, Table 2.1 represents a fairly typical good/bad definition, and in practice many lenders use something similar to this for loans, credit cards, motor finance and other forms of lending. Current or recent delinquency of three or more months (90+ days past due) is classified as bad, while those that are up-to-date or who have only a mild history of delinquency (less than one month or 30 days past due) are classified as good.[6] Those in the middle are usually classified as indeterminate. If you are new to model building and are thinking about what the good/bad definition should be, then this definition is a good place to start. If you are in doubt about how to classify a certain type of customer behaviour, or there is limited data available, then a simple question to ask yourself is: given what you know about the customers' behaviour now, would you grant them credit again? If you can answer this question, then use your answer to define cases as good or bad. If you really can't decide, then placing them in the indeterminate category may be more appropriate.

2.3.3 Profit based good/bad definitions

Common sense dictates that those classified as good should be profit making and those classified as bad should be loss making. In consumer credit markets current and historic delinquency status is highly correlated with profitability. This is why they are widely used when formulating good/bad definitions, but this is not always the case. Consequently, it is common for other criteria, such as the revenue generated by accounts, to be incorporated into the good/bad definition, in addition to delinquency status.

In theory, if an organization can establish the precise revenues and costs associated with each customer, allowing then to generate a measure of customer profitability, then the good/bad definition can be based entirely on a customer's profit contribution. Positive profit equates to good and negative profit equates to bad. If this is the case, then the actual delinquency status of accounts is largely irrelevant (Finlay 2010). However, one needs to be aware of wider business and social issues that may have a bearing on how good/bad definitions are defined. In the credit card market, customers who make little use of their cards or who always pay their bills in full and hence generate no interest revenue, tend to be unprofitable. Common sense suggests that these cases should be classified as bad because they are loss making. However, the negative publicity that can arise from rejecting "bad" customers who always pay their bills on time is not something that many organizations want to deal with, and if one takes a strategic perspective – the losses generated from such bad publicity may outweigh the short term benefits associated with classifying such customers as bad. As a consequence, cases like these will either be treated as good, or at best pushed into the indeterminate category, rather than classified as bad. An interesting case to bear in mind is that of the egg credit card in the UK. Egg was at one time a leading UK provider of credit cards, which made a name for itself as the first organization to provide purely on-line credit card accounts in the late 1990s. In 2007 the egg credit card portfolio was purchased by Citigroup. A short while later 160,000 people, representing 7 percent of all egg customers, were told that their credit agreements were to be terminated with 30 days notice. At the time it was claimed this was because they were high risk customers who were likely to default. However, the general view expressed in the media and by industry experts was that these were good paying customers who weren't profitable (Mathiason and Insley 2008). Now this may well have been the case, and some would argue that Citigroup had the right to terminate agreements it had with customers it identified as unprofitable. However, the case caused a huge amount of media attention, with questions about the matter raised in the Houses of Parliament. The chief executive of egg resigned a short while later[7] (Farrell 2008). The lesson to learn from the egg fiasco is that wider business and social issues need appropriate consideration when deciding how to classify and treat people, in addition to narrow considerations that focus solely on short term customer profitability.

2.3.4   Continuous modelling objectives

In my experience, classification models are the most popular type of model used within the financial services industry to predict consumer behaviour. However, in recent years there has been increasing focus on the use of regression models to predict continuous financial behaviours. In particular, models of revenue, loss and profitability. Models to predict event times, such as when someone will default on a loan or how long it can be expected before they respond to a mailing have also been gaining popularity. Often regression models will be used in conjunction with classification models to make decisions on the basis of two or more dimensions of customer behaviour. In Chapter 1 an example of a classification model to predict the likelihood of an insurance claim was introduced, along with a regression model to predict the value of claims. It was then shown how these two models could be used together to aid setting premiums. Another example is a response model that predicts the likelihood that someone responds to a mail shot, used in conjunction with a model of lifetime customer value. The two model scores are used in combination to come up with a direct marketing strategy that maximizes the overall return from customers, taking into account acquisition cost and the revenue generated from customers once they have been acquired.

The general principles for defining the modelling objective for a regression model are not that different from those that apply to classification models. The key is to make sure the modelling objective represents what the business is trying to achieve. When the modelling objective is a financial measure there will often be a requirement to calculate the value of the modelling objective using a number of component parts. For instance, a credit card provider may have a customer database containing detailed transactional information about each customer's credit card usage, month end balances, payments and so on. They want to use this to generate a measure of net revenue that is used as the modelling objective. To generate an accurate measure of net revenue it is necessary to establish how much each customer has spent against different transaction types such as cash withdrawals, retail purchases, balance transfers, and then apply the appropriate interest rates, not forgetting that if a customer paid their balance off in full, then no interest charges apply to retail purchases that month. Late fees and other charges also need to be added in to the equation, as do payment holidays and other features of the relationship. In particular, if one is measuring profitability or customer lifetime value, it is important to consider the following:

- Should the modelling objective include or exclude fixed costs? For example, will the model be used to predict the marginal contribution from credit card transactions, or the overall contribution of the customer taking into account cost of funds, infrastructure, call centre costs and so on?

- From what point in time does the cost component of profit begin to accrue? Is it the point at which someone was first contacted, the point at which they applied for the product or the point at which they became a customer?
- Should the modelling objective include or exclude provision charges? (for credit/insurance products).
- Should revenues and costs be subject to net present value adjustments?[8]

There is also a need to consider which part of the population should be used to construct the model. For most binary classification problems, nearly all available cases (with the exception of indeterminates) can potentially be used for model construction. When modelling continuous objectives a large number of cases may have zero or missing values. Better models generally result if these cases are excluded. It is probably best to illustrate this point with an example. Let's return to the insurance example introduced in Chapter 1. Imagine the goal is to predict claim values so that individuals who are expected to make large claims are excluded from direct marketing activity. The insurer has a mailing list that they previously used to target customers with insurance offers, and have information about the claim history of those that subsequently took up the offer. Assume, for arguments sake, 20 percent of customers made a claim. There are two ways to go about approaching this problem.

1. Construct a single model of claim value, using all those that took out insurance. For the 80 percent that didn't make a claim, the value of the modelling objective (the claim value) will be zero.
2. Construct two models. The first is a classification model predicting the likelihood of a claim, constructed using all those that took out insurance. The second is a regression model of claim value. For this model only the 20 percent of cases that made a claim are used. The expected claim value is then calculated by multiplying the probability of a claim by the expected value of the claim.

In my experience, the second approach yields better (more accurate) results than the first.

2.3.5   Product level or customer level forecasting?

These days many people have multiple product holdings with a single financial services organization. I, for example, have a current account and two credit cards provided by my bank. If I decided to apply to my bank for a personal loan, they would make an assessment of my creditworthiness using a credit scoring model to predict how likely I am to be a good or bad customer. If the chance of my being a bad customer is too high, then they will decline my application, but what should the bank do if it believes I am likely to be a good customer on the new loan, but a bad customer on my existing credit cards? Organizations generally approach this type of forecasting problem in one of three ways:

1. Take a product level view. The modelling objective is based solely on behaviour associated with the product in question. For the model used to assess my loan application, the good/bad definition would have been based solely on information about the repayment behaviour of other loans. Data about customers' behaviour when using other products and services would not form part of the good/bad definition.
2. Take a multi-level view. A set of product level models are constructed, as described in (1). These are then combined to produce a single estimate of customer behaviour. So for my loan application, the bank would have generated two separate forecasts about how I was likely to behave. One using its model of loan repayment behaviour, and the other using its model of credit card repayment behaviour. These two forecasts would then have been combined to generate an overall view of my creditworthiness.
3. Take a customer level view. The modelling objective incorporates information about customer behaviour when using two or more different products. So for the model used to assess my loan application, the good/bad definition used to construct the model would have been based on information about previous customers' card and loan repayment behaviour.

The above example refers to credit granting, but the same options exist in relation to direct marketing and insurance. For a long time the general view within the financial services industry has been that a customer level view is desirable. This is because it provides the most complete picture of how consumers behave, and hence aids in developing an integrated, customer centric, multi-product strategy. However, when considering which approach to take, it is very important to consider the business infrastructure that is currently in place. The operational and IT changes required to move from a product level view to a customer level view can be considerable, possibly requiring tens of millions of dollars of investment and many years effort to achieve. Consequently, the decision to make such a change is usually outside of the scope of a standard modelling project.

As Anderson (2007, p. 311) notes, a multi-level view is often the best option. It provides many of the benefits of a full customer level view, but often requires far fewer resources to implement. This is because all the base data required to construct the model remains at product level. Only the final model score is held at customer level.

A further point to note is that it is much more difficult to implement, monitor and maintain customer level and multi-level models. The development cycle for new and replacement models is also longer than for product level models. Upgrading to a multi-level or customer level view is only likely to be of benefit if the number of customers with multiple product holdings is considerable, and there are clear synergies to be gained from dealing with the customer from a multi-product perspective. I would suggest that if the proportion of customers with more than one of an organization's products is less than about 20 percent, then the cost/benefit case for upgrading the relevant systems to allow full customer level forecasting will be difficult to justify.

2.4   Forecast horizon (outcome period)

Over what period of time (known as the forecast horizon or the outcome period) should accounts be observed before the modelling objective is defined? Insurance policies often run for 12 months, and therefore, 12 months is the obvious choice of forecast horizon for insurance products of this type.[9] For many other types of consumer behaviour the choice of outcome period is more open to debate. There may be no fixed time as to when a customer event can occur, or the time is so far in the future it is impractical to use it. In credit scoring, where the goal is to predict if someone is a good or bad payer, the most obvious choice for the forecast horizon is the full term of the credit agreement. Someone is classified as good or bad on the basis of how well they repaid their loan. However, a residential mortgage agreement can span a period of 25 years or more, and it is impractical to go back and take a sample of accounts from 25 years ago – sufficient data to build reliable models just isn't available. Therefore, a shorter outcome period must be chosen. For products such as credit cards and overdrafts, the credit agreement may not have a fixed end date. Accounts remain active for as long as the customer continues to use them or for as long as the lender wishes to maintain a relationship with the customer. Likewise, for direct marketing, there is in theory no limit to the length of time between someone being sent a communication and their response to it.

Another issue is the longer the outcome period the worse any fore-cast is likely to be. In this respect, forecasting consumer behaviour is just like weather forecasting. Tomorrow's forecast is usually pretty good, but forecasts for a week or more ahead are little better then random guessing. Similarly, models that predict consumer behaviour over short timeframes tend to be more reliable than longer term forecasts.

In practice, the precise choice of outcome period is something of a compromise. It must be long enough to capture general patterns of consumer behaviour and yet short enough to be of practical use. Consider a credit card provider that is going to undertake a direct mail-ing campaign to recruit new customers. The organization undertakes a test mailing to a group of 50,000 potential customers. The results from the test mailing will then be used to construct a model to predict how likely people are to respond to a mailing. The model will then be applied to the full mailing list containing several million peoples' contact details. Only those the model predicts are likely to respond will be mailed as part of the full campaign. So the key question is: how long should the

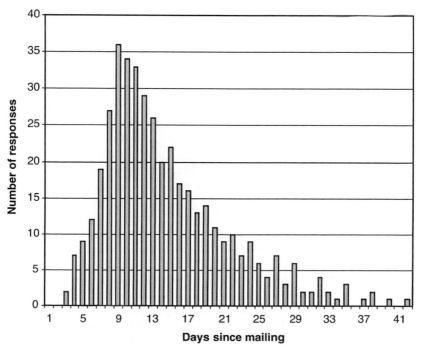

Figure 2.1   Mailing response over time

organization wait for responses from the test mailing before building the model? A simple approach is just to plot the number of responses over time, and then decide, on a somewhat arbitrary basis, what the forecast horizon should be, based on the pattern of responses that is observed. Consider the response pattern displayed in Figure 2.1.

In Figure 2.1, by the 42nd day following the mailing the number of responses has dropped to a very low level. Common sense says that very few additional responses are likely to be received after this time. Therefore, the data that has already been received is sufficient and model construction can commence without further delay. A general rule of thumb is that if you think that more than about 95 percent of all responses have been received, then this is sufficient to allow construction of a good quality model.

2.4.1   Bad rate (emergence) curves

For credit scoring, a similar approach to that presented in the previous section for mailing campaigns, is to produce bad rate curves,[10] based on historical account performance. A sample of accounts is taken at a point in time, and the good/bad definition is applied one month later, two months later, three months later and so on. An example of a bad rate curve is shown in Figure 2.2.

To produce Figure 2.2. it was necessary to take a sample of data from a considerable period of time in the past. In this case, credit applications from at least three years ago. The good/bad definition was then applied to accounts when they were aged one month, two months and so on, up to 36 months. The bad rate for accounts in the sample were then calculated and plotted against the age of the account. Note that in this example, the definition of bad is based on three months delinquent, and therefore, given that someone's first repayment is due one month after account opening, it takes a minimum of four months for someone to be classified as bad.

The principle underpinning the idea of the bad rate curve is that if a customer is going to "go bad" then they are more likely to do so within the first few months of the agreement, rather than towards the end, and this behaviour has been observed many times in consumer credit portfolios.[11] Once a customer has established a good repayment record for a period of time, then this is indicative that they will continue to make their repayments in future. The bad rate curve is used to select the time by which a considerable proportion of all bad cases have been observed. Choosing this point is somewhat arbitrary. For Figure 2.2, around 15 months would seem sensible, but a reasonable

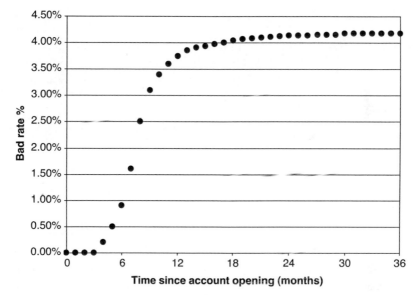

Figure 2.2 Bad rate curve

argument could probably be put forward for anything between 12 and 18 months.

The forecast horizon for any particular modelling objective will be problem and organization specific. In practice, most outcome periods for credit products tend to be in the region of 6–24 months, and in my experience 9–15 months is the norm for credit cards, mail order and short term lending. For mortgages and personal loans 18–24 months is more widely applied. While this is not sufficient time to fully evaluate repayment behaviour over the entire term of most credit agreements, it is sufficient to gain a reasonable picture of an individual's repayment behaviour.

2.4.2 Revenue/loss/value curves

The principles applied to produce bad rate curves for classification problems can also be applied to regression problems to predict measures such as loss given default, revenue and lifetime customer value. One simply plots average cumulative values over time, instead of cumulative bad rate over time. As for bad rate curves, one looks to identify where the graph begins to flatten, indicating that the majority of the behaviour has been exhibited by that time.

Typically, forecast horizons for models predicting revenue, loss and customer value are between 12 and 36 months.

2.5 Legal and ethical issues

Financial services, and credit granting in particular, have always been controversial. The earliest surviving legal code regulating credit agreements is contained within the Babylonian code of Hammurabi, dating to around 1750 BC. The Bible, the Koran and the Torah all contain prohibitions against lending practices and the charging of interest. In ancient Greece, debt caused such endemic problems that the people appointed a new ruler, Solon, in 594 BC, specifically to deal with it. He did this by banning the securitization of debt against one's person (thus preventing debtors and their family's being sold into slavery for unpaid debts) and using state funds to buy back debtors who had previously been sold abroad. Just prior to the start of the nineteenth century, it was estimated that half of the entire prison population of England were incarcerated solely for their inability (or unwillingness) to pay their debts (Finn 2003, pp. 111–12). Even today, there are stories in the media on an almost daily basis about the mis-selling of financial services products and the poor treatment that customer's have received.

Given credit's somewhat chequered history, it's not surprising that a host of legislation exists in many countries to protect consumers against what are considered unfair/unethical practices by the financial services industry. Each country has its own set of laws and regulations, but the general principles of financial services regulation tend to be very similar wherever you go in the world.

The vast majority of consumer legislation within retail financial services deals with the process by which financial agreements are entered into, the form and wording of advertisements and the processes that must be followed when someone breaches the terms of a credit agreement. There are however, a number of areas that need consideration when developing models of consumer behaviour. These are:

1. Restricted data. In many countries it is illegal to use information about Race, Gender, Sexual Orientation or Religion to make decisions about who to grant credit or insurance. In the US, Marital Status and Age are also subject to restriction. It is also illegal to use information that could be taken as proxy for these items. There is a well known credit industry story about an organization that tried to use the number of syllables in someone's name as a predictor variable in their models, as a surrogate for ethnic origin. This would be illegal in the UK or US today.
2. Data protection. EU data protection law requires organizations operating within the EU to gain someone's permission before holding or

using data about them.[12] This means it is illegal to apply models to people who have not given their permission to have decisions made about them in that way. In the UK, every credit application and insurance quotation contains a data protection statement. This states the purposes for which information provided by the applicant will be used. The applicant gives permission for their data to be used for the stated purposes by signing the application form.

3. Explicability of score based decisions. In the US, there is a requirement to be able to say explicitly why someone had their application for credit declined. If a credit scoring system is used to make lending decisions, it must be possible to say why someone received the score they did. For this reason lenders tend to favour simple linear models over more complex model forms, such as neural networks.

4. Redlining. Some countries prohibit making decisions about how to treat people on the basis of the zip code/postcode in which they live. Redlining is often seen as a proxy for race, because people of the same ethnic origin often live together. This is not to say that postcode/zip code level data cannot be used as predictor variables in models, but that it can't form the major component of the score someone receives.

In countries with less well developed financial systems, legislation around the use of data may be less restrictive than that described here. However, even if its legal for you to use information such as gender, race and religion in your region, I ask you to consider if it is ethical to do so.

2.6   Data sources and predictor variables

Models of consumer behaviour are created by determining the relationships that exist between a set of predictor variables and the modelling objective, using a large and representative sample of data. The more data available and the better the quality of data, the more predictive the model will be.

In recent years many organizations have come to realize the value of good data. As a consequence, the quality of the databases maintained by many financial services organizations and their data management practices have improved significantly. However, it is still the case that the data used for model building often comes from a variety of sources that need matching together. In addition, many items of data may be redundant, contain garbage, be unstable over time or otherwise be unsuitable for model construction.

The starting point to address these shortcomings is to carry out a scoping exercise to determine which predictor variables are going to be considered for model development. This involves coming up with a list of databases and data tables that the organization holds, and then reviewing the data held on each one to decide which items of data are suitable candidates for model construction. In particular, it is important to determine if data available for model development will also be available at the point of model application. If a credit scoring model is going be implemented within a bank's application processing system, then all the predictor variables that might feature in the model must be available within the application processing system. If a variable is not available, there needs to be a discussion about whether making the necessary changes to the application processing system is within the project's scope. If it is decided that such changes are out of scope, then there is little point in including that data within the model development sample. I have come across more than one modelling project where much time and effort were wasted because the team building the model did not consider the data available within the implementation platform. The result was that the models had to be rebuilt, with the offending predictor variables removed.

The output of the scoping exercise should be a data dictionary. This is a list detailing which data items are going to be considered for model construction and from where they will be sourced. As well as potential predictor variables taken from the sample point, the data dictionary should also include the outcome point variables that will be used to define the modelling objective (such as current and historic delinquency states for a credit scoring project). Unique match keys, such as account and customer numbers, should also be identified so that additional information can be attached to the sample at a later date, if required.

A simple short textual description of the data should be included in the data dictionary, along with any technical field names and format information. If there is a data item on a database called A196 that holds details about an individual's residential status (home owner, renter, living with their parents and so on), then there should be an explanatory statement to that effect. At the project planning stage it is not necessary to spend a lot of time evaluating every individual item of data in great detail, or determining the full range of values that an item of data may take. Instead, the goal is to come up with a list of variables that *might* feature in the model. These are going to be carried forward to the data gathering/preparation/pre-processing stages of the project

Table 2.3   Data dictionary

Ref.	Variable name	Source table	Format	Description
Sample point data				
1	A001	Application form	Text	Application ID (Match key)
2	A002	Application form	Text	Customer ID (Match key)
3	A003	Application form	Numeric	Age of applicant
4	A004	Application form	Numeric	Applicant gross annual income
5	A005	Application form	Text	Residential status
6	A006	Application form	Numeric	Time in current employment
...	...	...	...	...
...	...	...	...	...
29	A029	Application form	Numeric	Loan amount requested
30	A030	Application form	Numeric	Term of loan requested
...	...	...	...	...
...	...	...	...	...
90	B001	Credit report	Numeric	Worst current delinquency status for all active credit accounts
91	B002	Credit report	Numeric	Total outstanding balance on all revolving credit accounts
92	B003	Credit report	Numeric	Number of credit searches in last six months
...	...	...	...	...
...	...	...	...	...
187	Credit score	Decision	Numeric	Applicant's credit score
188	InitialDec	Decision	Text	Initial decision code, indicating the preliminary score based decision
189	Reason4	Decision	Text	Final decision code, indicating if the loan application was granted or declined.
Outcome point data				
190	CurrBal	Performance	Numeric	Current account balance
191	CurrDelstat	Performance	Numeric	Current delinquency status
192	DelStat1_12	Performance	Numeric	Worst delinquency status in the last 12 months

where more detailed analysis will be undertaken. As a rough guide, it shouldn't be necessary to spend more than 2–3 days, and perhaps less, to undertake a scoping exercise of this type. An extract from a data dictionary for a personal loan credit scoring project is shown in Table 2.3.

The second and third columns in Table 2.3 show the variable name and the table in the organization's data warehouse from which the data is sourced. The fourth column shows the data format (numeric or text) and the fifth column contains a short explanatory description. The two main sources of predictor variables (taken from the sample point at the start of the forecast horizon) are the Application form table and the Credit report table. Relevant information is also taken from the Decision table. Decision table information won't be used for model construction, but provides details of the existing credit score and the actual decisions that were taken about loan applications. This information will be used for comparing the performance of the new model against the existing credit scoring system. Outcome point data used to define the modelling objective (taken from the end of the forecast horizon) comes from the Performance table, which includes current and historic delinquency status, as well as the outstanding balance on the account.

Sometimes new variables, derived as functions of existing variables will also be considered, and these should also be listed within the data dictionary. For example, income and household expenditure may be two data items that are available for model construction, but an experienced analyst will know that the ratio of income to household expenditure is likely to be a better predictor of someone's creditworthiness than either variable on its own. If this ratio is not on any existing data table then it needs to be calculated. As with other items of data, consideration needs to be given to the resources required to implement derived characteristics at the point of model application.

For a small project, the data dictionary may contain fewer than 20 variables. For a large modelling project, it is not unusual for the data dictionary to contain 400–500 variables or more.

2.7   Resource planning

Delivery dates and budgets will often be set by senior management before the more detailed aspects of the project are decided. It then becomes a case of delivering the best possible model, given the time and cost constraints that have been imposed.

2.7.1 Costs

The largest cost of most modelling projects is the salary and administrative costs of those working on the project. A typical individual is only
productive for around 200 days a year, once holiday, staff development,
administration, illness and so on are taken into account. The cost to
an organization of employing someone is typically 1.5–2.0 times salary
taking into account taxes, pension, health care and so on. So for an
employee earning $100,000 a year, the day rate cost of that person will be
in the region of $750–$1,000 a day.

Using the $1,000 a day figure, project costs may range from less than
$5,000 for a one-off "quick and dirty" model taking just a few days
to produce, to around $1,000,000–2,000,000 for larger projects, such as
the redevelopment of a bank's entire suite of behavioural scoring models,
taking into account testing, implementation and monitoring.

Another cost associated with modelling projects is the cost of data
acquisition. This may be very little if all data can be sourced internally.
However, if it is necessary to purchase information from an external
source then the cost could be significant. In the UK for example, acquiring historic credit reports from a credit reference agency is likely to cost in
the region of $35,000 for a sample containing 50,000 records.

IT costs (other than person time involved in testing and implementation) are only likely to be significant if additional hardware or
software is required to implement the model. It is important to remember
that even relatively small changes to IT systems, such as adding a new
item of data to a database, can incur considerable costs and take many
weeks to complete once testing and risk assessments are taken into
account. This is particularly true for the legacy systems that some large
banks maintain and which may not be well documented.

If model implementation results in changes to operational processes
undertaken by customer services staff – such as changes to what they
see on their computer terminals, then staff education costs also need to
be considered. This cost can be considerable if a large number of staff
are involved, even though the time required to educate each individual
may only be a few minutes.

2.7.2 Project plan

Once the project requirements have been gathered a project plan can
be produced. A professional tool, such as Microsoft Project can be used
to produce the project plan, but given the scale of a typical modelling
project, it is perfectly feasible to produce something using Microsoft
Word or Excel, or even by hand using nothing more than pen and paper.

Most projects tend to be pretty linear in nature, with eight or nine main stages that occur sequentially – as discussed in the previous chapter in relation to Figure 1.5.

It is important to remember that members of the project team may have other duties and responsibilities. This requires the project manager to plan ahead to ensure people are available when required and the project schedule takes into account their other commitments. In my experience, perhaps the biggest single cause of project delays has been when key signatories/stakeholders have not been available to sign-off project deliverables and/or make decisions about the direction of the project. One cannot expect to finish some analysis on a Monday evening, and then have everyone round a table first thing Tuesday morning to review it. Even if the meeting has been planned well in advance, people need time to review materials prior to meetings – usually at least 24 hours and ideally several days. It's a poor project manager who only circulates a document an hour before the meeting to review it.

With some types of project it is relatively easy to shorten the overall project plan by splitting the project into several sub-projects, each of which is tackled by a separate team. The sub-projects are then integrated together towards the end of the project. If you are building a ten mile stretch of road, you could have one team working on the entire road. Alternatively, you could have ten teams each working on a one mile stretch, which in theory will result in a ten times reduction in the project's length. This is an example of a project that is highly parallel in nature. Model building projects on the other hand are essentially sequential in nature. Many tasks logically follow on from one another and cannot start until the preceding task is complete. It is also true that better models tend to result if the analyst who operates the statistical software that generates the model has also been involved in gathering and preparing the data. This is so that they develop an intuitive understanding of the data they are working with. Consequently, throwing more bodies at a modelling project is not likely to result in a massive reduction in model development time. Instead, if faster delivery times are required then it is generally a case of overtime for the analyst or fewer/lower quality deliverables. That's not to say that *some* gains can't be made from employing more analysts. If the project scope encompasses several different models, then a different analyst may be able to work on each one. Similarly, if data is coming from a number of different databases, it may be possible to assign the data pre-processing associated with each database to a separate analyst.

2.8   Risks and issues

An issue is something that stands in the way of the project delivering its objects on time and to cost, and therefore, needs to be dealt with. If there is no one within the business technically qualified to construct the model, then this is an issue that needs to be addressed. One solution is to recruit someone with the required skills or to have someone trained. Another option is to contract out the analyst role to an external supplier.

A risk on the other hand, is something that could happen, but it's not certain. If there is only one analyst with the technical knowledge to construct a model, there is a risk that they will leave mid-project to take up alternative employment. Something needs to be done to mitigate the risk. This could be by doing something to reduce the chance of the risk occurring to an acceptable level, or to put in place a plan to minimize the effect of the risk, should it occur. One strategy to reduce the risk would be to offer the analyst an incentive to stay, such as a bonus, if they complete their part of the project successfully. Alternatively, a second analyst could be trained or recruited, thus reducing the impact to the project should the analyst leave. A third option would be to pay a retainer to an external supplier who guarantees to provide the necessary analytical resource if the analyst leaves.

Good practice is to hold an open session as part of the project planning process, where project team members can talk freely about what they see as risk and issues. Risks are then prioritized by the likelihood of the risk occurring and its potential magnitude. Often this is done in a fairly arbitrary/ad-hoc way based on expert opinion or simple statistics. For example, the risk of the analyst leaving for alternative employment may be set at 15 percent, based on staff turnover figures for the previous year.

It is the project manager's responsibility to decide upon the magnitude and likelihood of each risk/issue, and then manage the process of dealing with each one in turn. The reader should be aware that it is very easy to get bogged down with issues and potential risks and it is easy to come up with all sorts of potential disasters that would be catastrophic for the project, but very unlikely to occur. The analyst could get eaten by a lion – a tragedy no doubt, but the chance of it happening is so small that it's not worth thinking about. My own rule of thumb is to only spend time thinking about a risk if I believe the chance of it occurring is more than about 5 percent *and* the cost to the project, should the risk occur, is more than 5 percent of the total project cost.

2.9   Documentation and reporting

For large and complex IT/construction projects hundreds of documents will be produced throughout the course of the project. As discussed earlier in the chapter, even a large modelling project is not on this scale, but there is still a need for good quality documentation. In credit and insurance markets in particular, models used to make hundreds of millions of dollars worth of lending and insurance decisions, are increasingly subject to external audit by the regulatory authorities in compliance with regulations such as BASEL II and Solvency II. Having a good clear record of the decisions that were made and why, a log of risk and issues, performance metrics and so on will help the model pass the audit process.

Organizations with mature decision making systems will have built and rebuilt their models many times. Consequently, there will often be template documents available. If this is the case, then it makes sense to use the templates that are available because they will have been seen and approved by auditors and senior managers in the past.

For small scale projects that are not subject to such stringent documentary/ audit requirements, then it is still good practice to have project documentation, but less is required and it can be maintained in a much more informal way. For a single use mailing selection model, documentation could just be a set of e-mails between the project sponsor and the project manager and/or the analyst doing the work.

Sadly, another reason for maintaining good documentation is that people have notoriously selective memories, particularly when blame is about to be proportioned for something that went wrong. Having documentary evidence of what occurred is good practice so that it is clear what was done and why. This will help to ensure lessons are learnt for next time, and if blame does need to be proportioned for any shortcomings with the project, then it's directed at the right people.

2.9.1   Project requirements document

A project requirements document is somewhat analogous to what an IT professional would refer to as a "business requirements document". Its purpose is to capture all the key project planning decisions and to communicate these to the members of the project team. The project manager should have responsibility for its production towards the beginning of the project, and it should be signed off by the project sponsor, project manager and the decision makers before the project moves beyond the project planning phase. This ensures there is a formal record confirming that the project manager was happy with the project plan and that it was approved by senior management.

The project requirements document should not be too long winded, and does not necessarily need to go into every single aspect of the project in minute detail, but it should capture all the important aspects of the project. As a guide, all the project requirements documents that I have seen or produced have been between five and 50 pages in length, possibly with one or two appendices. The average length is about 20 pages. The project requirements document should contain a separate section for each of the main areas of project planning, as discussed in the previous sections of this chapter. For example, a section for roles and responsibilities, a section covering business objectives and scope, a section on modelling objectives, details of the data dictionary, the forecast horizon to be applied and so on.

When writing a project requirements document there are two things to bear in mind. First, much of the information in the document will be reused to produce the final documentation at the end of the project. In theory, the final project documentation should be just the project requirements document with details of the model and relevant performance metrics tacked on the end as additional sections. Second, if at some point in the future someone asks why a particular decision was made, such as a 15 month forecast horizon was chosen for credit scoring model for a store card instead of a more common 12 month one, then the document should contain sufficient information to answer the question as to why 15 months was chosen. There could, for example, be a copy of a bad rate curve and any other documentation that was produced, together with some descriptive text explaining the decision.

The project requirements document should be viewed as a "Living document" that, subject to approval by the original signatories, can be amended or added to should the requirements of the project change during the course of the project. In this way the document should remain current and not become out-of-date as the project progresses.

2.9.2 Interim documentation

A typical project will generate a good deal of output in the form of meeting minutes, ad-hoc analysis, preliminary results and so on. Some of this may be important, but much of it will be only of temporary use and can be discarded once the project is complete. As a rule, if it is important enough to keep, then it should go into the final documentation at the end of the project.

2.9.3   Final project documentation (documentation manual)

Once the project is complete, full details of the project should be recorded for prosperity. This will aid learning for future projects, and act as a reference point should questions be raised about the project at some point in the future. So, if after several months of operation there is reason to suspect the model is not performing as intended, it is possible to go back and check that the model has been implemented correctly, as specified in the documentation manual. In particular, the documentation manual will act as a reference point for internal and external auditors wishing to establish whether the models are working as intended and have been developed and applied in accordance with any regulatory requirements.

As discussed previously, the documentation manual should contain most, if not all, of the information captured in the project requirements document. It should also contain the following:

* The structure of the final model (the predictor variables and weights).
* Details of the statistical process used to derive the model. For example output produced from the software used to produce the model, such as SAS or SPSS.
* Univariate analysis reports (as discussed in Chapter 5).
* A record of the pre-processing that was applied.
* Performance metrics and score distributions.
* Details of the decision rules to be employed in conjunction with the model.
* Coding instructions (scoring instructions). These explain to the person responsible for implementing the model how the structure of the model should be interpreted. More about coding instructions is covered in Chapter 10.

If the original project requirements document was of a good standard and kept up-to-date throughout the project, and high quality documentation was produced as the project progressed, then only about 4–5 days should be required at the end of a project to produce the final project documentation.

2.10   Chapter summary

Without good project planning there is a significant risk of a project running out of control, missing its target delivery date, costing more than expected and ultimately, failing to deliver any business benefit because the project deliverables were not aligned with the business objectives of the organization that commissioned it.

The essence of good project planning is about understanding how a model is intended to be used and what benefits it will bring. Only once this has been established can the resources required and the processes that need to be undertaken to deliver the project be determined with any accuracy.

For a modelling project, project planning should cover both the business and technical requirements of the project. Technical requirements deal with things that are directly relevant to the ability of the model to predict consumer behaviour. This covers things such as what behaviour the model is going to predict, the forecast horizon, the data sources that will be utilized and model form and method of construction. Business requirements are things the project must take into account to ensure that the model is acceptable to the business. Typical business requirements include: identifying roles and responsibilities, defining the project's objectives and scope, legal compliance, a plan for delivery and implementation of the model, risk and issue mitigation, and documentation and reporting requirements.

Having good project management processes in place does not necessarily mean a huge amount of oversight is required, particularly for small projects that are not business critical. The main thing is that there is someone (the project manager) who oversees the project and ensures that it's well planned and executed, and meets the requirements of the project's stakeholders.

3
Sample Selection

The databases available for model construction can be vast. Some customer databases contain tens of millions of records (observations) and thousands of predictor variables. Even with modern computing facilities it may not be practical to use all of the data available. There will also be cases that are not suitable for model construction, and these need to be identified and dealt with. The data used for model construction should also be as similar as possible to the data that will exist when the completed model is put into service – which usually means that the sample used to construct the model should be as recent as possible to mitigate against changes in the patterns of behaviour that accumulate over time. For these reasons it is common for models to be constructed using a sub-set (a sample) of the available data, rather than the full population.

In this chapter sample selection is discussed. In particular, we consider which sub-set of the available data should be selected for use in the model construction process.

3.1   Sample window (sample period)

If a 12 month forecast horizon has been agreed, then what one would ideally like to do is gather data about people from exactly 12 months ago so that the sample used to construct the model is as recent as possible. The modelling objective would then be defined as at today, based on behaviour observed in the 12 months since the sample was taken. Sometimes this is possible. However, for many modelling projects data is taken from across a period of time, referred to as a sample window (or sample period), as shown in Figure 3.1.

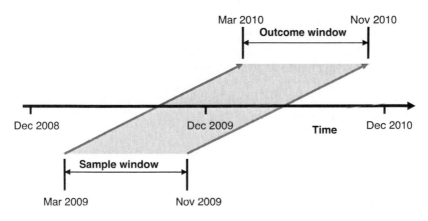

Figure 3.1 Sample window

In Figure 3.1 the sample window covers a period of nine months from March 2009 to November 2009. There is a corresponding nine month outcome window from March 2010 to November 2010, so that all observations have 12 months of observed behaviour. There are a number of reasons why data may need to be taken from across a sample window rather than from a single point in time. These include:

- Seasonality effects. Many types of consumer behaviour vary over the course of a month, quarter or year. Spending on credit cards, for example, is always higher in December than in January due to the Christmas holiday, with a corresponding rise in delinquency rates a couple of months later. Having a long sample window smoothes out these effects.
- Operational effects. Patterns of customer behaviour may have been disrupted for short periods of time due to IT issues/errors/changes. Data from these periods may be unreliable or not representative of general patterns of customer behaviour, and should therefore, be excluded. However, not all such events may be known about. Taking a long sample window will help reduce the impact of such events.
- Short term strategy initiatives. Customers may have been treated in a non-standard way for a period of time in order to meet organizational objectives. The result is a distorted picture of behaviour during this period.
- Lack of data. A customer database may be very large in totality, but there may be insufficient data at any single point in time to construct a model. An insurer may have many millions of customers,

but only a few hundred new insurance policies are underwritten each day. Of these, only a few subsequently go on to make a claim. As discussed in the next section, this is an insufficient number to build a robust model.

For credit scoring and insurance rating, sample windows of between three and 12 months are common.

3.2   Sample size

To construct a good quality model a large sample of data is required. For classification problems what is important is that there are sufficient numbers of each class; that is, a large number of goods and a large number of bads. There is little point having a sample containing many thousands of goods if there are only a few dozen bads. A widely used rule of thumb is a sample of around 1,500–2,000 cases of each class is a reasonable number[1] to aim for (Lewis 1992; Siddiqi 2006, p. 29). Models can be constructed using samples containing as few as 2–300 cases of each class, but in my experience, once the sample size falls below about 1,000 cases of each class model performance deteriorates rapidly.

These days, a modern PC can easily deal with samples containing 100,000 cases or more and several hundred predictor variables, and many organizations use samples of this size when developing their models. The general advice is that larger sample sizes are better, but the reader should be aware that it's very much a case of diminishing returns. The benefit from increasing the sample size from say, 2,000 to 5,000 cases of each class, is probably greater than the benefit of increasing the sample from 5,000 to 50,000 cases of each class. To give some idea of the effects of sample size on model performance, Figure 3.2 shows the results of some experiments that I undertook in conjunction with one of my colleagues, Dr Sven Crone, at Lancaster University in the UK.

The data in Figure 3.2 comes from two credit scoring data sets. Data set A is an application scoring data set provided by Experian UK. It contains details about a sample of people applying for a variety of unsecured loan and card products. Data set B is a behavioural scoring data set provided by an organization offering revolving credit.[2] In both cases these are real data sets that each organization had used previously for constructing credit scoring models. The baseline performance (100%) is the performance observed when using a sample size of 2,000

Figure 3.2   Sample size and performance

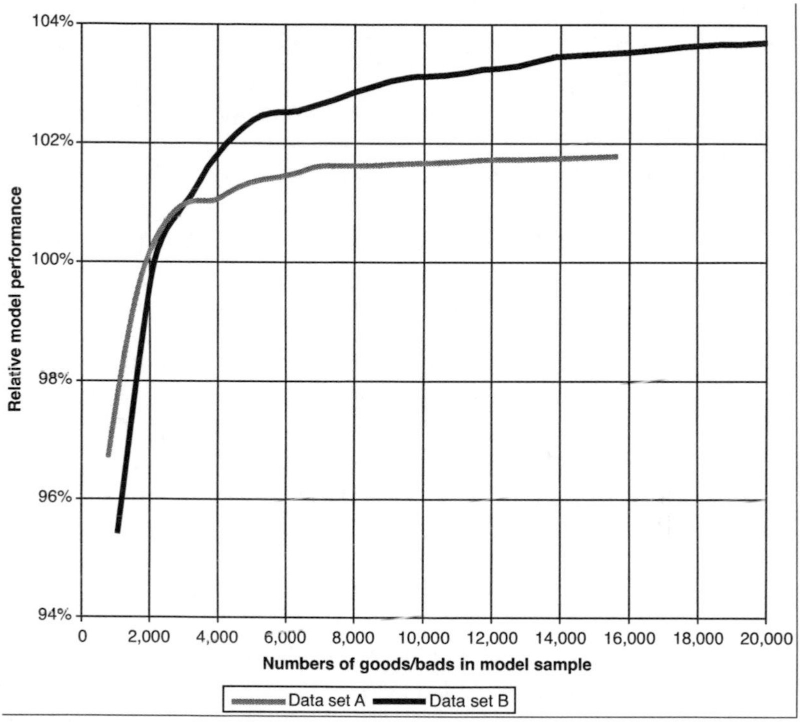

Notes:
1. The performance measure is the GINI coefficient. See Chapter 8 for more information about GINI.
2. Relative performance is calculated as 100 * B/A where A is the GINI coefficient for a model constructed using a sample size of approximately 2,000 cases of each class and B is the GINI coefficient of the model constructed using the comparison sample size.
3. The numbers reported on the graph represent development and holdout samples, assuming an 80/20 development/holdout split. So 2,000 goods/bads means that 1,600 cases of each class were used to derive the parameters of the model. The other 400 cases were assigned to the holdout sample and used to measure performance.
4. Data set A contained 39 predictor variables. Data set B contained 54 predictor variables. These were pre-processed to create 218 and 402 dummy variables respectively for data sets A and B. Preliminary variable selection was performed using the full data set using stepwise linear regression with a 1% criteria for model entry.
5. Experimental results have been calculated using 50 fold cross validation. See Chapter 11 for further information about k-fold cross validation.

cases of each class to construct a linear scoring model using logistic regression. (As discussed in Chapter 7, logistic regression is the most popular method for constructing classification models.) The lines on the graphs show the relative difference in performance from using sample sizes other than this. As Figure 3.2 shows, using more than 2,000 cases of each class yields performance gains. However, performance begins to tail-off once the sample sizes exceed around 5,000–6,000 cases. If one extrapolates the trends, it is reasonable to conclude that even if the samples contained hundreds of thousands of goods and bads, the improvement over and above that from using a sample containing 2,000 goods and bads is unlikely to be more than about 2 percent for data set A and 4 percent for data set B. These results are only for two data sets from one application domain, but I have little reason to believe that other data sets would show significantly different trends.

For regression models similar sample size issues apply. In my experience a sample of around 2,000 cases will be sufficient to yield good models, but reasonable benefits are likely to be seen from using samples that are two or three times larger than this.

3.2.1   Stratified random sampling

It is very important that the sample used to construct a model is representative of the population from which it was taken. By this, I mean it is important that the sample is not in some way biased towards individuals with specific traits, resulting in some types of people being under-represented or excluded from the sample. Consider a provider of home insurance that wants to construct a classification model to see which customers are likely to renew their insurance and which are not (an attrition model). Assume the insurer has a database containing 500,000 live policies within the sample window. Of these, 10,000 are to be sampled for model construction (5,000 that renewed their insurance by the outcome point and 5,000 that didn't). If the database is sorted in ascending order, by the date when someone first took out home insurance, then those at the start of the database will have been on the books for a considerable period of time and renewed their insurance policies many times. Those at the other end will be new customers for who this is the first policy they have taken out. If the sample is taken from the start of the database, then it will be biased towards people with a tendency to renew, and the model will overestimate the probability of renewal. If the sample is taken from the end of the database the bias will be in the opposite direction, and the model will underestimate the chance of renewal.

To counter such problems it is good practice to use a random process to select cases to include in the model development sample. The simplest way to do this is to attach a random number to the database. The database is then sorted in random number order and the first *N* cases selected, where *N* is the desired sample size.

For classification problems it is good practice to use stratified random sampling by good/bad status. The database from which data is to be taken is stratified (segmented) into two groups, one containing goods the other bads. Random sampling is applied to each group separately to select goods and bads for the model development sample.

3.2.2 Adaptive sampling

Stratified random sampling is standard practice and generally leads to the production of good quality models. However, because of its random nature, random sampling will naturally select more cases of one type than another, and sometimes certain types of cases will be over or under-represented in the sample. Let's say, for arguments sake, that a population contains 98,000 home owners and 2,000 renters. For model development, a random 1 in 100 sample is taken. The expectation is there will be 980 home owners and 20 renters. However, to get 990 home owners and only ten renters is not unlikely, given the random nature of the selection process, and if you are very unlucky, then you may not get any renters at all. If this occurs, then the sample used to construct the model will not be representative of population from which it was taken and the resulting model will be sub-optimal. In practice, if a sample contains many thousands of observations, these discrepancies will be minor and are not something to be unduly concerned about. However, if a small sample is taken from a very large population then the impact on model performance may be more significant.[3]

Adaptive sampling (active learning) is where some control is placed over the sample selection process so that the sample is more representative of the population from which it is taken (Cohn et al. 1994). In some situations the sampling process is adapted as it goes along. The choice of which observation to sample next is determined by the properties of the observations that have already been selected. In other situations, a pre-sampling exercise may be performed to provide guidance about the sampling strategy to adopt. One simple way to apply adaptive sampling of this type is to use a procedure known as clustering, and then apply stratified random sampling to the clusters that result (Kang et al. 2004; Yen and Lee 2006). A cluster is a group of observations (people in our context) that have similar attributes. Consider Figure 3.3.

In Figure 3.3, each observation has two variables associated with it: Income and Age. There would appear to be three distinct groupings (clusters). Young people with low incomes, older people with low incomes and older people with high incomes. Therefore, to obtain a representative

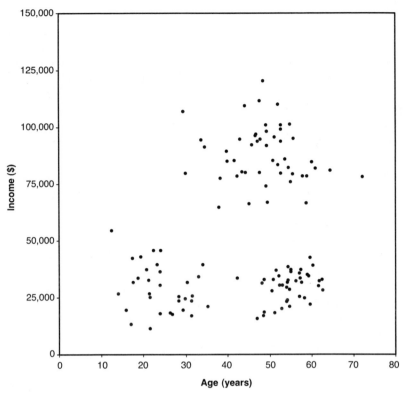

Figure 3.3   Clustered data

sample, it would be sensible to sample separately from each of these three groups.

Many software packages, including SAS and SPSS, provide clustering tools to enable a population to be automatically grouped into two or more clusters. Ideally, if you intend to take a sample of *n* cases from a population of *N*, then the best solution is to have *N/n* clusters and sample one case from each cluster. In practice, the number of clusters can be chosen with a degree of latitude and somewhere between five and 50 clusters is adequate for most problems. Once observations have been assigned to a cluster, stratified random sampling is applied to each cluster.

Clustering is a formal approach, but adaptive sampling principles can be applied in a more ad-hoc way based on univariate properties of the population or expert opinion. For example, if you know it's important to have a representative number of people from each category of residential status (renter, home owner and so on), then a separate sampling exercise can be applied to each category.

3.3 Development and holdout samples

Sometimes the process used to derive a model will pick out relationships that are spurious, or the strength of the relationships that exist will be overestimated. This is a problem known as over-fitting, and can be particularly acute if the sample used to develop a model is small in relation to the number of predictor variables used in the modelling process. A rule of thumb for classification problems is, if the ratio of goods (or bads) to the number of predictor variables is less than ten, then there is a risk of significant over-fitting occurring (Harrell et al. 1996).

One effect of over-fitting is that if the data used to construct a model is also used to evaluate how well the model predicts behaviour, the results will be over-optimistic. To gain a true picture about how well a model performs, standard practice is to split the data used for model development into two parts. A development sample and a holdout sample. The development sample is used to derive the parameters of the model. After model construction is complete, the finished model is used to calculate scores for the holdout sample, and the model is evaluated on the basis of how well it predicts behaviour for this sample.

Sometimes it can also be useful to calculate performance metrics for the development sample. This allows the results to be compared to those for the holdout sample to see if, and by how much, over-fitting has occurred. If model performance for the two samples is very different indeed, this suggests it would be prudent to repeat the model construction process in an attempt to reduce the over-fitting that has occurred.

Stratified random sampling should be applied to split the data into development and holdout samples so that the good:bad odds in each sample are the same. As a rule, fewer observations are required for the holdout sample than for the development sample. Common practice is to segment the population 80/20 percent or 70/30 percent development/ holdout.

3.4 Out-of-time and recent samples

Models of customer behaviour have a tendency to deteriorate over time (Hand and Jacka 1998, pp. 75–6). This means that a model constructed using a sample window 1–2 years in the past may not perform as well as the performance metrics calculated using the holdout sample suggest. It is also common to see score misalignment and population shifts over time. Score misalignment means the model ranks customers correctly, but gives everyone scores that are consistently too high or too low. Any decision rules derived from the properties of the holdout sample will be incorrect for the current population. Given that in order to construct a model to predict future behaviour, data must be taken from the past, there is no way to fully get around this problem. However, if the nature and trend in the changes that have occurred since the sample window can be identified, then a certain level of mitigating action can be taken.

One strategy to mitigate score misalignment is to take an additional "out-of-time" sample, towards the end of the model construction process. It may take many months from the time when the development and holdout samples were taken before a final signed-off model is ready for implementation. Therefore, a more recent sample of data can be taken just prior to model implementation. The performance of the model can then be evaluated using the out-of-time sample. If the score profile has changed compared to the holdout sample, then it is possible to adjust the decision rules that use the score to take the recent changes into account. Some organizations will also use censored (shorter) forecast horizons in conjunction with out-of-time samples. The model may have been developed to predict customer behaviour over 12 months, but an additional six or nine month forecast horizon is used to define a second good/bad status for the purpose of comparing the out-of-time sample with the holdout sample. In this way it is possible to use an out-of-time sample that is up to six months more recent than if a 12 month forecast horizon was used. The (rather large but commonly made) assumption is that any score misalignment seen using a six or nine month forecast horizon is the same as one would see if a 12 month horizon was used.

Population shifts are when there are changes to the geo-demographic profile of the population over time. Population shifts can cause score misalignment, but often the model will be well aligned and score people accurately – it's just that the number of people getting specific scores changes.

Population shifts can occur as the result of social and economic change, or because of changes to an organization's marketing strategy, resulting in the model being applied to different types of people. A typical example is where a credit scoring model is going to be used to decide which mortgage applications to accept. Following model development, analysis of the holdout sample led to a decision rule that resulted in 60 percent of mortgage applications being approved. However, in the time between the holdout sample being taken and the model going live the organization's marketing strategy has changed, resulting in a greater number of uncreditworthy people being targeted. When the model is put live only 40 percent of cases are approved. From a credit risk perspective, as long as the score gives each mortgage applicant a score representative of their likelihood of defaulting on their loan, then no problem, but from marketing and operational perspectives, forecasts for the number of new customers will have been based on the 60 percent figure generated from the holdout sample. Therefore, people from these areas of the organization are likely to be upset when they discover that only 40 percent of applicants are considered creditworthy.

A strategy to examine population shifts, which can be used in conjunction with the out-of-time approach, is to take a very recent sample of data. For the previous example, perhaps mortgage applications in the month immediately prior to model implementation. This data is too recent to allow a good/bad definition to be applied, but as long as the predictor variables are present a score can be calculated. It is then possible to compare the distribution of model scores generated using the recent sample with the distribution of model scores generated using the holdout sample. If a shift in scores is observed, and it is believed that the model is not misaligned, then the decision rules based on the model score do not need to be adjusted. Instead, the operational areas affected by the population shift need to be informed so that they can adjust their resource plans appropriately. The exception to this is if the business objectives are volume based and the population shift results in a different proportion of cases scoring above/below certain scores. In this case, the decision rules can be adjusted to ensure the expected volumes are delivered.

Sometimes the decision whether or not to take out-of-time and recent samples can be put off until the model is close to completion. However, if data needs to be sourced from third parties, such as credit reference agencies, then there may be a requirement to generate these samples (or at least have a plan for generating them) at the same time as the main development/holdout samples are taken. Otherwise, additional costs and delays could be incurred while the additional samples are processed by the data provider.

3.5 Multi-segment (sub-population) sampling

The sample sizes discussed in section 3.2 refer to a single model. Sometimes separate models are constructed for different population segments (sub-populations). For a personal loan product an organization may have one credit scoring model for the under 30s and another for the over 30s, and/or separate models for people who are retired, in full-time employment, students and so on. If sub-population models are going to be considered, then it's important the sampling strategy takes this into account so that there are sufficient numbers within each sub-population. If only 10 percent of the population are aged under 30, then a random sample of 5,000 cases can only be expected to contain 500 cases under 30. This is unlikely to be sufficient for constructing a robust model. An alternative strategy is to sample 2,500 cases from each age group.

The more models an organization has, the more complex and expensive the process of developing, monitoring and maintaining them. There is also no guarantee that a single model won't generate better forecasts than a multi-model solution (Banasik et al. 1996). Therefore, my recommendation is that sub-population modelling should generally be avoided unless there is good reason to think otherwise. However, two situations that I have come across where constructing multiple models has given better results than a single model are where:

- Different relationships exist within the data. If the underlying relationships between the predictor variables and the modelling objective are significantly different for different groups, then having separate models may generate better forecasts. CART and artificial neural network models are less prone to this issue than linear models. Consequently, multiple models are less likely to be needed if these forms of model are being constructed.
- Thick/Thin data exists for different groups. This is where there are lots of predictor variables for some segments of the population (thick data), but relatively few for others (thin data). Sometimes this occurs because cases originated from different media channels, where different variables are captured for each channel. Alternatively, data provided from an external source may only be available for a proportion of cases.[4] In this case, it is sensible to construct two separate models, based on the amount of data available.

It is very difficult to determine before a model is constructed if, and by how much, the predictive ability of a modelling system will be improved by using several models instead of one. Good practice is to build a single model first. This is then used to benchmark the performance of models built on separate sub-populations. Another problem is that deciding which segments to consider can be problematic. For example, if one is considering building models for applicants of different ages, is it better to segment over/under 30 or over/under 40? In general there are three approaches that can be adopted to determining sub-populations for model development.

1. Come up with a list of potential sub-population models based on expert opinion. For example, past experience may have taught us that better models result if we build separate models for people who have made an insurance claim within the last five years compared to those that have not. Sampling is undertaken separately for each group.
2. Take a relatively large sample of data, perhaps 50,000 cases or more of each class, and look for significant sub-groups within the sample. A very common approach is to combine a CART model with another form of model. A CART model is constructed first. The high level splits within the CART model are then used to define the populations used to construct linear models, artificial neural networks and so on.
3. Apply residual (error) analysis. As a rule, there will be no pattern to the residuals for an efficient model. The errors should be randomly distributed with a mean of zero. If there are patterns within the residuals, this suggests a better solution can be obtained. Consider a response model. The score, S, takes values in the range 0–1, representing the likelihood of a response being received. Behaviour is coded 1 to represent a response and 0 otherwise. If a response is received the error, $e, = 1 - S$. If no response is received, $e = 0 - S$. If the model consistently under or over predicts the likelihood of response for say, the under 30s, then the average value of e for this group will be non-zero. Therefore, under 30s would be a candidate for a separate model.

3.6 Balancing

A balanced population is one where the number of goods and bads are approximately the same. The good:bad odds are 1:1 or thereabouts. For many classification problems populations are naturally unbalanced. In credit scoring the good:bad odds of a credit portfolio can range from less than 2:1 to over 200:1. For response modelling the response:non response odds may be 1:100 or more, and if one is building models for fraud prediction, then good/bad odds (non fraud:fraud odds) of 1,000:1 are not unheard of.

There are several ways samples can be taken and/or adjusted when a population is unbalanced and several different scenarios to consider.

Table 3.1   Sampling schema

Sampling schema	Sample size		Development sample		Holdout sample	
	Number of goods	Number of bads	Weight (goods)	Weight (bads)	Weight (goods)	Weight (bads)
1. Unbalanced	48,000	2,000	1	1	1	1
2. Balanced (undersampled, weighted)	25,000	25,000	24	1	24	1
3. Balanced (undersampled, unweighted)	25,000	25,000	1	1	24	1

To illustrate the balancing strategies that can be applied let's consider two examples. For the first example, consider a credit card portfolio containing two million customers. Of these, 1,920,000 are good customers and 80,000 are bad, giving population odds of 24:1. Due to the size of the population and the costs of acquiring data, it has been decided that the maximum possible sample size is 50,000. Table 3.1 shows three ways the credit card provider could undertake sampling.

The first sampling schema in Table 3.1 is to take an unbalanced sample. An unbalanced sample is where the proportion of goods and bads in the sample is identical to that of the parent population. To put it another way, the sample good:bad odds and the population good:bad odds are both 24:1.

The second sampling schema is to create a balanced sample via undersampling, and then applying a weighting factor. Undersampling means the sampling procedure generates a sample whose good:bad odds are lower than the parent population. To put it another way, the sample contains fewer cases of the more commonly occurring class than would be expected from a completely random sampling procedure. In Table 3.1 25,000 cases of each class have been taken so that the sample good:bad odds are 1:1. A weight of 24 is then assigned for each good, and weight of 1 for each bad. A weight of 24 means that when it comes to model construction each case is treated as if it appears 24 times in the sample.

The third sampling schema is undersampling without weighting. The sample is identical to the second option, but the weighting is not used for model construction (Which is the same as saying all the weights are equal to one). The weight is however, required for calculating performance metrics using the holdout sample and any out-of-time or recent samples.

This is important because if the holdout sample good:bad odds are different from population good:bad odds, then the statistics used to determine how the model performs will be misleading and yield over-optimistic results.

Academic research into the effect of balancing has concluded that models constructed using balanced samples are usually more predictive that those using unbalanced samples (Weiss 2004). Consequently, in situations like the one illustrated in Table 3.1 my recommendation is to use a balanced sample for model development. This is regardless of the form of model developed or the modelling technique applied to find the model parameters. If you are using logistic regression or neural networks I suggest using a weighted sample (schema 2). However, if you are using discriminant analysis, linear regression or CART modelling approaches then a weighting factor should not be applied for model development.

Let's now move on to consider the second example. A mortgage provider wants to construct a model to predict the likelihood of having to foreclose on its existing customers. Within the sample window there are 300,000 mortgage customers who, by the end of the outcome period, have not had their homes repossessed (these are good) and 2,000 who have (these are bad). This gives population odds of 150:1. Again, the maximum possible sample size is set at 50,000. The main difference between this example and the previous one is that in this case it's feasible to include all available bads in the sample. Sampling is only required for the goods. There are now four potential sampling strategies as illustrated in Table 3.2.

Table 3.2   Revised sampling schema

Sampling schema	Sample size		Development sample		Holdout sample	
	Number of goods	Number of bads	Weight (goods)	Weight (bads)	Weight (goods)	Weight (bads)
1. Unbalanced with weighting	48,000	2,000	6.25	1	6.25	1
2. Balanced (undersampled, weighted)	2,000	2,000	150	1	150	1
3. Balanced (undersampled, unweighted)	2,000	2,000	1	1	150	1
4. Oversampled	48,000	2,000	6.25	150	6.25	1

The first three sampling schema in Table 3.2 are similar to those in Table 3.1. The main difference is that the weighting of observations in each of the samples has become a little more complex. For the first sampling schema a weight of 6.25 is required for the goods, to ensure the sample odds are the same as the population odds of 150:1. With sampling schema 2 and 3, undersampling has been applied, but because all available bads have been sampled, just 2,000 goods are required to create a balanced sample giving a total sample size of 4,000.

The fourth sampling schema is called "oversampling". First, an unbalanced sample is taken, which is the same as the first sampling schema. For model construction a weight is assigned to cases in the minority class (the bads in this example) so that the weighted numbers of goods and bads are the same. Note that as for undersampling, the good:bad odds of the weighted holdout sample must equal the population good:bad odds, otherwise biased results will be produced when it comes to evaluating the model's performance.

For problems like this, the effect of the chosen sampling schema on the performance of the model depends on three factors:

1. The degree of imbalance. The higher the good:bad odds of the population the more pronounced the differences in the performance of models using different sampling schema.
2. Sample size. A model constructed using a large sample is less sensitive to balancing than a model constructed using smaller samples, particularly when undersampling is applied. This is because for small samples the benefit gained from undersampling is offset by the reduced number of cases of the majority class. In Table 3.2, 48,000 goods could have been used for model construction if an unbalanced sample was taken or oversampling applied, but only 2,000 goods if undersampling was applied. However, if the population was ten times as large, then the effect of reducing the number of goods from 480,000 to 20,000 would be far less pronounced.
3. Method of model construction. The sensitivity of different modelling techniques varies greatly. For classification models, logistic regression is relatively insensitive to balancing. Linear regression/discriminant analysis on the other hand (probably the second most popular methods for constructing classification models after logistic regression) are more sensitive to the balancing of the sample, and CART is the most sensitive of all.

To give an idea of the magnitude of the effect different balancing strategies can have on model performance, Table 3.3 shows the results

Table 3.3   Result of balancing experiments

Sampling schema	Data Set A			
	Model form and method of model construction			
	Linear model (Logistic regression)	Linear model (Linear regression)	Neural network	CART
1. Unbalanced	+1.15%	–0.08%	+1.84	–2.18%
2. Undersampled (unweighted)	0.00%	0.00%	0.00%	0.00%
3. Oversampled	+1.15%	+0.12%	+1.11%	+1.69

Sampling schema	Data Set B			
	Model form and method of model construction			
	Linear model (Logistic regression)	Linear model (Linear regression)	Neural network	CART
1. Unbalanced	+0.24%	–1.97%	+0.99%	–12.12%
2. Undersampled (unweighted)	0.00%	0.00%	0.00%	0.00%
3. Oversampled	+0.21%	+0.22%	+0.75%	+3.80%

Notes:
1. The performance measure was the GINI coefficient. GINI is explained in more detail in Chapter 8.
2. Performance was calculated relative to the baseline schema (Schema 2). It was calculated as $(100 * M/N - 100)$. N is the GINI coefficient for the baseline sampling schema (Schema 2). M is the GINI coefficient of the sampling schema the baseline is being compared to.
3. For data set A the original unbalanced data set contained 75,528 goods and 13,261 bads. For data set B the original unbalanced data set contained 120,508 goods and 18,098 bads.
4. For undersampling, a sample of goods was created using random sampling without replacement. All bads where used, and therefore, no sampling of bads was required.
5. For oversampling (Schema 3) all goods and all bads were included in the sample. The bads were then weighted so the number of weighted bads was equal to the number of goods.
6. Experiments were performed using 50 fold cross validation. See Chapter 11 for an explanation of k-fold cross validation.

of some further experiments I conducted in collaboration with Dr Crone at Lancaster University.

The experiments examined the effect on model performance of three different sampling schema, applied to two moderately unbalanced credit scoring data sets. The baseline for comparison in Table 3.3 is sampling schema 2 – balanced (unweighted) samples created via undersampling. The figures in the other cells of a given column show the relative improvement in model performance for that method of model construction. For example, when logistic regression was applied to data set B, using an unbalanced sample, this resulted in a model that was 0.24 percent better than the baseline. Likewise, over sampling resulted in a model that was 0.21 percent better than the baseline.

What these results suggest, is that for large, moderately unbalanced data sets, the impact of balanced/unbalanced samples when using logistic regression or neural networks is of the order of 1–2 percent. This is not a huge margin of difference, but for a bank with a large consumer credit portfolio, this level of improvement could be worth several million dollars a year to the bottom line. The results also suggest that using unbalanced and oversampled data sets (schema 1 and 3) result in very similar levels of performance when using logistic regression or neural networks. If anything, the unbalanced samples lead to slightly better models than oversampling for these methods – although the differences are not statistically significant. Another point to note is that unbalanced and oversampled samples yield better models than undersampling. I would at this point stress again, that if you undertake any experimentation of your own regarding balancing, then the results should only be based on an unbalanced holdout sample. If you use the development sample to calculate performance metrics, or have applied balancing to the holdout sample, then you are at serious risk of getting biased results.

For linear regression and CART the story is somewhat different. The impact of different balancing strategies is more pronounced. For these methods using unbalanced samples leads to the worst performance and oversampling the best.

I would very much stress that these results should be taken as indicative only, and for populations displaying a greater degree of imbalance than these, it would be reasonable to expect more pronounced differences to be seen.

A final note of caution about using balanced samples created via undersampling (without weighting) or oversampling. If the score is meant to be a direct estimate of the probability of good/bad behaviour, then the probability estimates produced by the model for the hold-out (or other) samples will be marginally lower than they should be (Weiss 2004). However, this can be corrected relatively easily using a calibration factor. Calibration is discussed in more detail in Chapter 7.

3.7 Non-performance

Sometimes customer behaviour will not be known. Hence, the modelling objective cannot be defined. Some common reasons why behaviour may be unknown are:

- Offer not taken up. Someone may apply for a personal loan or a mortgage, be sent an acceptance letter and a credit agreement to sign, but they never return the signed agreement. Likewise, many people obtain insurance quotations but don't take out insurance.
- Rejects. For consumer credit products it's not unusual for anywhere between 20 and 80 percent of applications to be declined. These cases will therefore, not have any repayment behaviour associated with them. For insurance products, reject rates tend to be much lower, with only the most risky cases being declined because premiums are priced to reflect claim propensity.
- Early account closure. A customer relationship may end before the end of the forecast horizon. Therefore, it may not be possible to apply the good/bad definition at that point. In such cases it is common for the good/bad definition to be based on the most recent data available; that is, at the point when the account closed. Note that this may be linked to account transfer, which is discussed in section 3.8.

As a rule, non-performance cases are excluded from model construction because they don't contribute to the parameter estimation process. However, it is good practice to take a sample of each type of non-performance so that their score profile can be examined once the model has been constructed. The main exception to this rule is in credit scoring where it is common practice to apply reject inference – a process that attempts to estimate how those that had their application rejected would have behaved, if they had in fact been given a loan. These "inferred rejects" can then be used for model construction. Reject inference is discussed in detail in Chapter 9.

3.8 Exclusions

There are often cases where customer behaviour is known, but for one reason or another it should not be used for model construction. If there is something wrong with the data, or you are not going to be able to use information about certain types of people going forward within your decision making processes, then that data should be excluded. The effect of including such cases is to weaken the observable relationships, and hence produce a less effective forecasting model. It is however, good practice to retain a sample of excluded cases so their score profile can be examined after the model has been constructed. Some exclusions will be based on the properties of accounts at the sample point, while others will be based on outcome point data. Every organization will have their own set of exclusion criteria, but some common reasons to apply exclusions include:

- Marketing suppressions. For direct marketing there will be some people who should not be targeted. In many countries, if someone states they don't want to receive unsolicited communications, then organizations are legally required to exclude them from their campaigns. It also makes sense to exclude people who are deceased and people with whom the organization had a previous relationship that ended unsatisfactorily. For example, most credit card providers will not want to target someone who recently wrote-off thousands of dollars of debt on another credit card.
- Dormant accounts. If a behavioural credit scoring model is being developed, the predictor variables will tend to relate to spending and repayment patterns in the 6–12 months prior to the sample point. If an account has been dormant for this period, all balance and payment data will be zero. Therefore, there will be little information to use for modelling purposes.
- Staff/VIP accounts. Many organizations treat staff differently from normal customers. It is generally good practice to exclude staff accounts from model construction.
- Corrupt data. If data for some individuals is incorrect, this information is not going to help predict behaviour. For example, if some cases in the sample originated from fraudsters, who lied about their income, age or other personal details, then these cases should be excluded.
- Modelling objective known at sample point (already bad). In consumer credit markets, once a customer is classified as bad due to a poor repayment record, it is extremely rare for their account to recover and be reclassified as good. Therefore, if the customer is bad at the sample point, they will invariably be bad at the outcome point. There is no need for a model to predict this.
- Policy rules. A policy rule is similar to a marketing suppression. If you know people with certain characteristics are going to be treated in a certain way, then there is no need for a model to predict their

behaviour. For example, an insurer constructing a model to predict claims may have a policy to only provide car insurance to people aged 21 and over. Therefore, there's no point including anyone under 21 in the sample.

- Account Transfer. A feature of credit card portfolios is lost/stolen cards. When a customer reports their card as lost or stolen, standard practice is to create a new account and copy over all the data from the original account to the new account. The original account is closed and a marker, indicating account transfer has occurred, is placed on the account. To avoid double counting only the new account should be included.

3.9   Population flow (waterfall) diagram

When the sampling strategy has been determined, a good way of presenting it to stakeholders is to produce a population flow (waterfall) diagram. This shows the numbers falling into each state, how many exclusions there are, how many cases of non-performance and so on. Standard practice is to produce two diagrams. One for the entire population and one for the sampled population. Figure 3.4 shows the population flows associated with a project to construct an application scoring model for a personal loan portfolio.

The top half of the diagram provides a breakdown of all loan applications made within the sample window. Of the 240,010 loans applications that were made, 109,949 – around 46 percent, were rejected. Of those that were accepted, 5,227 were defined as exclusions. For this project, exclusions were predominately cases of known fraud, bankrupts and staff accounts, as well as a sample of about 100 test cases that were processed through the live system to evaluate an IT change that happened to occur within the sample window. As these do not represent real loan agreements it was prudent to exclude them. Just under 22 percent (27,106) of the remaining accepts have no performance associated with them. The majority of these are where applicants did not go on to sign and return a copy of the credit agreement, but this group also contains a few dozen cases where individuals did sign the agreement, but then exercised their legal right to terminate it before making any repayments.[5] This leaves a population of 97,728. Of these 90,005 were classified as good, 5,890 as bad and 1,833 as indeterminate using the organizations good/bad definition.

The lower part of Figure 3.4 shows the sampling strategy applied to produce the model development sample. For this project, the cost of

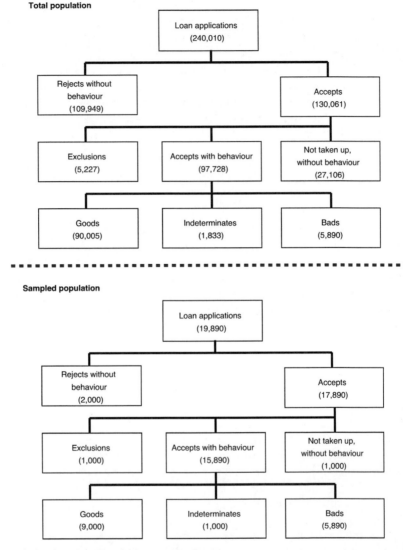

Figure 3.4   Population and sample flows

acquiring external data for the model development placed an upper limit on the sample size of 20,000 cases. This led to a decision to sample all bad cases and a somewhat larger number of goods. A sample of 2,000 rejected cases was also taken to allow reject inference (as discussed in Chapter 9) to be performed. Other account types (indeterminates, exclusions and not taken ups) were not used for model construction, but a reasonable number of each type were included within the sample in order to examine how they would be scored by the new model.

3.10   Chapter summary

A model developer will often be faced with a vast amount of data that can potentially be used for model construction. Even with a modern computer it may not be feasible to use all of the available data – it will just take too long to process or require too much memory. Alternatively, there may be cost implications that restrict the amount of data that can be used, particularly if data needs to be purchased from an external supplier. In situations like this it is usual to sample the data to create a representative sub-set of the population. The goal is to produce a sample that allows models to be built in a reasonable time and at reasonable cost, while at the same time facilitating the generation of a model that is as good, or as nearly as good, as would result from using the full population.

When deciding how to sample there are a number of factors to bear in mind:

1. Sample size. All other things being equal, the larger the sample the better model. However, once samples contain more than about 10,000 cases (5,000 of each class for a classification problem) then the benefits of even larger samples tend to be relatively small.
2. Segmentation of sample into development, holdout and out-of-time samples.
3. Balancing. For classification problems, better models may result if undersampling or oversampling is applied to create a balanced sample. However, it is not universally true that a balanced sample will always lead to a better model. The method used to construct the model and the size of the sample employed will have a bearing on how much balancing affects the quality of the model that is produced.
4. Adaptive sampling. If there are time/cost constraints that mean that only a small sample can be taken from a large population, then applying adaptive sampling techniques can provide benefits.
5. Missing (non) performance. Sometimes behaviour for some cases is not available. These cases therefore, need to be dealt with appropriately.

Another issue facing model developers is that there are often cases within the population which should not be used for model construction. This is because they are not representative of the data that will be available when the model is implemented, the data is corrupt or can otherwise not be relied upon. There is also no point including observations where deterministic behaviour exists. If you can say categorically how someone will behave in future, then there is no reason to build a model to predict their behaviour. Excluding these cases generally leads to better (more predictive) models for the remainder of the population.

4
Gathering and Preparing Data

If you have done any data analysis or modelling as part of a statistics course at university, then you were probably given a file containing a set of predictor variables and a dependent variable. All you had to do was read the data into the modelling software and worry about which data analysis and modelling procedures to apply. You probably didn't have to give any thought to where the data came from or how it was prepared. In practice, it is rare for data to be provided in such a readily usable format. The data required for model building, more often than not, is scattered across multiple databases/data tables/IT systems and may be held in a variety of different formats. Work is required to extract relevant data from each source, and then match it together to produce a single data set that can be used for data analysis and model construction.

All consumer databases also contain errors, inconsistencies and omissions. This may be due to mistakes made by data entry staff, hardware failures, incorrect information supplied by individuals themselves or incorrect calculations/transformations that have been applied by the computer systems that process the data. Databases also change and evolve over time. New items of data are added as new business requirements emerge, and redundant data items cease to be maintained or are deleted when they are no longer required. Sometimes the same item of data, such as someone's income, may be held on two different systems and there are discrepancies between them. These discrepancies may be due to any one of a number of reasons. Perhaps the data was captured at different points in time, or subject to different data cleaning algorithms before being stored within the organization's systems. Maybe there are two income fields. One income field has been adjusted to take into account inflation, but the other has not. Perhaps both fields are

89

described as containing "income" but actually contain different data. One holds individual income, the other household income. In situations like this a decision needs to be made about which (or both) of the two income values to use.

Alternatively, people coming through different media channels may provide different information about themselves. Someone who fills in a paper application form is asked if they own their own home, but someone applying via the internet is not. Consequently, information about home ownership is available for some cases but missing for others. Other people may simply not have filled in the question about home ownership. Therefore, this type of missing data may indicate something very different about someone's behaviour than missing due to the question not being asked. Many organizations buy data from third party suppliers such as credit reference agencies (credit bureaus) or list providers, and these data sources are subject to their own set of changes, errors and omissions.

The overall result is that the model development sample is imperfect. This makes it difficult to fully establish the relationships that exist between the predictor variables and the modelling objective. Another problem is that some predictor variables may have become redundant and will not be available in the future. These should be excluded from model construction because they won't be available when the model is implemented. Matters are further complicated because the deficiencies in the data can vary over time, reflecting upgrades, bug fixes, changes to business practices and so on.

It may be impossible to retrospectively obtain missing data or restore data that has been corrupted, but a great deal can be done to "clean up" a sample to remove some of the inconsistencies, correct errors and exclude any data that is obviously unreliable. This process is known as data preparation, data cleaning or data cleansing. The objectives of data preparation are twofold. The first is to produce a sample that is representative of the data available at the point where the model is applied. The second objective is to format the data so that it yields the most predictive model possible. Data preparation won't generate a perfect sample, but good data preparation will lead to a far more useful model than would otherwise result.

4.1   Gathering data

Modern organizations hold their customer data within a "data warehouse". This is a central repository of information, available for the

Quotation table										
Quote ID	Request date	Name	Date of birth	.....	Claims in last 5 yrs	Car manufacturer	Model	Engine size	Trim	Quote ($)
00000416	29/05/2004	Simon Bateman	04/07/1976	.....	0	BMW	320d	2.0	ES	$907
00000417	29/05/2004	Sarah Lee	17/07/1958	.....	0	Ford	Focus	1.6	Zetec	$552
00000418	30/05/2004	Steven Finlay	12/12/1972	.....	3	Volvo	XC80	3.0	SE	$2,950
.....	.....	.....	.....	.....	.....	.....	.....	.....	.....	.....
00700807	25/12/2010	Jenny Kid	30/10/1959	.....	0	Volvo	XC60	3.0	SE	$404
00700808	25/12/2010	Ruth Timms	03/09/1988	.....	1	BMW	320d	2.0	ES	$1,554
00700809	25/12/2010	Paul Carey	22/11/1963	.....	0	Toyota	Prius	1.8	VVT-i	$410

Figure 4.1   Insurance quotation table

production of management reports, data analysis and modelling.[1] Most data warehouses are constructed using a relational database structure. A relational structure means the warehouse comprises a number of two dimensional tables (relations) that allow entries within the tables to be matched together. Each table in the data warehouse can be thought of as containing observations (also referred to as rows or records) and fields (columns or variables). This is similar to how data is represented in a spreadsheet such as Microsoft Excel. An example of a table is illustrated in Figure 4.1.

In Figure 4.1, each observation in the Quotation table contains information about one request for a motor insurance quote. Each field contains one piece of information about each quote. The QuoteID field, for example, contains a reference number that can be used to uniquely identify each quotation and the table is sorted in QuoteID order. Other fields on the table include the date the quotation was requested, the applicant's date of birth, number of claims in the last five years, car manufacturer, model, engine size, trim and so on. The final column contains the premium quoted to the customer.

In theory, there could be one large table, with each row containing all information that is known about an individual, but in practice this leads to large cumbersome tables with much redundancy. Imagine an insurer, that holds details about one million motor insurance quotations, and there are 5,000 types of vehicle that the organization is willing to provide quotes for. The organization could have a single large table, similar to Figure 4.1. As well as fields containing applicants' personal details the table also contains vehicle information. If, as in Figure 4.1, there are four fields containing information about vehicles,

Quotation table							
Quote ID	Request date	Name	Date of birth	.....	Claims in last 5 yrs	VehicleID	Quote ($)
00000416	29/05/2004	Simon Bateman	04/07/1976	.....	0	000194	$907
00000417	29/05/2004	Sarah Lee	17/07/1958	.....	0	001276	$552
00000418	30/05/2004	Steven Finlay	12/12/1972	.....	3	004941	$2,950
.....	.....	.....	.....	.....	.....	.....	.....
00700807	25/12/2010	Jenny Kid	30/10/1959	.....	0	004941	$404
00700808	25/12/2010	Ruth Timms	03/09/1988	.....	1	000194	$1,554
00700809	25/12/2010	Paul Carey	22/11/1963	.....	0	003802	$410

Many

1

Vehicle table				
Vehicle ID	Vehicle manufacturer	Model	Engine size	Trim
.....	.....	.....	.....	.....
000192	BMW	318d	2.0	ES
000193	BMW	318d	2.0	SE
000194	BMW	320d	2.0	ES
.....	.....	.....	.....	.....
001276	Ford	Focus	1.6	Zetec
001277	Ford	Focus	1.8	Zetec
.....	.....	.....	.....	.....
003802	Toyota	Prius	1.8	VVT-i
.....	.....	.....	.....	.....
004941	Volvo	XC60	3.0	SE
.....	.....	.....	.....	.....

Figure 4.2   Many to one relationship

this means 4,000,000 cells are needed to hold the information. Given that there are only 5,000 different types of vehicle, the vehicle details for many individuals will be identical. A more efficient method of storing the data is to have two tables. One holds quotation information, the other holds vehicle details – as illustrated in Figure 4.2.

In Figure 4.2, the Quotation table from Figure 4.1 has been modified so that all fields containing vehicle details have been replaced with a single "VehicleID" field, and a second Vehicle table created. The VehicleID can then be used to match between the two tables. Having two tables results in a considerable reduction in the amount of data. Instead of having 4,000,000 cells containing information about vehicles (1,000,000 customers * 4 cells of vehicle data), there is now just 1,025,000 cells of information. One field containing the VehicleID for each of the million customers on the Quotation table, and 5,000 observations and five fields (25,000 cells) of information in the Vehicle table. Given that many individuals all have the same type of car, there is said to be a "Many to one" relationship between the Quotation table and the Vehicle table.

Storing data across multiple tables enables it to be held and managed efficiently and avoids duplication. Duplication of data is something all database managers seek to avoid, and in a well constructed database any given piece of information is only ever held in one place. As well as being inefficient in terms of storage space, what you also tend to find is that if an item of data is stored in several different tables, maybe across several different databases, then over time differences arise. This occurs because people make amendments to the data or change the way it's processed, and they usually only update the table of interest to them. If the same information is stored on another table then this won't be updated.

To make use of information across tables there must be at least one field (or combination of fields) in each table that has a unique value for each observation. This is referred to as a match key (or primary key in database terminology). In Figure 4.2, a primary key for the Quotation table is QuoteID because each quotation has a different QuoteID. The primary key for the Vehicle table is VehicleID. The VehicleID field in the Quotation table is referred to as a "foreign key". This means it is not a key for the Quotation table, but is a key for another table. Therefore, it is possible to match records in the two tables together.

Match keys can be derived in a number of ways. Sometimes they are based on the order table entries are created. The first person to ever ask for an insurance quote is given QuoteID "00000001", the next "00000002" and so on. In other situations a match key may be based on pre-existing information, such as someone's national insurance number (social security number) which in theory uniquely identifies them. Alternatively, a match key may be derived from several fields that are not unique themselves, but when combined together generate what is assumed to be a unique key. Many people share the same name, date of birth or postcode (zip code). However, it is very unlikely that two people have the same name, date of birth and postcode. So combining these three items of information together – such as STEVENFINLAY140775NG27BP – will create a unique key. Sometimes, if one is dealing with non-relational databases, or information that comes from an external source, there won't be a natural match key. Therefore, combining columns to create a match key is precisely what needs to be done to enable data matching to occur.

An entity relationship diagram is one way of representing the relationships between different tables within a database. Figure 4.3 provides an example of an entity relationship diagram that was used to inform the data gathering for a project used to construct a claim propensity model for a motor insurer.

In Figure 4.3 there are four tables. The Quotation and Vehicle tables have already been introduced, and the predictor variables for the model will be sourced from these two tables. The Policy table contains details of all policies the company has underwritten. For example, when the policy started, when it ended (or will end), the annual

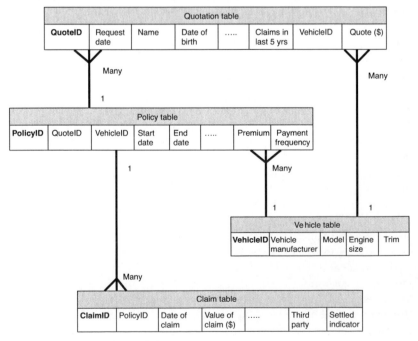

Figure 4.3   Entity relationship diagram

premium, frequency of payments so on. The Claim table contains information about the nature and value of claims that have been made against policies in the past. The Claim table provides the outcome point data that will be used to define the modelling objective. For a single policy there can be any number of claims made during the period of cover. This means that a "one-to-many" relationship exists between policies and claims.

During the project planning phase, the decision was taken to build a model using a sample of 10,000 policies (5,000 polices against which no claims were made and 5,000 policies where one or more claims were made). The sample window was defined as between one and two years ago, with a 12 month outcome period. To take an appropriate sample, the analyst begins by extracting all policies that were opened during the sample window from the Policy table. These are then matched to the Claim table using PolicyID as the match key. Most policies have no claims against them, which means that these policies will not have a corresponding observation on the Claim table. After the match has occurred,[2] the fields for these cases will be empty (unpopulated). Conversely, for some policies, several claim observations exist. To be of use the analyst needs to accumulate the data across the claims to create a single observation for each policy. If a policy has three claims associated with it, with claim values of $925, $5,000 and $7,000, then it would make sense for the analyst to create two new fields – one containing the total number of claims (3) and the other the total value of claims ($12,925). Once claim information has been accumulated and matched to the policy table a good/bad definition can be defined, based on the number and value of claims for each policy. Once this is complete, the sample of 5,000 goods and 5,000 bads can be taken using stratified random sampling. The next task is to match to the Quotation table, and then the Vehicle table, to obtain the predictor variables that will be used for model construction.

4.1.1 Mismatches

Sometimes you may expect all observations in one table to match observations in another, but the actual match rate is significantly less than 100 percent. The project from which Figure 4.3 was taken provides a good example of where this occurred. The analyst working on the project began by taking data from the Policy and Claim tables, and this was used to define the good/bad definition. After taking a sample of goods and bads, the data was matched to the Quotation table to obtain the predictor variables. In theory, every customer with an insurance policy had to have had a quotation before taking out their policy. Therefore, the project team naturally assumed there would be a 100 percent match rate between the Policy table and the Quotation table. However, only 67 percent of policy's could be matched to the Quotation table using QuoteID as the match key. After some digging around and making enquiries with colleagues from the risk and IT functions, the analyst was able to determine that:

- 0.25 percent of observations on the Policy table were artificially created test cases – not real policies. These were used within the IT department to test the operation of the system that maintained policy information following any changes/bug fixes, and did not have a corresponding quotation associated with them. The test cases on the Policy table could be identified by the product code ("TEST").
- Nine percent of observations related to cases where the original policy had been revised. If someone changed their car or wanted to change the details of their insurance cover for some other reason, then standard practice was to create a new policy and copy over key details from the existing policy. The old policy was then flagged as closed. For some reason details of the original quotation (the QuoteID) were not copied over to the new policy record when this process occurred.
- Seventeen percent of policies originated with a different insurance company, that was taken over a few months ago. Following the takeover, details of all active policies were transferred to the organization's systems. The QuoteID for these policies originated with the company that was taken over, and therefore, they do not have a corresponding record on the organization's Quotation table.
- Six percent of cases on the Policy table had what appeared to be invalid QuoteIDs, with only a seven digit QuoteID, instead of the eight digits that all quotations should have.
- For 0.75 percent of cases no explanation could be found for the missing QuoteID.

As a result of what the analyst uncovered, the following actions were taken:

- The test cases were deleted from the sample.
- In the 9 percent of cases where the policy had been revised, it was possible to use an additional key held on the policy table to match the new policy to the original policy and retrieve the QuoteID.

- For the policies that had originated with another insurer, the analyst obtained a copy of the original quotation table. This was held on a backup tape that was provided to the IT department when the takeover occurred.
- The policies with seven digit QuoteIDs were traced to an IT change which occurred towards the beginning of the sample window. Originally, QuoteIDs were seven digit numbers. However, as the company grew it realized it would soon run out of unique QuoteIDs. Therefore, all new QuoteIDs were amended to be eight digit numbers. All existing cases on the quotation table had a leading zero added to their QuoteID. So QuoteID "0945292" became "00945292". However, this change was never made to existing records on the Policy table. To get these cases to match, a leading zero was added to the match key on the Policy table.

The result of all this effort was to improve the match rate from 67 percent to 99.25 percent. For the 0.75 percent of cases for which no explanation could be found, a decision was taken to exclude these cases from the development. There was no obvious pattern to these last few cases, and therefore, given that they represented less than 1 percent of the sample, it was difficult to cost justify further investigation.

4.1.2   Sample first or gather first?

In Chapter 3 sampling strategies were discussed. Guidance was provided about the type of sample one should take, but very little was said about the physical process of taking the sample.

When sampling from large database(s) across many different tables, one is often faced with something of a dilemma. With no time or resource constraints, one would ideally match all of the data together from across the relevant tables, and then undertake sampling. If you have the resources available to do this then this is recommended because it means you have all the data you are ever going to need in one place, and won't need to go back and repeat the process if you decide you need more later. In practice, if one is dealing with millions or tens of millions of records then this may not be feasible due to the amount of processing time required or constraints on computer memory. If this is the case, then one way to undertake sampling is as follows:

1. Define the modelling objective (i.e. the good/bad definition for a classification model or the quantity of interest for a regression model). This is done using only the table(s) containing behavioural information

gathered over the outcome period for observations within the sample window. If you recall, for the insurance example of Figure 4.3, information from the policy and claims tables were used to define the good/bad definition before the rest of the sampling process was applied.[3]

2. Select the sample. Sample selection is based on the modelling objective that has been defined in step 1.

3. Match to obtain predictor variables. Only observations within the sample are matched to tables that contain predictor variables, decision codes, and so on.

4. Apply exclusions. Most exclusions are based on sample point information, and therefore, can only be applied after step 3 has occurred.

5. Top-up the sample. This step is only required if the number of exclusions defined in step 4 results in there being insufficient goods or bads for model development. An alternative strategy is to take a slightly larger sample than you think you are going to need in step 2, in anticipation that these numbers will be reduced once exclusions have been applied. If this leads to a sample that has too many observations, then it is a trivial task to delete some of them.

4.1.3   Basic data checks

During the project planning phase consideration should have been given to the list of predictor variables that will be used for model construction, together with the relevant data tables/files/databases where the data will come from. However, at that point, all one normally knows is the names of the fields and the databases/tables from which they will come. What isn't known are the precise details of the information each field contains. There may, for example, be a field called "Total household income", but it has never been populated, and therefore, contains zero's for every observation by default.

Once the model development sample has been created, it is prudent to carry out some basic checks to see what the data looks like. If certain fields are poorly populated or filled with meaningless rubbish, then there is no point taking them forward, and one should revisit the project requirements document and remove them from the data dictionary.

The simplest way to examine the data is to produce a frequency report for every variable in the data dictionary, to see the range of values each predictor variable takes and how the values are distributed. For numeric data, simple statistics such as the mean, minimum and maximum values can also be informative. All professional modelling/data analysis soft-

1. Employment status			
Value	Meaning	Number	%
1	Full-time	5,812	58.1%
2	Part-time	1,606	16.1%
3	Retired	1,005	10.1%
4	Student	430	4.3%
5	Homemaker	590	5.9%
6	Unemployed	557	5.6%
Total		10,000	100.0%
Mean	N/A		
SD	N/A		

2. Time in current employment			
Value	Meaning	Number	%
−1	No data	2,582	25.8%
1	1 month	76	0.8%
2	2 months	103	1.0%
...	...	...	...
486	40 yrs 6m	2	0.0%
487	40 yrs 7m	1	0.0%
Total		10,000	100.0%
Mean	40.8		
SD	82.3		

3. Age of applicant			
Value	Meaning	Number	%
0	No data	41	0.4%
18	18 years	167	1.7%
19	19 years	244	2.4%
...	...	...	...
98	98 years	7	0.1%
99	99+ years	28	0.3%
Total		10,000	100.0%
Mean	37.2		
SD	22.5		

4. Vehicle type			
Value	Meaning	Number	%
Audi	Audi	428	4.3%
BMW	BMW	733	7.3%
...	...	...	...
Vauxall	Vauxall	1,017	10.2%
Volvo	Volvo	301	3.0%
XXXXXXXX	No data	477	4.8%
Total		10,000	100.0%
Mean	N/A		
SD	N/A		

5. Council tax band			
Value	Meaning	Number	%
A	Band A	44	0.4%
B	Band B	58	0.6%
C	Band C	122	1.2%
D	Band D	12	0.1%
E	Band E	11	0.1%
F	Band F	77	0.8%
G	Band G	9	0.1%
H	Band H	8	0.1%
X	No data	9,667	96.7%
Total		10,000	100.0%
Mean	N/A		
SD	N/A		

6. Income band			
Value	Meaning	Number	%
1	<$25K	882	8.8%
2	$25–50K	3,279	32.8%
3	$51–100K	4,503	45.0%
4	$101–150K	884	8.8%
5	>$150K	358	3.6%
99	No data	94	0.9%
Total		10,000	100.0%
Mean	N/A		
SD	N/A		

Figure 4.4　Basic data checks

ware such as SAS and SPSS provide tools to do this quickly and easily. Figure 4.4 shows examples of some reports produced for six variables: Employment Status, Time in Current Employment, Age of Applicant, Vehicle Type, Council Tax Band[4] and Income Band.

Figure 4.4 shows the values that each variable can take and the proportion of cases that take each value. A description is also provided for each value, explaining what it means. However, it is important to note that in very many real life situations one may start from a position of not knowing what the values represent. Therefore, it may be necessary to trawl through documentation or to seek out people who know what the values mean.

Five out of the six variables in Figure 4.4 appear to be well populated with sensible values, but for Council Tax Band more than 95 percent of cases are missing. In theory, every UK dwelling should have a council tax band assigned to it, which suggests it is probably not worth taking this variable forward to the later stages of model development. For Time in Current Employment, around 25 percent of values are missing. This is a significant proportion, but is not unexpected. This is because for people who are not in employment (retired, student, homemaker and unemployed) Time in Current Employment has no meaning. Missing in this case can be interpreted as meaning "not in full or part-time employment". If anything, it would be suspicious if there weren't any missing (or default) values. If this were to be the case, then the analyst should question why values exist for people who are reported as not working.

All of the other four variables have some missing values associated with them, but the proportion of missing values is relatively low. In general, having a handful of missing values (say less than 5%) is not a problem for real world model building and not something to be unduly worried about.

Another thing to note is that many of the variables in Figure 4.4 have different coding schema. The same values have different meanings depending upon the variable – even when they hold values on a similar scale. For Time in Employment the values represent months. For age the values represent years. In an ideal world it would make things simpler if standard coding conventions are adopted for all variables that use a similar scale. Age and Time in Current Employment would both be held as months, or as years. However, in the real world it is common to find fields containing similar data to be coded in different ways. Similarly, it's common for missing and default values to be represented by different values. In Figure 4.4 missing values for age are represented by values of 0, but missing values for Time in Current Employment are coded as –1.

Another thing to watch out for is when missing cases are coded as plausible values. I remember one project I worked on where the data suggested that more than 50 percent of applicant's who had applied for a store card were classified as unemployed. This seemed strange, especially given that the card was for an up-market department store. Querying the data led to the conclusion that if the employment status was not provided, then the IT system set the employment status as unemployed. So what I thought meant unemployed, actually meant unemployed or employment status not provided. The way around this problem was to use time in current employment to distinguish between unemployed and not provided. All cases without a time in current employment were assumed to be unemployed, while those with a valid time in current employment were assumed to be where employment status was not provided. Another example, associated with a different project, was where there were large numbers of loan applicants who appeared to be in their 90s. In reality, if an operator couldn't be bothered to ask the question or the applicant was unwilling to provide a date of birth, then the system let the operator enter 11/11/11. Therefore, these cases were recoded as default values for modelling purposes.

The data in Figure 4.4 covers a number of different types. Some are numeric, others textual. The idea of predictor variables being either numeric or textual was introduced in Chapter 2, albeit very briefly, when describing the data dictionary. However, data can be further classified into the following types.

- Interval. This is where the values can be interpreted as lying along a numeric scale. In consumer behavior modelling, time and value variables are usually classified as interval. In a practical context, continuous numeric variables such as the loan to value ratio for a mortgage or the percentage of someone's credit card limit that has been utilized are also treated as interval. Time in Current Employment and Age of Applicant in Figure 4.4 are examples of interval variables.
- Categorical (nominal). A categorical variable is where each value represents a different attribute and there is no ranking or trend that can be inferred from the attributes. The variable Vehicle Type in Figure 4.4 is an example of a categorical variable that has attributes "Ford", "Volvo", "BMW" and so on. Employment Status is another example. It takes numeric values of 1–6 for full-time, part-time, retired, student, homemaker and unemployed respectively, but it would be non-sensical to say that because "student" is represented by a value of 4 it is equal to twice "part-time", represented by a value of 2.
- Ordinal. An ordinal variable is similar to a categorical variable, but the values can be interpreted as some form of ranking. Council tax band and income band in Figure 4.4 are both examples of ordinal variables.
- Free form. This is where someone has been able to enter a string of numbers, characters or symbols. There is not a predefined set of values that someone can enter. Examples of free form text are people's

names, e-mail addresses and the purpose of a loan that someone has applied for.

Interval data is nearly always numeric[5] and free form data is usually held as text. Categorical and ordinal variables may be stored as either numbers or text, depending upon the characters used to define each attribute. Whether a variable is stored as numeric or text, and whether it is classified as interval, categorical, ordinal or free form is important because it has implications about how the data is analysed and pre-processed prior to modelling. These are subjects that are discussed in more detail in Chapter 5 and 6.

4.2   Cleaning and preparing data

4.2.1   Dealing with missing, corrupt and invalid data

As illustrated in Figure 4.4, missing corrupt or otherwise invalid data is a common problem (note that going forward the term "missing" is used as a catchall for missing, corrupt and/or invalid). For example, you may find that you only have age for 80 percent of observations. Alternatively 5 percent of cases may have *negative* ages, or there might be people who appear to be unfeasibly old. If all or nearly all observations have missing values then the usual course of action is to consider the data to be unreliable and exclude the predictor variable from further analysis. However, if only a proportion of cases are missing then you may wish to retain that variable because what data there is may contain predictive information about consumer behaviour. Instead, action is taken to deal with the observations that contain missing data.

If only a small percentage of observations have missing values or there is no pattern to the missing values; that is, they are *missing completely at random* (MCAR), the simplest option is just to delete them. One problem with this approach is that missing values are often spread across different predictor variables and observations. Perhaps 5 percent of age values are missing, a different 5 percent of time in employment values are missing, 3 percent of incomes values are missing and so on. The overall result is that all, or almost all, observations have some data missing for one or more predictor variables. Therefore, deleting these cases won't leave a big enough sample for model development, or leave a reduced sample that delivers usable, but not optimal, models.

The major problem however, is that for real world problems data is not missing completely at random.[6] The data is missing because some action resulted in the data not being recorded. Often, the very fact that data is missing is in itself predictive of behaviour. Therefore, to delete observations with missing data leads to a biased model that does not provide the best possible predictions.

A second option for dealing with missing data is to impute the missing values; that is, to make an educated guess about what the missing data should be. Basic imputation can be carried out using simple univariate (one variable) procedures. For example, for a variable such as age, the mean age is calculated using cases where age is known. Cases where age is missing are then assigned the mean value. More complex multivariate (many variable) procedures consider how missing values co-vary with other predictor variables, and generally provide superior results than simple univariate methods. Most software packages, including SAS and SPSS provide a range of automated procedures for the analysis and imputation of missing data.

A third option is to code the missing values to a default value. For example, in Figure 4.4, missing ages have been coded as 0 and missing Vehicle types as "XXXXXXXXXX".

Whether to apply imputation or assign default values depends on the nature of the problem and the type of pre-processing that is going to be applied – as discussed in Chapter 6. If dummy variables or weight of evidence transformations are used to pre-process the data, which are the most popular pre-processing methods applied to consumer behaviour modelling, then using default values is often the most practical method to apply. If functional transformations are applied to pre-process the data[7] or no pre-processing is applied, then I recommend applying some form of multivariate imputation (regression or expectation maximization).

An important factor to consider before using imputation is how missing data will be dealt with operationally; that is, what value should be used to calculate the model score for cases where data is missing? If a default category has been assigned and a model generated using the default category, then where data is missing a parameter coefficient will exist, allowing a score to be calculated. However, if imputation has been applied to the development sample and missing values occur operationally, then it will be necessary to apply the imputation process within the operational system where the score is calculated. In many areas of financial services, including credit scoring and insurance rating, the systems used to implement models do not have the ability to apply imputation without a programmer being employed to write the necessary code, and most organizations won't want to spend the time or effort to do this. An alternative to upgrading the system is to assign some average or default score when cases are missing, but this is not ideal.

Imputation is of greatest value when the missing values to be imputed *only* exist within the development sample, and operationally the data will be available when the model is implemented. For example, income values are missing for 25 percent of quotations within a sample used to construct a claims model. However, the organization's policy going forward is not to allow quotations to be made unless an individual provides full details of their income. Imputation is therefore applied to the 25 percent of missing income cases, so that the model development data is more representative of the data that will be available when the model is deployed.

If you want to know more about missing data and the methods that can be applied to deal with it, then I recommend the book "Statistical Analysis with Missing Data" by Roderick J. A. Little and Donald B. Rubin (2002), which is widely acknowledged as the definitive text on the subject of missing data.

4.2.2   Creating derived variables

It is quite common to create new "derived" variables as part of a modelling project, by combining two or more predictor variables together in some way. Generally, there are three types of derived variables analysts create:

- Ratio variables. Often there will be two variables, such as credit card balance and credit card limit. Each may be a useful predictor variable on its own, but dividing card balance by card limit to create a measure of limit utilization will often provide additional insight into behavior.
- Accumulated variables. This is where variables of the same type exist across different categories or time periods. The variables are combined together in some way, such as by taking an average, the minimum or maximum value. Consider a data set that contains credit card expenditure this month, credit card expenditure last month, the month before that and so on. These fields can be used to create a variety of new variables. For example, average expenditure in the last three months, the maximum expenditure in the last 12 months, the difference between average expenditure in the last three months and the last six months and so on.
- Extracted variables. Free form text often contains useful information, but cannot be used directly in the model construction process. It first needs to be processed in some way to transform it into categorical, ordinal or interval form. Consider a personal loan application where

there is a field called "loan purpose". Common words or phrases may be present that can be used to derive loan purpose categories. For example "take a holiday" "go on holiday" "have a holiday" are all cases where the loan is obviously going to be used for a holiday.

The creation of ratio variables invariably results in missing/invalid values for cases where the ratio can't be calculated. Typically, there are several different reasons why a ratio can't be calculated. Consider Table 4.1.

In Table 4.1, the value of "Raw ratio" has been calculated by dividing the card balance by the card limit. "Missing" is used to represent cases where data is not available or can not be calculated. Observations 1 and 2 are examples of where the ratio can be calculated.[8] For observations 3 through 7 the ratio can't be calculated and hence, a "missing" status is assigned. However, in each case the ratio can't be calculated for a different reason. Observation 4 is missing because the value of the card limit is missing, while observation 5 is missing because the card limit is zero and so on. Therefore, for the cleaned version of the ratio a different default value is assigned to represent each possible scenario.

With accumulated variables, missing values can also cause problems. If you are calculating average balances over a period of time and some balances are missing, then you need to decide whether to set a default category to represent missing data, or calculate the average value with the missing values excluded. Likewise, if you have a credit card account that has been on the books for only three months, if you try and calculate a field such as "total monthly spend in the last 12 months", then this will not have the same meaning as for an account that has been on the books for 12 months or more. A decision needs to be taken whether to a) calculate the 12 month ratio using three months of data,

Table 4.1   Missing values for ratio variables

Observation	Card balance	Card limit	"Raw" ratio	Cleaned ratio
1	$9,000.00	$20,000.00	+0.450	+0.450
2	–$100.00	$15,000.00	–0.067	–0.067
3	Missing	Missing	Missing	–9,999,999
4	$0.00	Missing	Missing	–9,999,998
5	£0.00	£0.00	Missing	–9,999,997
6	$9,000.00	£0.00	Missing	–9,999,996
7	Missing	$20,000.00	Missing	–9,999,995

or b) assign a default to the value of the variable for all accounts that have been on the books for less than 12 months.

4.2.3   Outliers

An outlier is something outside the range of usual or expected values. If a value is infeasible – such as someone having an age of –57 or 8,754, then it should be treated in the same way as a missing value, as discussed earlier in the chapter. However, sometimes extreme values may be theoretically possible; that is, they are valid data, but very unlikely to occur. These days there are quite a lot of people who are more than 100 years old, but to receive a mortgage application from someone who is more than 100 is a most unusual event. When dealing with populations containing millions of observations and many predictor variables, then one can expect to get quite a lot of cases that have unusual values, and the difference between a value that is somewhat unusual and one that is clearly exceptional (an outlier) is not necessarily easy to discern. Consequently, the definition of what constitutes an outlier is often based on expert opinion. A more quantitative rule of thumb is to define outliers to be values that lie more than 3–4 standard deviations from the average value.[9] Assuming values are normally distributed, this roughly translates to 1:1000–1:10,000 observations being treated as outliers for any given variable.

As with missing data, I would recommend coding genuine outliers (as opposed bizarre values due to corrupt/incorrect data) with a single default value rather than excluding them.

4.2.4   Inconsistent coding schema

If data has been gathered from across a period of time, or different samples have been taken from different databases that are then combined together, then variables will often have more than one coding schema associated with them. By this I mean that a certain value may mean something for some observations, but a different value is used for others to mean the same thing. Consider Table 4.2 which was produced as part of the basic data checking undertaken for the variable residential status.

In Table 4.2 there are two different values used to represent each type of residential status. A character representation is used for some while a numbering system has been employed for others. There are several reasons why this might have occurred. Maybe there used to be two different IT systems that were used to process applications from different sources, each with their own coding schema. At some point

Table 4.2   Values for residential status

Value	Meaning
O	Home owner
T	Tenant
L	Living with parent
1	Home owner
2	Tenant
3	Living with parent

the data from each system was combined. Maybe some observations were added to the database as a result of a merger or acquisition, or it may be the case that a change was made at some time in the past to align the coding schema with that used for other variables. The change was applied to new data going forward, but for existing accounts no changes to the original coding schema were made.

As Siddiqi notes (2006, p. 66) many changes to systems and data-bases are not well documented, and one is often required to talk to people from relevant areas of the business in order to try and under-stand when and why changes to a coding schema occurred. Sometimes the reasons why different schemas have been employed can't be found. While frustrating, this is not necessarily a show stopper as long as it is clear what the different coding schema means, and one knows what coding schema will be employed going forward, when the model is implemented.

4.2.5   Coding of the dependent variable (modelling objective)

For binary classification problems, the goal is to predict into which of two classes (good or bad) an observation falls. The dependent variable therefore, needs to be coded so that observations can take only one of two values. In Chapter 2, classifying observations as good or bad was discussed, but how these values should be coded for modelling was not covered at that point. Conventions vary, but assigning goods a value of 1 and bads a value of 0 (or vice versa) is common practice. Alternatively, some practitioners use a +1/–1 coding for good and bad. For the model-ling techniques discussed in the main part of this book, it is assumed that goods are coded as 1 and bads as 0.

The model will only be constructed using good and bad cases, but there may be additional classes represented within the development sample such as, indeterminates, exclusions and non-performance. The dependent variable for these cases may be coded to a default value, say

–99, or left undefined. If any examples of these additional classes exist, I recommend creating an additional "Good/Bad Flag" to represent them. A typical Good/Bad Flag might take values such as:

G: Good
B: Bad
I: Indeterminate
E: Exclusions
N: Non-performance (Accepted applications without behaviour)
R: Non-performance (Rejected applications without behaviour)
X: Other (any cases that don't fall into the above categories)

A good/bad flag is not a requirement for modelling, but having a simple indicator of this type is often very useful and saves time when it comes to specifying sub-sets of a sample for modelling, reporting and general ad-hoc analysis.

For continuous modelling objectives the dependent variable will be a numeric value, whose derivation was discussed in section 2.3.4. Although there is no concept of "Good" and "Bad" with a continuous variable, it can still be useful to define an additional indicator variable to allow exclusions, non-performance cases and so on, to be easily identified.

4.2.6   The final data set

After data has been gathered, cleaned and prepared, there should be a single data set containing the predictor variables and the dependent variable. Table 4.3 provides an example of a data set containing a sample of 10,000 accounts that are going to be used to build a claim propensity model.

In Table 4.3 predictor variables such as applicant age, income and residential status, taken at the sample point, are shown on the left hand side, as well as other sample point information such as QuoteID and the sample date. Information about the sampling process and outcome point information, calculated at the end of the outcome period, are held in the right most columns. This includes the dependent variable (modelling objective), coded 0/1 for customers who did/did not make a claim as well as a weighting field. A good/bad flag and sample indicator, to identify whether an observation forms part of the development sample, holdout sample or out-of-time sample, are also present.

Note that in Table 4.3 the data set contains data from all three samples that are going to be used to build and validate the model; that is, development, validation and out-of-time samples. I recommend that, if

Table 4.3 The final data set

Ref.	QuoteID	Sample date	Applicant Age (yrs)	Income ($000)	Residential status[1]	Vehicle make[2]	...	Weight	Sample[3]	Good/Bad Flag[4]	Dependent variable[5]
1	0079345	12-Jan-09	29	35	T	56	...	8	D	G	1
2	0079995	16-Jan-09	62	112	O	32	...	1	D	B	0
3	1008765	26-Feb-09	42	79	O	12	...	20	H	X	.
4	1009045	28-Feb-09	55	160	O	2	...	8	D	G	1
5	1009755	07-Mar-09	49	42	T	3	...	8	H	G	1
...	...	...	...	...	...	...	...	...	...	...	...
9,998	1296607	17-May-09	19	29	X	56	...	8	O	B	1
9,999	1296712	17-May-09	49	60	L	12	...	1	O	B	0
10,000	1308766	18-May-09	31	54	O	8	...	8	O	G	1

Notes:

1. O = Owner, T = Tenant, L = Living with parent, X = unknown/other
2. Each number represents a make of car. e.g. 2 = Audi, 3 = BMW, 4 = Citroen.
3. D = development sample, H = Holdout sample, O = Out-of-time sample
4. X = Exclusion, G = Good, B = Bad
5. 1 = Good; i.e. no claims in last 12 months. 0 = bad i.e. one or more claims in the last 12 months.

possible,[10] one carries out the data gathering and preparation process as a single exercise, rather than separately for each sample. This is to ensure each sample has been subject to the same data processing. In the past I have come across situations where an initial data gathering exercise was undertaken to produce the development sample. Then, at a later stage of the project, the exercise was repeated to generate holdout and out-of-time samples. However, prior to taking the holdout and out-of-time samples the analyst made corrections to the code used to gather and prepare the data to improve match rates and better deal with missing/corrupt data, but they did not apply the changes to the development sample. The result was that some of the predictor variables contained somewhat different representations of the data depending upon which sample one was dealing with, making it impossible to make a true comparison of model performance across the different samples.

4.3   Familiarization with the data

One advantage of having the model developer gather and prepare data, rather than having someone else do it, is it begins the process of familiarizing them with the data they are going to use to construct the model. By the time data preparation is complete the analyst should have a good feel for where the data has come from, which variables contain meaningful information, the form the data is held in and how well each variable is populated. As a former analyst I know how easy it is to get tied up with the statistics without giving much thought to the context within which the model will be applied. In many modelling contexts it is important to have a good understanding of what the data represents, where it comes from, and why it contains the values it does. For any credit scoring model, for example, implementation of the model will almost certainly not be authorized if an adequate explanation of the source and meaning of the predictor variables in the model cannot be provided, because of the risk that such unknowns represent.

If you are an analyst discussing the model you are planning to construct with senior members of the project team, then you should be able to answer the following questions about any item of data that you are considering taking forward to the next stage of the model development process:

- What is it? So you've got a variable called CvalToPrem. Someone who doesn't work closely with data asks you what data this variable

contains – You need to be able to say "Ah – that means the ratio of claim value to premiums paid, expressed as a percentage."
- What do the values mean? If a variable called residential status takes values of O, L, P, C or U, can you explain what all of these mean; for example, home (O)wner, (L)iving with parent, (P)rivate tenant, (C)ouncil tenant, (U)nknown?
- Its past origin? What system or database did the data come from? For example, for a credit scoring model was it captured directly from the applicant via the customer interface, supplied by a credit reference agency or taken from the prospects database?[11]
- Its future origin? What system or database will data come from when the model is implemented? This may be different from the system that provided the data for modelling purposes. For example, for a model of claim propensity, the data may come from an insurer's data warehouse, but the model is going to be implemented within the organization's on-line quotation system.

If you can't answer any of these questions then you should seriously consider not taking that item of data any further; that is, excluding it from model development altogether because you won't be able to attach any business meaning to the data. Consequently, you may struggle to provide satisfactory assurance to relevant stakeholders that the data will be available at the time and location of model implementation. From a management perspective, if the analyst(s) building the model can't answer questions such as these, then what level of confidence do you have in their ability to develop a business usable model that will deliver what you want?

4.4   Chapter summary

For many projects the data required for model development is scattered across different databases and IT systems. This data needs to be matched together to produce a single data set that is suitable for analysis and modelling. Data may also be sourced from external suppliers and this too will need to be matched to the model development sample.

Consumer data tends to be messy. For some individuals data will be missing. For others extreme values (outliers) may exist. Alternatively, the data for some individuals just doesn't make any business sense. For example, dates of birth set sometime in the future, or people with a negative number of children. Consequently, decisions need to be taken about how to deal with such cases.

If there are relatively few observations for which missing/corrupt/ extreme data exists, and there does not seem to be any pattern to the missing data, then the best option may be just to delete these observations from the data set. However, data will often be missing for a reason and/or the number of exclusions would mean that too little data would be left for model development. In general, a better option is to retain observations and assign default values, with different default values assigned if there are different reasons for the data to be missing. It is also possible to apply imputation algorithms to infer what the value of missing values would likely have been, but in general this does not lead to better models that those created using default values. In addition, if imputation is applied, then additional work is required to ensure that the imputation process can be applied at the point where the final model will be implemented, to impute values for new observations going forward.

The time taken to gather and prepare data should not be underestimated. It can take anything from a few hours to many weeks to gather, clean data and prepare data, depending upon the number of databases/ tables from which data is sourced, and the quality and format of the data obtained.

5
Understanding Relationships in Data

By the end of the data gathering and preparation process there should be a single, clean and well formatted data set ready for detailed analysis. The file will contain all predictor variables that are going to be considered for inclusion within the model, as well as the dependent variable (the modelling objective). Potential predictor variables that may have been suggested during the project planning phase, but which have subsequently been shown to contain no meaningful data or data that is obviously incorrect will also have been excluded. For those predictor variables that have been retained, missing and spurious values will have been coded to default values and so on.

At this stage, one is ready to begin analysing and understand the relationships between the predictor variables and the dependent variable. If a relationship is sensible and significant then the variable is retained. This does not necessarily mean the variable will feature in the final model, but that it will be considered within the model construction process. If a relationship is not deemed to be significant, then the variable will not be considered further.

Sometimes a statistically significant relationship exists between a predictor variable and the dependent variable, but the relationship is counter to what common sense or expert opinion says it should be. For some types of model these variables may be retained, but more often than not, the relationship will be considered spurious and that variable will also be excluded from model construction.

Preliminary analysis of the relationships between predictor variables and the dependent variable is usually undertaken one predictor variable at a time – a process referred to as univariate analysis or characteristic analysis. Sometimes it can be worthwhile undertaking multivariate analysis of the relationships between two (or more) predictor variables and the dependent variable at the same time. This is done to identify where predictor variables interact with each other. Interaction means the relationships that predictor variables have with the dependent variable are to some extent dependent upon the relationships that exist with other predictor variables. In general, univariate analysis is sufficient to identify the most significant relationships that exist in the data. Therefore, the main focus in this chapter is on univariate analysis of data. Where interaction effects do exist, usually they contribute only marginally to the predictive ability of a model. However, there are some cases where suitable treatment of interaction effects can lead to small but worthwhile improvements in model performance. Therefore, interaction is discussed towards the end of the chapter.

5.1   Fine classed univariate (characteristic) analysis

A traditional, simple and effective way to examine the relationship between a predictor variable and the dependent variable is to under-

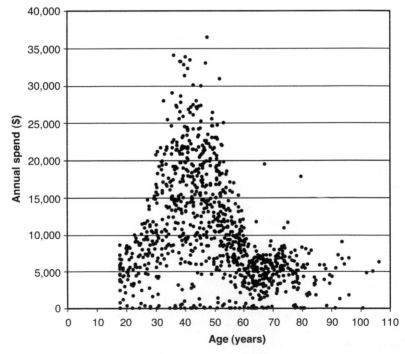

Figure 5.1   Relationship between age and card spend

take visual analysis of the data. The values of each predictor variable and the dependent variable are plotted against each other on a graph. Consider a project where the objective is to predict how much someone spends on their credit card in the next year. One predictor variable under consideration is the age of the card holder. A scatter graph, showing the relationship between age and card spend for the 2,000 cases in the sample, is shown in Figure 5.1.

In Figure 5.1 credit card spend appears to be related to the age of the account holder. The relationship follows a curve, indicating this is a non-linear relationship. For the youngest customers, average card spend is low, but rises quickly with age. However, above about 40 years of age, card spend declines until about 60, when spend levels off. The graph is also skewed to the left. Peak spend occurs in relatively young card holders (the average age of cardholders in this sample is 51[1]). Another feature of the graph is that there are quite a few cases with zero spend, representing dormant account holders who did not use their cards over the forecast horizon.

There are various statistical tests that can be applied to establish if a relationship exists between age and card spend, but as a rule – if you can clearly see a pattern in the data – as in Figure 5.1, then the relationship will be statistically significant. Any statistical test of significance acts merely to confirm what you can see. With large data sets containing thousands of observations, tests of statistical significance tend to be more useful where the patterns are not so obvious, indicating at best a marginal relationship between the variables, or as we shall discuss later, the magnitude of the test statistic is used as a ranking tool to determine which predictor variables have the strongest relationship with the dependent variable. Tests of significance can also be useful in situations where there are hundreds or thousands of predictor variables, making it somewhat time consuming to manually examine every relationship in detail. Automated procedures are used to produce measures of significance for each predictor variable, and only those with the strongest association with the dependent variable are examined in greater detail.

Let's look at a second example. Consider a classification problem where the behaviour of interest is response to a mail shot. The dependent variable can take one of two values representing a response or non-response event. The sample contains 180,000 cases, of which 3,721 responded and the rest did not. This equates to a good rate (response rate) of 1.82 percent and a corresponding bad rate (non-response rate) of 98.18 percent. A plot of age vs response is shown in Figure 5.2.

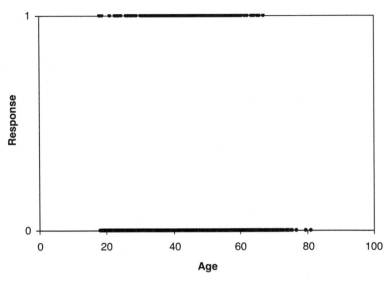

Figure 5.2   Relationship between age and response

In Figure 5.2 a response to the mail shot is coded as 1 and non-response as 0. The graph does not really tell you very much. All you get is two smudged lines, one for each value of the dependent variable. If you also go back and reconsider Figure 5.1, while a pattern can be discerned, the graph is somewhat "messy" due to the high number of data points and the variation in spend for a given age. Often a better way to observe patterns in large data sets is to discretize the data (also known as fine classing[2] or binning). Observations are classed into one of a finite number of intervals based on the value of the predictor variable. The average values of the predictor variable and the dependent variable are then calculated for each interval. Consider Figure 5.3 and Figure 5.4.

Figures 5.3 and 5.4 use the same data as Figures 5.1 and 5.2, but this time observations have been grouped into 20 intervals, each containing 5 percent of the sample population. This leads to a much clearer picture of the patterns present in the data. For example, in Figure 5.4 a trend between age and response is now clearly visible. The older someone is, the more likely they are to respond. The trend is also approximately linear. You can draw a straight line through the points, with most points lying on or very close to the line. A further feature of the relationship between age and response is it displays a "monotonically increasing trend". This means the average response rate always increases the older people are.

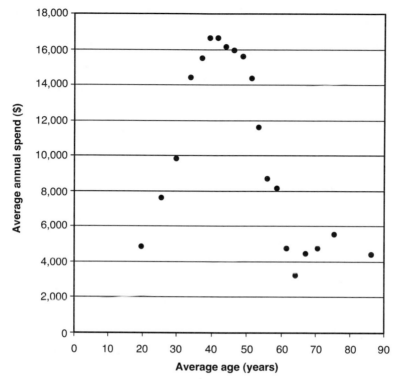

Figure 5.3   Classed relationship between age and card spend

Note that for classification problems, if under or over sampling has been applied to create the development sample, then an appropriate weighting should be applied. This is to ensure that patterns observed in the univariate analysis reports are representative of the population from which the sample was taken.

For categorical and ordinal variables, such as residential status and number of dependants, it naturally makes sense to calculate the average value of the dependent variable for each possible value (each attribute) of the predictor variable (note that going forward attributes and intervals are referred to interchangeably). For interval variables however, there are many ways that classing can be undertaken. A good place to start is to have intervals of equal size; that is, intervals that all contain approximately the same number of observations. For most problems having between ten and 25 intervals is sufficient for any major patterns in the data to be discerned, but there is no reason why there can't be more than

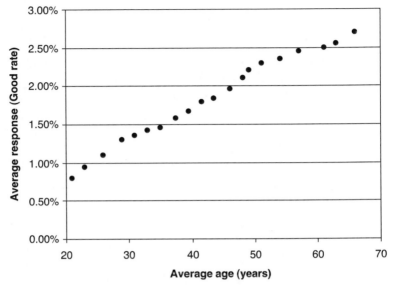

Figure 5.4 Classed relationship between age and response

25 intervals if the data set is large enough. However, each interval needs to contain sufficient numbers of observations so that the average interval value is stable. If an interval contains too few observations, then it is unlikely to provide as much useful information as it could. As a general rule, I recommend that at this stage (prior to pre-processing), to try and ensure that as a *minimum*, each interval contains at least 50 observations in total, and *at least* ten cases of each class.

There are many ways to present univariate analysis. Graphical representations of the data – such as those in Figures 5.3 and 5.4 are useful, but it can be difficult to present more than two or three aspects of the data using a single graph. An alternative is to present univariate analysis as a tabular report. Table 5.1 is a tabular version of the univariate analysis report for the relationship between age and mailing response from Figure 5.4.

Table 5.1 contains columns for the number of goods, the number of bads and the total number of cases within each interval. There are also columns showing the bad rate and the good:bad odds, which were introduced in section 2.3.1. Note that the good rate (1 – bad rate) has been included in Table 5.1, but going forward only bad rates are presented in later examples to keep matters simple and consistent. If you wish to use

Table 5.1 Univariate analysis report for age

Interval	Attribute	Number of goods	Number of bads	Total number	% of total	Good rate (response rate)	Bad rate (non-response rate)	Good:bad odds	Weight of evidence	Z-statistic
1	<= 21	72	8,928	9,000	5.00	0.80%	99.20%	0.008	-0.831	-7.414
2	22–24	85	8,915	9,000	5.00	0.94%	99.06%	0.010	-0.667	-6.385
3	25–27	99	8,901	9,000	5.00	1.10%	98.90%	0.011	-0.509	-5.228
4	28–30	117	8,883	9,000	5.00	1.30%	98.70%	0.013	-0.340	-3.770
5	31–32	122	8,879	9,000	5.00	1.35%	98.65%	0.014	-0.302	-3.406
6	33–34	128	8,872	9,000	5.00	1.42%	98.58%	0.014	-0.251	-2.896
7	35–36	131	8,870	9,000	5.00	1.45%	98.55%	0.015	-0.230	-2.677
8	37–38	142	8,858	9,000	5.00	1.58%	98.42%	0.016	-0.141	-1.708
9	39–40	150	8,850	9,000	5.00	1.67%	98.33%	0.017	-0.086	-1.074
10	41–42	161	8,839	9,000	5.00	1.79%	98.21%	0.018	-0.016	-0.200
11	43–44	166	8,834	9,000	5.00	1.84%	98.16%	0.019	0.013	0.164
12	45–46	176	8,824	9,000	5.00	1.96%	98.05%	0.020	0.074	1.002
13	47–48	189	8,811	9,000	5.00	2.10%	97.90%	0.021	0.147	2.059
14	49–50	198	8,802	9,000	5.00	2.20%	97.80%	0.022	0.195	2.787
15	51–52	207	8,793	9,000	5.00	2.30%	97.70%	0.024	0.240	3.516
16	53–55	212	8,789	9,000	5.00	2.35%	97.65%	0.024	0.262	3.880
17	56–59	221	8,780	9,000	5.00	2.45%	97.55%	0.025	0.305	4.609
18	60–62	225	8,775	9,000	5.00	2.50%	97.50%	0.026	0.326	4.973
19	63–66	230	8,771	9,000	5.00	2.55%	97.45%	0.026	0.346	5.338
20	>=67	243	8,757	9,000	5.00	2.70%	97.30%	0.028	0.405	6.431
Total		3,271	176,729	180,000	100.00	1.82%	98.18%	0.019	0.000	

good rates instead of bad rates for your own projects, then that is not an issue.

Looking at the bad rate or odds it can be seen that there is clearly a monotonic trend of decreasing bad rate/increasing odds as age increases.

One of the advantages of a tabular report is it has the potential to provide more information than a graph. If additional classification types exist, such as indeterminates and non-performance, then columns can be included for these categories. Likewise, if you want to display additional outcome point information, such revenue or write-off amounts, then columns for these can also be included. If you want to generate graphs, then these can be produced easily from the relevant columns.

The second to last column in Table 5.1 is the Weight of Evidence (WoE). The WoE for an interval is calculated as:

$$WoE = Ln\left(\frac{g_i/G}{b_i/B}\right)$$

where:

g_i is the number of goods within the interval.
b_i is the number of bads within the interval.
G is the total number of goods in the whole population.
B is the total number of bads in the whole population.

So for the first row of Table 5.1, the weight of evidence is calculated as:

$$WoE = Ln\left(\frac{72/3,271}{8,928/176,729}\right) = -0.831$$

The WoE is a standardized way of comparing the interval good:bad odds with the average good:bad odds of the sample. Any interval that has a higher proportion of goods than average will have a positive weight of evidence, and any interval that has a higher than average proportion of bads will have a negative WoE. A WoE of 1 means the good:bad odds are e^1 (2.718) times average, a value of 2 e^2 (7.389) times average and so on. Likewise, a value of –1 means the odds are 2.718 times smaller than average.

A useful property of WoE is that it always displays a linear relationship with the natural log of the good:bad odds (*Ln(odds)*). This is very useful for pre-processing data, particularly when linear models are being constructed.

The final column in Table 5.1 is the Z-statistic. The Z-statistic (sometimes referred to as a Z-score)[3] provides a measure of how likely it is that the bad rates of two populations are different. The Z-statistic for an interval is calculated as follows:

$$Z\text{-statistic} = \frac{BR_{\neq i} - BR_i}{\sqrt{\dfrac{BR_{all}\,(1 - BR_{all})}{n_{\neq i}} + \dfrac{BR_{all}\,(1 - BR_{all})}{n_i}}}$$

where:

$BR_{\neq i}$ is the bad rate for observations in all intervals except interval i.
BR_i is the bad rate for interval i.
BR_{all} is the overall bad rate for the entire sample.
n_i is the number of observations in interval i.
$n_{\neq i}$ is the number of observations in all intervals except interval i.

So for the first row in Table 5.1 the Z-statistic has been calculated as:

$$Z\text{-statistic} = \frac{98.13 - 99.20}{\sqrt{\dfrac{98.18\,(1 - 98.18)}{171,000} + \dfrac{98.18\,(1 - 98.18)}{9,000}}} = -7.414$$

In Table 5.1 the Z-statistic is used to compare the proportion of bads in each interval with the rest of the sample. The larger the absolute value of the Z-statistic, then the more confident one can be that there is a genuine difference between the bad rates of the two groups. Any given value of the Z-statistic translates to a level of confidence that the observed difference is genuine and not some random feature of the process used to produce the sample. A Z-statistic with an absolute value greater than 3.58 can be taken to mean a very strong (>99.9%) level of confidence that the bad rate of the interval is different from the bad rate of the rest of the sample. Absolute values between 1.96 and 3.58 indicate a moderate degree of confidence (somewhere between 95 percent and 99.9 percent) that the bad rate within the interval is significantly different. So in Table 5.1 it is possible to say that intervals 1–4 and 16–20 all have bad rates that are very significantly different from the rest of the sample and intervals 5–7 and 13–15 are moderately different. To put it another way, there is a strong case for saying that the response rates of people in these intervals is significantly different from the people in the other intervals.

Often it is insightful to use WoE and the Z-statistic in combination. WoE gives a measure of the magnitude of difference between the interval bad rate and the average bad rate, while the Z-statistic tells you whether or not the difference is statistically significant. Generally, the relationship will need to be both large and statistically significant if it is going to add to the predictive ability of the model.[4]

For regression problems, the WOE can not be calculated directly, but a similar standardized measure is :

$$WoE = \frac{a_i - a}{s}$$

where:

a_i is the mean value of the dependent variable calculated using observations in interval i.

a is the mean value of the dependent variable calculated using the whole sample.

s is the standard deviation[5] of the dependent variable, calculated using the whole sample.

A slightly different version of the Z-test can also be performed:

$$Z = \frac{a_{\neq i} - a_i}{\sqrt{+\dfrac{s_{\neq i}^2}{n_{\neq i}} + \dfrac{s_i^2}{n_i}}}$$

where:

a_i is the mean value of the dependent variable calculated using observations in interval i.

$a_{\neq i}$ is the mean value of the dependent variable calculated using observations in all intervals except interval i.

s_i is the standard deviation of the dependent variable calculated using observations in interval i.

$s_{\neq i}$ is the standard deviation of the dependent variable calculated using observations in all intervals except interval i.

n_i is the number of observations in interval i.

$n_{\neq i}$ is the number of observations in all intervals except interval i.

As before, a Z-statistic with an absolute value greater than 3.58 can be taken to mean a very strong (>99.9%) level of confidence that average value of the interval is different from the rest of the population.

5.2   Measures of association

Weights of Evidence and the Z-statistic can be useful when looking at individual attributes within a variable, but what is often of greater interest are combined measures of association that take into account all of the individual attributes that a predictor variable contains. In this section the most common of these combined measures of association are described.

5.2.1   Information value

Probably the most popular measure of association used for classification problems is the information value (IV). The information value for a classed variable is calculated as:

$$IV = \sum_{i=1}^{I} \left(\frac{g_i}{G} - \frac{b_i}{B} \right) Ln \left(\frac{g_i/G}{b_i/B} \right)$$

where:

> I is the number of intervals that the variable has been classed into.
> g_i is the number of goods in the ith interval.
> b_i is the number of bads in the ith interval.
> G is the total number of goods in the whole sample.
> B is the total number of bads in the whole sample.

Information values can range from zero to infinity, but values in the range 0–1 are most common. A value below about 0.05 indicates little association, and therefore, the variable is unlikely to be predictive of behaviour. A value of between 0.05–0.25 indicates a moderate relationship, and anything over about 0.25 indicates a fairly strong relationship. Consider Table 5.2.

Table 5.2 shows the univariate analysis report for employment status. This is a categorical variable. Therefore, no additional classing of the variable is required at this stage, with one row in the report for each employment status. The report has been produced using the same data used to produce Figure 5.4 and Table 5.1. Visual examination of Table 5.2 shows that those classified as self-employed or students are the two groups that are most likely to respond, with the good:bad odds for people in these groups more than three times higher than those for other groups. The significance of these relationships is support by the value of the Z-statistic. The rightmost column in Table 5.2 shows the contribution each attribute makes to the information value of

Table 5.2   Calculating information value for employment status

Interval	Classing	Number of goods	Number of bads	Total number	% of total	Bad rate (non-response rate)	Good:bad odds	Weight of evidence	Z-statistic	Information value
						Employment status				
1	Full-time employed	1,954	111,582	113,536	63.08	98.28%	0.018	−0.055	−4.002	0.002
2	Part-time employed	228	15,870	16,098	8.94	98.58%	0.014	−0.253	−3.993	0.005
3	Self-employed	515	8,482	8,997	5.00	94.28%	0.061	1.188	28.460	0.130
4	Student	170	2,886	3,056	1.70	94.44%	0.059	1.158	15.633	0.041
5	Homemaker	168	12,815	12,983	7.21	98.71%	0.013	−0.345	−4.635	0.007
6	Retired	117	13,744	13,861	7.70	99.16%	0.009	−0.777	−8.929	0.033
7	Unemployed	119	11,350	11,469	6.37	98.96%	0.011	−0.565	−6.431	0.016
Total		3,271	176,729	180,000	100.00	98.18%	0.019	0.00		0.234

0.234. This indicates there is a moderate degree of association between employment status and mailing response.

5.2.2 Chi-squared statistic

Another popular measure applied to classification problems is the chi-squared (test) statistic. The chi-squared statistic is calculated as

$$\text{chi-squared statistic } (\chi^2) = \sum_{i=1}^{I} \left(\frac{g_i - \hat{g}_i}{\hat{g}_i} \right)^2 + \left(\frac{b_i - \hat{b}_i}{\hat{b}_i} \right)^2$$

where:

each predictor variable is classed into I intervals.
g_i is the number of goods in the ith interval.
b_i is the number of bads in the ith interval.
$\hat{g}_i$ is the expected number of goods in the interval if the distribution was completely uniform and $\hat{b}_i$ is the expected number of bads in the interval if the distribution was completely uniform. These are calculated as

$$\hat{g}_i = \frac{(g_i + b_i)G}{G + B} \quad \text{and} \quad \hat{b}_i = \frac{(g_i + b_i)B}{G + B}$$

where:

G is the total number of goods in the sample.
B is the total number of bads in the sample.

In general usage the chi-squared test is used to decide if there is sufficient evidence to conclude that two distributions, classed into a number of discrete intervals, are the same or different. In predictive analytics, as described here, the usage is slightly different. The test itself is not important. Instead, the size of the test statistic is used to provide a measure of the relative strength of the relationship between a predictor variable and the dependent variable, in a similar manner to information value. Chi-squared values can range from zero to infinity. Values greater than about 30 generally indicate a moderate relationship, with values greater than 150 indicating a strong relationship.

5.2.3 Efficiency (GINI coefficient)

A third measure of association for classification problems is efficiency (GINI coefficient). First, all of the intervals for a given variable are sorted in bad rate order from high to low. The efficiency is then calculated using the Brown formula (or Trapezium rule):

$$\text{Efficiency} = 1 - \sum_{i=2}^{I} [G(i) + G(i-1)][B(i) - B(i-1)]$$

where:

    I is the number of intervals the variable has been classed into.
    $G(i)$ is the cumulative proportion of goods in the ith interval.
    $B(i)$ is the cumulative proportion of bads in the ith interval.

Efficiency values lie in the range 0–1. Any value greater than about 0.05 indicates a moderate relationship with the dependent variable, with values greater than about 0.25 indicating a strong relationship.

5.2.4   Correlation

Information value, the Chi-square statistic and efficiency are all measures commonly applied to binary classification problems, where the predictor variables have been classed into a number of discrete intervals. For regression problems, where the dependent variable can take a range of values, alternative measures of association can be used. One popular measure is Spearman's Rank Correlation Coefficient.[6] Spearman's Rank Correlation Coefficient provides a measure of the relative ranking of observations between two variables – in this case a predictor variable and the dependent variable. It can therefore, be applied to ordinal and interval variables, but not categorical (nominal) variables. Each variable is sorted in order from low to high (or vice versa). Observations are then assigned a rank from 1...n where n is the number of observations. The coefficient is calculated as:

$$\text{Spearman's rank correlation coefficient} = 1 - \frac{6\sum_{1}^{n}(v_i - d_i)^2}{n(n^2 - 1)}$$

where

    v_i is the rank of observation i in terms of the predictor variable.
    d_i is the rank of observation i in terms of the dependent variable.

If the rankings are in perfect agreement, the coefficient takes a value of 1. If they are in perfect disagreement (with the lowest value of the predictor variable matching with the highest value of the dependent variable and vice versa), the value of the coefficient is –1. Spearman's

Table 5.3   Calculating Spearman's rank correlation coefficient

Interval	Attribute	Number of cases	Average spend	Weight of evidence	Z-statistic	Rank of age (v)	Rank of average spend (d)	Difference between ranks ($v-d$)	Difference squared ($v-d$)^2
					Age of customer				
1	<= 20	100	4,812	−0.745	7.406	1	6	−5	25
2	21–26	100	7,595	−0.289	3.394	2	8	−6	36
3	27–30	100	9,795	−0.034	0.386	3	11	−8	64
4	31–34	100	14,385	0.350	−4.725	4	14	−10	100
5	35–37	100	15,468	0.423	−4.993	5	15	−10	100
6	38–40	100	16,611	0.494	−6.170	6	20	−14	196
7	41–42	100	16,601	0.493	−6.303	7	19	−12	144
8	43–44	100	16,130	0.465	−5.970	8	18	−10	100
9	45–46	100	15,941	0.453	−6.170	9	17	−8	64
10	47–49	100	15,577	0.430	−5.746	10	16	−6	36
11	50–51	100	14,327	0.346	−4.586	11	13	−2	4
12	52–53	100	11,610	0.136	−1.750	12	12	0	0
13	54–56	100	8,691	−0.154	1.811	13	10	3	9
14	57–59	100	8,141	−0.219	2.664	14	9	5	25
15	60–64	100	4,757	−0.757	7.407	15	4	11	121
16	65–67	100	3,226	−1.145	8.535	16	1	15	225
17	68–71	100	4,431	−0.827	7.861	17	3	14	196
18	72–75	100	4,758	−0.756	7.285	18	5	13	169
19	76–86	100	5,506	−0.610	6.414	19	7	12	144
20	87+	100	4,382	−0.839	7.734	20	2	18	324
Total		2,000	10,137	0.000					2,082

Spearman's rank correlation coefficient = −0.5654

Rank Correlation Coefficient can be calculated using the raw values of the two variables, or alternatively, using the average interval values after classing has been applied (so I intervals in the above equation instead of n observations). As a rule, a value of anything greater than about ±0.05 indicates some level of association, with values above about ±0.30 indicating a high level of association.

Table 5.3 provides an example of the calculation of Spearman's Rank Correlation Coefficient for the predictor variable age and the dependent variable credit card spend, that were introduced previously in relation to Figure 5.1 and Figure 5.3.

In Table 5.3 age has been classed into 20 intervals. Each age interval is naturally ranked from low to high (1 to 20). The ranking of card spend has then been calculated, using the average card spend for each age interval. The two right most columns contain the difference and the square of the difference between each rank respectively. Putting these values into the Spearman correlation coefficient equation gives a value of –0.5654. This supports the case that there is a relationship between increasing age and decreasing card spend. If you refer back to Figure 5.1, you will see that it is in agreement with the observed trend.

Correlation coefficients can also be calculated for classification problems. Spearman's Rank Correlation Coefficient can be applied to classed data using the ranking of the average interval values, but for binary classification problems it is not appropriate to calculate it using raw (unclassed) data. This is because for each observation the dependent variable can only be assigned one of two ranks. All goods are assigned to one rank and all bads to another. A more appropriate correlation measure to apply to unclassed data is Pearson's Correlation Coefficient. This is calculated as:

$$\text{Pearson's Correlation Coefficient} = \frac{\sum_{1}^{n}(x_i - \bar{x})(y_i - \bar{y})}{\sqrt{\sum_{1}^{n}(x_i - \bar{x})^2}\,\sqrt{\sum_{1}^{n}(y_i - \bar{y})^2}}$$

where

x_i is the value of the predictor variable for the ith observation.
y_i is the value of the dependent variable for the ith observation.
$\bar{x}$ is the mean value of the predictor variable.
$\bar{y}$ is the mean value of the dependent variable.
n is the number of observations in the sample.

Pearson's Correlation Coefficient only measures linear relationships in the data for ordinal and interval variables. Two variables may be strongly associated, resulting in a high information value, chi-squared statistic or efficiency, but have a zero correlation coefficient if the relationship is highly non-linear. Due to this limitation, it is more common to calculate measures of correlation after data pre-processing has been applied, to transform the data.

5.3 Alternative methods for classing interval variables

Classing an interval variable into say, 20, equally sized groups will usually be sufficient to allow useful insights into the relationship between a predictor variable and the dependant variable to be drawn. However, sometimes a little bit of additional information can be teased from the data by applying more complex procedures to define intervals. Similarly, much may be gained by applying expert opinion to adjust interval definitions, drawing on the experiences gained from working on other projects.

5.3.1 Automated segmentation procedures

One view is that the best (most informative) classing is where intervals are chosen to maximize a measure of association, such as information value, the Chi-squared statistic or efficiency.[7] One approach is to recursively split a population into smaller and smaller groups. Each time a split is made, the split is selected that maximizes the chosen measure of association. For the variable Age in Table 5.1, the process would begin by looking at all possible splits; that is, 18 in one interval and 19+ in the other, then 18–19 in one interval and 20+ in the other and so on. For each possible split the information value (or other statistic) is calculated and the split that yields the highest information value is chosen. The process is then repeated for each of the two groups created from the first split. The process terminates after a pre-set number of intervals have been defined, when splitting does not lead to any significant increase in information value or the intervals contain less than a specified minimum number of observations (say 100–200). Note that this is identical to the process used to construct a CART model as discussed in Chapter 7, but the process is restricted to using only a single predictor variable to construct the tree.

5.3.2 The application of expert opinion to interval definitions

However the initial classing has been undertaken, after the intervals have been defined they should be reviewed. If necessary, the interval boundaries should be adjusted so that they are sensible from a business perspective and take into account expert knowledge about where natural breaks in the data occur. Consider the univariate analysis report in Table 5.4.

Table 5.4 Univariate analysis report for credit limit utilization

										Credit limit utilization

Interval	Range			Number of goods	Number of bads	Total number	% of total	Bad rate	Good:bad odds	Weight of evidence	Z-statistic	Information value
1	−45.6% to	2.2%		7,846	154	8,000	10.00	1.93%	50.95	1.111	15.140	0.077
2	2.2% to	5.5%		7,716	284	8,000	10.00	3.55%	27.17	0.482	8.491	0.019
3	5.6% to	9.8%		7,703	297	8,000	10.00	3.71%	25.94	0.436	7.826	0.016
4	9.9% to	14.7%		7,677	323	8,000	10.00	4.04%	23.77	0.348	6.496	0.010
5	14.8% to	19.8%		7,623	377	8,000	10.00	4.71%	20.22	0.187	3.734	0.003
6	19.9% to	24.5%		7,572	428	8,000	10.00	5.35%	17.69	0.053	1.125	0.000
7	24.6% to	49.1%		7,469	531	8,000	10.00	6.64%	14.07	−0.176	−4.143	0.003
8	49.2% to	75.9%		7,399	601	8,000	10.00	7.51%	12.31	−0.310	−7.724	0.011
9	76.0% to	88.4%		7,339	661	8,000	10.00	8.26%	11.10	−0.413	−10.793	0.021
10	88.5% to	157.8%		7,156	844	8,000	10.00	10.55%	8.48	−0.683	−20.153	0.063
Total				75,500	4,500	80,000	100.00	5.63%	16.78	0.000		0.224

Table 5.4 is taken from a credit scoring project. The objective is to construct a classification model to predict good/bad repayment behaviour of existing credit card customers. The dependent variable is assigned a value of 1 for goods and a value of 0 for bads. The variable credit limit utilization (defined as 100 * card balance/card limit) has been classed into ten equally sized intervals, each containing 10 percent of the population. The first interval starts at –45.6 percent. This means there is at least one account in the sample with a negative balance, indicating the account is in credit. The final interval ends with 157.8 percent, indicating that there is at least one account that has a balance above its credit limit. Anyone with experience of working with credit card data should know there are certain values of credit utilization that give important information about the behaviour of an account. Someone with a negative balance (who is in credit) is likely to display different behaviour than someone with a positive balance. Likewise, having a zero balance is indicative of different behaviour than having a very small positive or negative balance. Another difference occurs at 100 percent utilization. People who are within their credit limit usually behave very differently from those who have exceeded their credit limit. Armed with this additional information, a better representation of the intervals is given in Table 5.5.

The new classing introduced in Table 5.5 clearly brings out some additional information about the relationship between utilization and good/bad repayment behaviour. In particular, the zero interval is very significantly better in terms of bad rate, than the adjacent intervals. Similarly, those with a credit limit utilization in excess of 100 percent are significantly worse than the adjacent interval. Further evidence that the revised classing provides a better representation of the relationship between card utilization and good/bad repayment behaviour is given by the information value, which has risen from 0.224 to 0.271.

5.4 Correlation between predictor variables

In section 5.2.4 the idea of correlation was introduced as a way of measuring the strength of association between a predictor variable and the dependent variable. Correlation measures can also be useful for examining the relationships between predictor variables. This is important because if two predictor variables are perfectly correlated, then in effect the two variables contain the same information. Therefore, only one needs to be included in the modelling process and the other can be discarded. Consider a situation where age and date of birth are two potential predictor variables. To all intents and purposes, age and date of

132

Table 5.5   Revised univariate analysis report for credit limit utilization

						Credit limit utilization				
Interval	Range	Number of goods	Number of bads	Total number	% of total	Bad rate	Good:bad odds	Weight of evidence	Z-statistic	Information value
1	-45.6% to -0.1%	1,297	47	1,344	1.68	3.50%	27.60	0.498	3.415	0.003
2	0.0%	4,904	48	4,952	6.19	0.97%	102.17	1.807	14.681	0.098
3	0.1% to 2.1%	1,645	59	1,704	2.13	3.46%	27.88	0.508	3.916	0.004
4	2.2% to 5.5%	7,716	284	8,000	10.00	3.55%	27.17	0.482	8.491	0.019
5	5.6% to 9.8%	7,703	297	8,000	10.00	3.71%	25.94	0.436	7.826	0.016
6	9.9% to 14.7%	7,677	323	8,000	10.00	4.04%	23.77	0.348	6.496	0.010
7	14.8% to 19.8%	7,623	377	8,000	10.00	4.71%	20.22	0.187	3.734	0.003
8	19.9% to 24.5%	7,572	428	8,000	10.00	5.35%	17.69	0.053	1.125	0.000
9	24.6% to 49.1%	7,469	531	8,000	10.00	6.64%	14.07	-0.176	-4.143	0.003
10	49.2% to 75.9%	7,399	601	8,000	10.00	7.51%	12.31	-0.310	-7.724	0.011
11	76.0% to 88.4%	7,339	661	8,000	10.00	8.26%	11.10	-0.413	-10.793	0.021
12	88.5% to 100.0%	5,228	472	5,700	7.13	8.28%	11.08	-0.415	-9.030	0.015
13	100.1% to 157.8%	1,928	372	2,300	2.88	16.17%	5.18	-1.175	-22.280	0.067
Total		75,500	4,500	80,000	100.00	5.63	16.78	0.000		0.271

birth provide the same information – there is no reason to have them both. One way to think about this is that if you tell me how old someone is, then I can determine their date of birth and vice versa. So as long as one piece of information is known, then the other can be determined, and is therefore, not required. For some (but not all) types of modelling technique (such as linear regression and logistic regression), the mathematics underpinning them breaks down if an attempt is made to construct a model containing two perfectly correlated variables, such as age and date of birth. Therefore, one must be removed to allow modelling to proceed.

When faced with two (or more) variables that are perfectly correlated most software packages will automatically select one of the variables to include in the modelling process and ignore the other(s) so that model parameters can be derived. What causes greater concern is when two predictor variables are very highly correlated, but not perfectly correlated. Perhaps the correlation coefficient is ±0.9 or more, but less than ±1. In these situations it is possible to generate models, but there is a danger that the model's parameters are unstable (have high variance). This means that the parameter estimates can vary substantially if the data used to construct the model changes by even a very small amount. So if you try and generate a model several times using slightly different samples – may be by randomly assigning different observations to the development and holdout samples, then each time a model with very different parameter coefficients will be generated. In general, modelling techniques that incorporate stepwise selection procedures, which are discussed in detail in Chapter 7, deal with most (but not all) correlation issues automatically. If necessary, one can carry out checks after the model parameters have been derived to confirm that parameter estimates are stable and to see if correlation between predictor variables is causing problems.

It is worth bearing in mind that for predictive modelling, having highly correlated variables within a model is not an issue in itself, as long as the model generates good quality predictions. However, many model builders believe it is good practice to examine the correlations between predictor variables, and if very high levels of correlation are found, then to exclude relevant variables from the modelling process. What constitutes high correlation is open to debate. Personally I subscribe to the view that correlation is not something to be overly concerned about at this stage, and I would generally allow an automated stepwise procedure to be applied by the modelling software to remove most of the correlation issues. I would then review the information provided by the modelling software, which will highlight where high correlation exists between the variables that feature in the model.[8] I then consider removing a predictor variable only if the parameter estimate is shown to have a very large variance and does not conform with business expectation. Others take the view that any correlation above about ±0.6 is a problem, and as a result, one or more variables need to be excluded from the later stages of model development.

5.5   Interaction variables

Sometimes the nature of the relationship between predictor variables and the dependent variable are, to some extent, dependent upon the relationship that the predictor variables have with each other. This effect is termed "interaction" and should not be confused with the correlation issues discussed in section 5.4. To illustrate the effect of interaction, consider Figure 5.5.

Figure 5.5a shows the relationship between annual income and good/bad behaviour. There is clearly a monotonic trend in the relationship – the greater income someone has the lower the bad rate. Similarly, Figure 5.5b shows the relationship between residential status and good/bad behaviour. There are three categories of residential status. Tenants have the highest bad rate, owners the lowest and people living with their parents are somewhere in the middle. Now, consider the relationship between income and good/bad behaviour for each individual category of residential status, as shown in Figure 5.6.

Figure 5.6 shows that the relationship between income and good/bad behaviour is very different, depending upon the residential status. For home owners, the trend is similar to that seen in Figure 5.5a, but the line is steeper and the information value is higher. This indicates there is a stronger relationship between income and good/bad behaviour for home owners than for the population as a whole. For tenants, the relationship is counter to that in Figure 5.5a. Those with high incomes who rent have significantly higher bad rates than those with low incomes who rent. For those living with parents, the trend is flat. There is no obvious relationship between income and good/bad behaviour. This is supported by the very low information value of just 0.01.

One way of dealing with interactions is to create new "interaction variables". If one variable is numeric and the other is categorical, as in this example, then one option is to create three new variables. For the first, the value of income is assigned a default value, of say – 9999999, unless the individual is a home owner. Likewise for the second and

Figure 5.5a

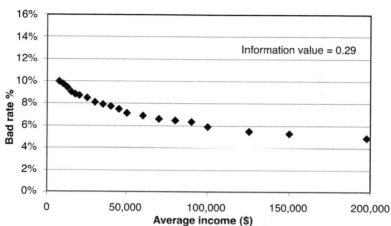

Figure 5.5b

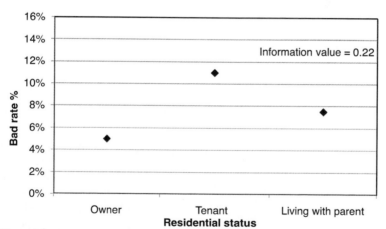

Figure 5.5 Interaction variables

third variables, default values are set for anyone who is not a tenant or not living with parents respectively. This approach can also be applied to situations where both variables are categorical. An alternative approach is to create a single new variable which has one category for each possible combination of categories. So, for employment status with five categories (employed, unemployed, retired, student, homemaker) and marital status with four categories (Married, single, divorced, widowed) the interaction variable will have 20 categories (employed and married, employed and single, and so on).

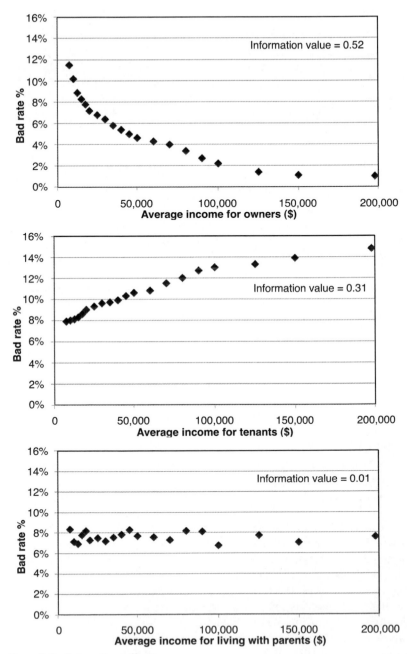

Figure 5.6   Interaction effects

If both interaction variables are interval or ordinal, then an interaction variable can be created by multiplying the two values together.

What has been described so far are two way interactions; that is, the effects of two predictor variables are considered in combination. In theory, one can have three, four, ..., N way interactions (where N is the number of predictor variables). For example, there could be three way interaction effects between income, residential status and marital status. In practice, two way interactions only occasionally have an impact on model performance, and I have never come across a situation where having more than a two way interaction variable has been required.

On a practical note, while one can carry out interaction analysis at this point in the model development process, I generally recommend leaving interaction analysis (if undertaken at all) until after preliminary variable selection and data pre-processing (as discussed in the next chapter) have been undertaken. This is for three reasons:

1. After preliminary variable selection there will be fewer variables to deal with which will save time and cost.
2. One issue with interaction analysis is that if there are many categories of data to consider, then even if one is dealing with large samples, there may be insufficient numbers within each interval of the interaction variable to allow significant conclusions about the data to be drawn. One function of data pre-processing is to generate more stable (larger) groupings of the data prior to modelling which will help alleviate this problem.
3. The most popular methods of data pre-processing (weights of evidence and dummy variables) transform all variables into an ordinal type – regardless of whether they were categorical, ordinal or interval to start with. Therefore, interaction terms can be created simply by multiplying the two variables together.

Most software packages can automatically create and apply interaction terms. However, if there are more than a few dozen predictor variables then the number of potential interactions quickly becomes too large for all interactions to be included due to computational requirements. Even if just two way interactions are considered, then the possible number of interaction variables is equal to $N * (N - 1)/2$, where N is the number of predictor variables. Consequently, some preliminary work is required to select the variables for which interactions might be important. Some software vendors provide tools to do this. Alternatively, a competent analyst should, with a few days of effort, be able to write code using software such as SAS or C++, that will generate all possible two-way interaction variables, and then rank them in order of information value or some other measure of association.

5.6   Preliminary variable selection

By this point in the model development process univariate analysis reports and measures of association may have been calculated for hundreds of predictor variables. Before going further, it is usually a good idea to discard any variables that do not display significant relationships with the dependent variable, or are otherwise unlikely to feature in the final model. There are a number of reasons why it is prudent to do this. These include:

- Development time. The more predictor variables retained, the more time it will take to complete subsequent steps of the model development process.
- Relationships inconsistent with business expectation. A predictor variable may contain sensible values and there may be a very strong relationship between a predictor variable and the modelling objective. However, if the relationship is counter intuitive then it may not be accepted by stakeholders.
- False predictors. Sometimes a variable appears to have an association with the dependent variable, but this association is as a result of previous decision making or reflects information that was obtained after the point where the score was applied. For example, when assessing creditworthiness for credit cards and personal loans, the variable "payment protection insurance requested" often has a very high information value. This is not because someone who decides to take out payment protection insurance is inherently uncreditworthy, but because after someone's credit score has been calculated, customer service staff are instructed to specifically target those people with low credit scores, to try and encourage them to take out insurance.
- Noise. Having lots of non-predictive variables within the modelling process can lead to reduced performance of the final model. This is particularly a problem for methods that generate the parameters for neural network models.

• Implementation. From an operational perspective, simple models containing few variables are best. Complex models are more difficult/ costly to implement and monitor, and there is more scope to make errors when the model is implemented.

While not a trivial task, it is relatively easy to fully automate the univariate analysis process and preliminary variable selection. Many software packages will automatically determine which variables are significant and which are not, based on one or more measures of association. Some will also carry out Z-tests or t-tests and identify individual attributes that are of particular significance. Likewise, most large financial services organizations have a suite of automated tools that can produce univariate analysis reports for all predictor variables and rank in order of information value or some other measure of association. It is therefore, possible to come up with some simple rules, based on information value or some other measure, as to which variables to retain and which to discard. Some modellers I know will discard any predictor variables where the information value is below about 0.05. Others take a more cautious approach and only discard variables where the information value is below 0.02. Another strategy is simply to select the 50 or so variables with the highest IV values and discard the rest – in the knowledge that it is very unusual in consumer behaviour modelling for more than about 30–40 variables to feature in a model. In my experience, all of these "rules of thumb" for discarding variables work reasonably well, and lead to models that provide similar levels of predictive ability. However, there are often benefits to combining an automated selection process, using quantitative rules, with qualitative decision making based on expert opinion. In particular, simple rules based purely on measures of association are unlikely to identify cases where the predictor variables display unexpected relationships with the dependent variable that are counter to business expectation, and should therefore, be discarded. Likewise, stakeholders often expect to see certain variables within some types of models. Therefore, it makes sense to retain these at this stage, even if they subsequently do not feature in the final model. For similar reasons, if one is building a new model to replace an existing one, it is prudent to retain any variables that featured in the old model, even if they no longer display a strong association with the dependent variable.

Univariate analysis, as described previously, works pretty well in most cases. However, an argument against looking at variables one at a time is that no account is taken of the interaction and correlation effects that may exist between predictor variables. Consequently, multi-variate approaches to variable selection have been developed which consider several predictor variables in combination. For example, some "wrapper" approaches to variable selection,[9] work on the basis of building lots of preliminary models using sub-sets of predictor variables – perhaps 10–15 at a time. Those variables that make a large contribution to any of the preliminary models are retained, while those that do not are discarded. Stepwise selection is the most popular wrapper method. With stepwise selection a model is constructed by adding variables to the model one at a time. At each iteration of the modelling process a relevant measure of association (called a partial measure) is recalculated for all predictor variables that do not currently feature in the model, taking into account the variables that are currently in the model. The variable that has the highest measure of association is then added into the model, if adding it provides a statistically better fit to the data. One of the benefits of stepwise selection is that most software packages allow stepwise procedures to be incorporated automatically within the model building process, which is discussed in greater detail in Chapter 7.

If one is going to employ linear or logistic regression, or any method of model construction that allows a stepwise procedure to be incorporated, then why bother with preliminary variable selection at all? Why not just let the stepwise process select the best set of predictor variables to use? Often this can be a valid way to proceed. However, one limitation of stepwise procedures is that when very many predictor variables are available, then the stepwise process (and other wrapper methods) can take a very long time to complete even with the most modern computer.[10] Another issue with stepwise procedures is that if the number of predictor variables is very high in relation to the number of observations in the data set, then spurious associations can be found, leading to a sub-optimal selection of variables. A third issue is that stepwise procedures, like any automated procedure, won't apply any business expertise to the variable selection process, and will retain variables that display statistically significant, but non-sensical relationships with the dependent variable. For these reasons it makes sense to carry out a preliminary variable selection exercise to reduce the number of variables and remove any where the relationships are clearly discordant with business expectation.

My own approach to preliminary variable selection varies from problem to problem, but is generally along the following lines:

- To start, I typically discard any variable where the information value (or rank correlation for regression problems) is below about 0.025, *unless* there is a very good business reason to retain it. For example, the variable featured in the old model that the new model will replace. Typically, this results in discarding between 10 and 50 percent of the variables under consideration.

- Of the variables that remain, I manually review the univariate analysis reports for each variable. This may seem like a daunting task if there are several hundred variables to review, but an experienced analyst may require less than a minute, on average, to review each report – so rarely more than about a day's effort in total. Manually reviewing the data is good practice because it allows the analyst to build up a mental picture of the relationships in the data and any anomalies or unusual patterns that exist.

- If I see a relationship that obviously does not conform to business expectation, then this variable is excluded. Likewise, if the vast majority of observations (more than about 98–99 percent) fall within a single category or have default values then I would tend to discard the variable regardless of the information value.

- If I am unsure about the nature of the relationship that is observed, then I would approach relevant stakeholders to seek their opinion before making a decision to retain or discard the variable.

- If for any reason it cannot be determined whether a variable should be retained or discarded, then I tend to err or side of caution and retain it for the time being. It can always be discarded later.

- I don't worry much about correlation at this stage, unless two variables are perfectly correlated, in which case I will discard one. Instead, any investigation of correlation between predictor variables will be driven by the outputs from the modelling process.

- I typically expect to discard between one third and two thirds of all potential variables during the preliminary variable selection stage.

- There are very few projects where I would expect to carry forward more than about 100 variables to the data pre-processing stage.

I admit that these rules are somewhat arbitrary, but they have served me well and many fellow model developers I know adopt a similar approach. For more information about some of the different variable section methods available, the paper "An introduction to variable and feature selection" by Isabelle Guyon and Andre Elisseeff (2003), published in the *Journal of Machine Learning*, is a good place to start.

Once univariate analysis has been undertaken, this is often a good time to hold a project meeting to review the univariate analysis reports. The objective is to draw upon the business expertise of stakeholders to gain a contextual understanding of the relationships that are observed, and to agree which variables will be taken forward to the next stage of model development. Often the project sponsor/stakeholders will have strong opinions about which variables should or should not feature in the final model, and this is an ideal time to discuss these to avoid unnecessary reworking later down the line.

5.7   Chapter summary

Once a cleaned and prepared sample of data is available, detailed analysis of the relationships in the data can begin. Typically, this means reviewing the relationship between each predictor variable and the dependent variable one variable at a time – a process referred to as univariate analysis or characteristic analysis.

When dealing with large data sets, visual analysis of the data is often aided by classing the data to remove noise and make any patterns in the data more readily discernible. Interval variables are classed into about 20 intervals and the average value of the dependent variable calculated for each interval. If large samples are available, then more than 20 intervals can be used, but about 20 is usually sufficient to allow the major patterns in the data to be observed.

In support of any qualitative visual analysis of the data, more quantitative measures of association between predictor variables and the dependent variable can be produced. The most popular measures for classification problems are the information value, the chi-squared statistic and efficiency. For regression problems correlation measures are more widely applied, such as Spearman's rank correlation coefficient.

Sometimes two predictor variables are highly correlated with each other. This means the variables, to some extent, contain the same information. High levels of correlation between predictor variables can cause problems for some model construction methods. Therefore, it may be prudent to exclude a variable if it displays a very high level of correlation with one or more other predictor variables. Correlation analysis can be performed prior to modelling, but many model development packages produce correlation measures automatically as part of the outputs produced from the modelling process. Therefore, one has the option to leave correlation analysis until after preliminary model construction has occurred.

Sometimes interaction effects may be present in the data. This means that a predictor variable displays significantly different relationships with the dependent variable, depending on the values taken by another predictor variable. As a rule, interaction effects do not play a large part in the majority of consumer behaviour models, but there are some cases where the creation of interaction variables can improve the performance of models in terms of their forecasting accuracy.

When dealing with large data sets containing hundreds of predictor variables, it can be useful to carry out preliminary variable selection, discarding some variables, to increase the speed of subsequent model development steps. Typically, one should be able to discard between one third and two thirds of all variables at this point, based on low information values combined with expert opinion, without any subsequent loss of model performance.

6
Data Pre-processing

Some model construction techniques are very flexible when it comes to the format of the predictor variables. However, many methods, and in particular the most popular methods for generating linear models, rely on the relationships between the predictor variables and the dependent variable being linear. This means that better models can be generated if any predictor variables that display non-linear relationships with the dependent variable can be pre-processed (transformed) so that the relationships are more linear.

A second objective of data pre-processing is standardization. If one predictor variable takes values in the range 10,000 to 1,000,000, and another takes values in the range 0.01 to 1, then the parameter coefficients (the model weights) will be very different, even if the two variables contribute equally to the final model. This isn't necessarily a problem for some modelling techniques, but as a rule, it is good practice to transform interval variables so that they all take values that lie on the same scale. For example, one common standardization technique is to calculate the mean and standard deviation of each predictor variable, then subtract the mean and divide by the standard deviation.

There are many ways that data pre-processing can be carried out. In this chapter the two most popular ways of pre-processing data for consumer behaviour modelling are introduced. These are: (1) dummy variables, and (2) weight of evidence transformed variables. Both of these methods generate a set of new variables that have linear (or log linear) relationships with the dependent variable and at the same time standardize the data. However, each method has its advantages and disadvantages, requiring the model developer to decide which to use on the basis of the data they have available for model construction.

The final part of the chapter discusses "Coarse classing". This is the process of merging together some of the intervals created during data pre-processing. Coarse classing is performed for two reasons. First, to ensure that all intervals within the pre-processed variables contain a good number of observations. Second, to smooth the data so that the relationships in the data are sensible from a business perspective.

6.1   Dummy variable transformed variables

One of the simplest methods of transforming data is to replace each predictor variable with a set of dummy (indicator) variables. A dummy variable can take only one of two values, typically 0 or 1. For categorical and ordinal variables, a separate dummy variable is created to represent each attribute. If an observation has a given attribute, then the dummy variable representing that attribute is assigned a value of 1, otherwise the dummy variable is set to 0. Consider residential status, which has four attributes: (O)wner, (T)enant, (L)iving with Parents and (U)nknown. Four dummy variables are created, as illustrated in Table 6.1.

Table 6.1 shows an extract of a model development sample containing 50,000 observations. The value of the variable Dummy 1 (Owner) has been set to 1 for all cases where the individual has a residential status of "Owner" and 0 otherwise. Likewise, for dummy variables 2, 3 and 4, the variable has been set to a value of 1 if an observation has the relevant attribute. For each observation, one and only one dummy variable takes a value of 1. All the other dummy variables associated with that variable take a value of zero.

The process of defining dummy variables for interval variables is broadly the same as for ordinal and categorical variables. However, the

Table 6.1   Dummy variable definitions

Ref	Residential status	Dummy 1 (Owner)	Dummy 2 (Tenant)	Dummy 3 (Living with parent)	Dummy 4 (Unknown)
1	O	1	0	0	0
2	O	1	0	0	0
3	T	0	1	0	0
4	U	0	0	0	1
...	...	...	...	...	...
49,998	L	0	0	1	0
49,999	T	0	1	0	0
50,000	O	1	0	0	0

variable is first classed into a number of intervals. Typically (prior to coarse classing), this will be the same set of intervals used to produce the fine classed univariate analysis reports, which were discussed in the previous chapter. Therefore, there will usually be somewhere between ten and 25 equally sized intervals, plus any additional intervals for default values or specific ranges that have been defined for business reasons. The number of intervals is then reviewed and coarse classing applied (as discussed in section 6.3), which acts to merge some of the intervals together.

In theory, when it comes to model construction, if N dummy variables have been defined to represent a predictor variable, then only $N–1$ dummy variables are required because it can be inferred from the $N–1$ dummies whether or not an observation falls into the Nth dummy. In fact, for some modelling approaches, such as logistic and linear regression, the mathematics used to derive the model break down if all N dummies are included. Therefore, one dummy must be excluded to allow the model construction process to occur. The choice of which dummy to exclude can be made manually,[1] but most software packages can automatically select a dummy variable to exclude as a preliminary step in the model construction process.

6.2   Weights of evidence transformed variables

A second approach to data pre-processing is to apply a "weight of evidence transformation". If you refer back to section 5.1, the weight of evidence was introduced as a standardized measure of the difference between the good:bad odds of an individual attribute and the overall good:bad odds of the sample. The principle underpinning the weight of evidence transformation is simply to replace the value of a predictor variable with the associated weight of evidence. The weight of evidence is then used within the modelling process instead of the observation's true value. Table 6.2a shows the univariate analysis report for residential status for a classification problem, and Table 6.2b illustrates the weight of evidence transformation applied to the data set of 50,000 observations that is going to be used for model development.

6.3   Coarse classing

For the modelling process to generate robust parameter coefficients, and to reduce the effects of over fitting, there needs to be sufficient numbers of observations within each interval used to define dummy variables

Table 6.2 Weight of evidence transformed variables

Table 6.2a *Univariate analysis report for residential status*

Interval	Attribute	Number of goods	Number of bads	Total number	% of total	Bad rate	Good: bad odds	Weight of evidence	Z-statistic	Information value
1	Owner	33,104	1,507	34,611	69.22	4.35%	21.967	0.344	23.683	0.071
2	Tenant	7,863	845	8,708	17.42	9.70%	9.305	-0.515	-15.814	0.058
3	Living with parents	3,900	474	4,374	8.75	10.84%	8.228	-0.638	-13.956	0.047
4	Unknown	2,115	192	2,307	4.61	8.32%	11.016	-0.346	-4.722	0.006
Total		46,982	3,018	50,000	100.00	6.04%	15.567	0.000		0.182

Table 6.2b *Model development sample*

Ref	Residential status	Weight of evidence (residential status)
1	O	0.344
2	O	0.344
3	T	-0.515
4	U	-0.346
...	...	
49,998	L	-0.638
49,999	T	-0.515
50,000	O	0.344

and/or calculate weights of evidence. What one means by "sufficient number" is debatable, but one rule of thumb is that each interval should contain at least 100 observations in total. For classification problems, an additional recommendation is that each interval should contain at least 25 goods *and* 25 bads.[2] These are minimum figures. Personally, I feel much more comfortable if each interval contains many hundreds of cases, and in excess of 100 goods and 100 bads for classification problems. The question then arises: what course of action should be taken if an interval contains too few observations? The answer is to "coarse classify" the variable; that is, to combine any interval with to few observations with another. Note that coarse classing is usually applied before dummy variable or weight of evidence transformations are applied, based on the trends observed within the fine classed univariate analysis reports.

6.3.1 Coarse classing categorical variables

Consider a home insurance problem. People are classified as bad or good respectively, if they do or do not make a claim on their household insurance during the policy. The univariate analysis report for the variable marital status is shown in Table 6.3.

In Table 6.3, the attribute "Separated" contains only 23 bads. It is therefore, sensible to consider combining it with one of the other intervals, but which one? One option is to combine it with the interval with which it is most similar in terms of bad rate (or good:bad odds or weight of evidence) which in this case would be the single category.

A more qualitative approach is to ask: which group are separated people most like in terms of their overall demographic profile? Personally, I would be tempted to say that people who are separated tend to be on the road to divorce and therefore, are probably better aligned with the divorced category than the single category. They are more likely to be of a similar age to divorced people, more likely to have dependent children, more likely to be in part-time work or homemakers and so on. If necessary, I could go away and look at things like average age or employment status for each group to confirm or refute my suspicions. Table 6.4 shows the result of the two possible coarse classifications that have been discussed so far.

The question as to which coarse classing in Table 6.4 is best is debatable. The answer will depend on the problem context, and as ever, business opinion may play its part regardless of what the numbers say. One thing to note is that in both cases the information value of the coarse classed variable is slightly lower than for the fine classed version. This is

Table 6.3 Univariate analysis report for marital status

					Marital status					
Interval	Attribute	Number of goods	Number of bads	Total number	% of total	Bad rate	Good:bad odds	Weight of evidence	Z-statistic	Information value
1	Single	6,069	841	6,910	27.44	12.17%	7.216	-0.358	-11.470	0.04064
2	Married	8,233	521	8,754	34.76	5.95%	15.802	0.426	11.769	0.05304
3	Divorced	2,984	486	3,470	13.78	14.01%	6.140	-0.519	-11.558	0.04592
4	Separated	155	23	178	0.71	12.92%	6.739	-0.426	-1.928	0.00153
5	Widowed	1,174	59	1,233	4.90	4.79%	19.898	0.657	5.138	0.01617
6	Cohabiting	4,344	295	4,639	18.42	6.36%	14.725	0.356	6.579	0.02014
Total		22,959	2,225	25,184	100.00	8.83%	10.319	0.000		0.17742

to be expected, given that the amount of information that one can gain about the relationships in the data decreases the fewer intervals there are.

All other things being equal, one way to make a decision about which coarse classing to apply is to choose the one that results in the lowest reduction in information value (or other measure of association). Using this criteria, the coarse classing in Table 6.4a that combines separated with singles would appear to be best, as the information value is 0.17738 compared to 0.17735 for the divorced option. However, in this example, the difference between the two alternatives is relatively small. Alternatively, multivariate tools based on clustering or factor analysis can be applied to provide more quantitative "distance" measures of how related two attributes are, but unless one has access to specialist software to carry out the relevant analysis this may prove very long winded if there are very many predictor variables to consider, and there is no guarantee that these methods will provide a significant uplift over simpler "common sense" approaches based on expert opinion and/or maximization of a univariate measures of association such as information value.

6.3.2   Coarse classing ordinal and interval variables

As for categorical variables, coarse classing should be undertaken for ordinal and interval variables to ensure that robust models are generated and the chance of over fitting the data is reduced. However, a second reason for applying coarse classing, which is particularly relevant for interval and ordinal variables, is to smooth the data so that monotonic trends are observed. This is not for statistical reasons, and the requirement to have monotonic trends in the data is not a requirement for all modelling projects, but in many cases stakeholders like to see trends in the data that conform to their expectations. Consider the univariate analysis report for Time Living at Current Address in Table 6.5, which comes from the same home insurance project discussed earlier in the chapter.

In Table 6.5 there is clearly a strong relationship between how long someone has lived at their address, and the likelihood of them making a claim on their home insurance. The chance of a claim decreases the longer they have lived there. This is supported by an information value of 0.44. However, the trend in the relationship is not monotonically decreasing. There is a "kink" at 23–37 months and another at 122–240 months, where the bad rate increases before continuing with its downward trend. To smooth the data, the relevant intervals are merged with another. Given that Time Living at Current Address is

Table 6.4 Alternative coarse classifications

Table 6.4a *Marital status with single/separated coarse classed*

Interval	Attribute	Number of goods	Number of bads	Total number	% of total	Bad rate	Good: bad odds	Weight of evidence	Z-statistic	Information value
1	Single/separated	6,224	864	7,088	28.14	12.19%	7.204	-0.359	-11.740	0.04212
2	Married	8,233	521	8,754	34.76	5.95%	15.802	0.426	11.769	0.05304
3	Divorced	2,984	486	3,470	13.78	14.01%	6.140	-0.519	-11.558	0.04592
5	Widowed	1,174	59	1,233	4.90	4.79%	19.898	0.657	5.138	0.01617
6	Cohabiting	4,344	295	4,639	18.42	6.36%	14.725	0.356	6.579	0.02014
Total		22,959	2,225	25,184	100.00	8.83%	10.319	0.000		0.17738

Table 6.4b *Marital status with divorced/separated coarse classed*

Interval	Attribute	Number of goods	Number of bads	Total number	% of total	Bad rate	Good: bad odds	Weight of evidence	Z-statistic	Information value
1	Single	6,069	841	6,910	27.44	12.17%	7.216	-0.358	-11.470	0.04064
2	Married	8,233	521	8,754	34.76	5.95%	15.802	0.426	11.769	0.05304
3	Divorced/separated	3,139	509	3,648	14.49	13.95%	6.167	-0.515	-11.778	0.04738
5	Widowed	1,174	59	1,233	4.90	4.79%	19.898	0.657	5.138	0.01617
6	Cohabiting	4,344	295	4,639	18.42	6.36%	14.725	0.356	6.579	0.02014
Total		22,959	2,225	25,184	100.00	8.83%	10.319	0.000		0.17735

Table 6.5 Univariate analysis report for time living at current address

Time living at current address

Interval	Range	Number of goods	Number of bads	Total number	% of total	Bad rate	Good:bad odds	Weight of evidence	Z-statistic	Information value
1	0–3 months	2,106	412	2,518	10.00	16.36%	5.11	-0.702	-5.928	0.066
2	4–6 months	2,147	372	2,519	10.00	14.77%	5.77	-0.581	-4.444	0.043
3	7–12 months	2,197	321	2,518	10.00	12.75%	6.84	-0.411	-2.726	0.020
4	13–22 months	2,245	273	2,518	10.00	10.84%	8.22	-0.227	-1.290	0.006
5	23–37 months	2,216	302	2,518	10.00	11.99%	7.34	-0.341	-2.135	0.013
6	38–60 months	2,312	207	2,519	10.00	8.22%	11.17	0.079	0.346	0.001
7	61–88 months	2,403	115	2,518	10.00	4.57%	20.90	0.706	1.787	0.037
8	89–121 months	2,446	73	2,519	10.00	2.90%	33.51	1.178	1.983	0.087
9	122–240 months	2,440	78	2,518	10.00	3.10%	31.28	1.109	1.980	0.079
10	241+ months	2,447	72	2,519	10.00	2.86%	33.99	1.192	1.982	0.088
Total		22,959	2,225	25,184	100.00	8.83%	10.32	0.000		0.440

an interval variable, it makes sense to combine intervals that are adjacent. So in this case the 23–37 months interval could be combined with the 13–22 month interval or the 38–60 month interval. As discussed previously in relation to coarse classing categorical variables, the decision as to which intervals to combine could be made on the basis of maximizing the information value of the resulting coarse classing, or on the basis of which combination makes most business sense. Note that you may find that the new coarse classed interval may still result in a kink in the trend, requiring a further iteration of coarse classing to be applied.

Another common practice is where two adjacent intervals have similar odds/bad rates, the two groups are combined. This is done to create larger and more robust intervals for modelling purposes. With regard to the kink at 122–240 months in Table 6.5, the two adjacent intervals both have very similar bad rates. In addition, while there are a reasonable number of bad cases in intervals 8, 9 and 10, there are considerably fewer than in intervals 1–7. My suggestion would be to combine intervals 8, 9 and 10 together.

The coarse classing process can be automated to some extent, based on more quantitative measures. Some software algorithms perform statistical tests (Z-test or t-test depending upon the number of observations) to establish if there is a statistically significant difference in the bad rates between two intervals, and if not, combine them together. The process is then repeated with the new set of intervals until no further combinations are made; that is, the bad rates for all remaining intervals are significantly different from one another. A similar approach is to repeatedly combine intervals as long as the information value does not drop by more than a pre-determined amount when two intervals are combined.

6.3.3 How many coarse classed intervals should there be?

From the academic and practitioner communities there has been relatively little published research exploring how many coarse classed intervals one should have and how intervals should be defined, with a few notable exceptions such as Hand and Adams (2000). Circumstantial evidence that I have gathered from my own model building exploits, together with informal discussions with other model developers, is that in general there is very little benefit to having more than about 5–10 coarse classed intervals for each predictor variable, and to have more than about 20 is unusual. In many cases just two or three coarse classed intervals are sufficient, particularly if a variable displays only a weak relationship with the dependent variable. Even if a very large data set is available and a predictor variable displays a very strong relationship with the dependent variable, then moving from say 20 to 40 coarse classed intervals is likely to provide, at best, only a marginal uplift in model performance.

6.3.4   Balancing issues

As discussed in section 3.6, for classification problems it is sometimes prudent to take a balanced sample from an unbalanced population. If a balanced sample has been created, then in order to gain a true picture of the relationships in the data at the univariate analysis stage, a weighting factor needs to be applied. Otherwise, any relationships in the data will appear distorted because they represent the balanced sample data, not the imbalanced population from which the sample was taken. However, when it comes to modelling the data, for some methods of model construction, and for CART/Linear regression/ Discriminant analysis in particular, better models generally result if a balanced model development sample is used. What this means in practice is it may be necessary to produce two versions of the initial (fine classed) univariate analysis reports. The first version of the reports is generated using a weight factor so that the numbers and patterns in the report reflect those of the population from which the sample was taken. This version of the reports is used to discuss the data with stakeholders and for preliminary variable selection. The second version of the reports are produced without the weighting factor applied, and this version is used to carry out coarse classing.

6.3.5   Pre-processing holdout, out-of-time and recent samples

The initial fine classed univariate analysis and subsequent coarse classing should be undertaken using only the development sample. Data within the holdout sample, out-of-time and recent samples should not be considered at this point. Otherwise, when it comes to validate the model, the validation process will not be wholly independent. This creates a risk that model performance will be overestimated. However, the data pre-processing that has been applied to the development sample will need to be applied to the holdout sample(s) to allow model scores to be calculated. If dummy variables have been defined for the development sample, then identical definitions need to be applied to the holdout sample(s). If weights of evidence transformations have been applied, then the weights of evidence calculated for the intervals within the development sample must be copied over to the holdout sample(s). The weights of evidence should not be calculated again, using the data in the holdout sample(s).

6.4 Which is best – weight of evidence or dummy variables?

Both dummy variable and weights of evidence transformed variables have their merits and drawbacks. One of the main criticisms against using dummies is the increase in the number of variables. Typically, anywhere from 2–20 dummy variables are required to represent each predictor variable. It's quite normal to end up with a development sample containing hundreds, and sometimes thousands, of dummy variables. Consequently, dummy variable based models take a lot more computer time to generate than models created using weight of evidence transformed variables. This used to be a very significant problem when computer processing power was more limited. However, these days computational effort is not so much of an issue when using standard modelling approaches such as linear or logistic regression, but it may be a problem for some methodologies including those that generate neural network models. This means that a second stage of variable selection may be required to reduce the number of dummy variables to a more manageable number.[3] However, one simple and quick way to do this is to use stepwise linear regression as discussed in Chapters 5 and 7.

6.4.1 Linear models

In terms of raw predictive ability, the performance of linear models developed using dummy variable and weights of evidence transformed variables tend to be very similar. In my experience dummy variable based models sometimes have a slight edge when large samples (greater than about 5,000 cases of each class for classification problems) are available, and weights of evidence based models tend to be more robust if samples are small, where there is greater chance of over fitting. This is particularly the case if a sample contains less than about 1,000 cases of each class.

Another issue with dummy variables is it is common for some parameter coefficients of the model to have values that do not conform with the relationships observed in the univariate analysis reports. A monotonic increasing or decreasing trend will have been seen in the relationship between a predictor variable and the dependent variable, but this pattern is not replicated by the parameter coefficients that

Table 6.6 Coarse classed univariate analysis report for time in employment

Time in current employment

Interval	Range	Number of goods	Number of bads	Total number	% of total	Bad rate	Good:bad odds	Weight of evidence	Z-statistic	Information value
1	0–1 years	1,438	495	1,933	7.68	25.61%	2.91	−1.268	−14.093	0.203
2	2–3 years	2,036	483	2,519	10.00	19.17%	4.22	−0.895	−8.803	0.115
3	4–5 years	3,038	418	3,456	13.72	12.09%	7.27	−0.350	−2.696	0.019
4	6–10 years	5,702	415	6,117	24.29	6.78%	13.74	0.286	1.923	0.018
5	11–15 years	4,652	224	4,876	19.36	4.59%	20.77	0.699	2.758	0.071
6	16+ years	6,093	190	6,283	24.95	3.02%	32.07	1.134	3.742	0.204
Total		22,959	2,225	25,184	100.00	8.83%	10.32	0.000		0.630

enter the model – even after coarse classing has been applied. Let us continue with our home insurance example introduced earlier in the chapter. Table 6.6. shows the coarse classed univariate analysis report for the variable "Time in current employment".

In Table 6.6 coarse classing has been applied so that the trend between time in employment and bad rate shows a monotonic decreasing trend. Six dummy variables were defined, each one representing one of the six intervals in the report. These were then used (along with other variables) to generate a linear model using an appropriate method, such as linear or logistic regression. The resulting model has the following parameter coefficients for time in employment:

– 0.022	(0–1 years)
+ 0.000	(2–3 years)
+ 0.051	(4–5 years)
+ 0.044	(6–10 years)
+ 0.094	(11–15 years)
+ 0.122	(16+ years)

Although the general trend is for people who have been in their employment longer to contribute more positively to the score, there is a "kink" for those who have been in their employment for 6–10 years. The expectation is that the parameter coefficient should be somewhere between +0.051 and +0.094 to ensure that the trend is monotonically increasing, but with a value of +0.044 this is clearly not the case. Why does this effect occur? The most likely reason is because of interaction and/or correlation effects between predictor variables. From a purely theoretical perspective this is not a problem for predictive modelling if the model accurately reflects the nature of the data. In practice however, many stakeholders will not accept a model that does not conform to their expectation, which is that the parameter coefficients should display the same trends as seen in the coarse classed univariate analysis reports. Therefore, it may be necessary to exclude certain variables or redefine the coarse classed intervals in order to force the parameter coefficients to follow the pattern that the user expects to see. So in this example, it may be appropriate to combine the dummy variables for the 6–10 year group with the 4–5 year group or the 11–15 year group and reproduce the model. The net result is that in order to produce a business acceptable model, the model may be sub-optimal in terms of predictive ability because of the compromises that have been made about which variables are allowed to enter the model and/or how dummy variables have been defined.

The major disadvantage of using weight of evidence transformed variables to construct linear models is that the relationships between the weight of evidence transformed predictor variable and the dependent variable are forced to be (log) linear. Dummy variables provide a more flexible representation of non-linear data than weights of evidence transformed variables. If interaction effects exist, then a weight of evidence based model can give scores that are higher than they should be to observations in some intervals, and scores that are too low in others – a problem referred to as misalignment in credit scoring terminology. Misalignment can also occur with dummy variable based models, but is generally of a lower order than that seen with weights of evidence based models.

One popular way to correct for misalignment is to introduce dummy variables for those intervals that are misaligned, and in general there is no reason why dummy variables and weight of evidence transformed variables cannot both be created and entered into the modelling process together.

My own favoured approach (time permitting) is to generate both sets of pre-processed variables, and construct three preliminary models. One using just dummy variables, one using just weight of evidence transformed variables and the third using a mixture of the two. I tend to favour weights of evidence based models, but I use the other two models to inform my decision as to which method of pre-processing to use. Alternatively, I will sometimes seek to build a model primarily based on weights of evidence transformed variables, but then see if I can improve on the model by including one of more dummy variables. This is often a process of trial and error, involving several iterations of modelling and evaluation before a final model is decided upon.

6.4.2   CART and neural network models

For techniques that generate CART and neural networks models (and other non-linear modelling techniques), I recommend using weight of evidence transformed variables, rather than dummy variables. This is for the following reasons:

- Most techniques used to generate non-linear models require far more computation time than common techniques for generating linear models. For large data sets with very many predictor variables, using dummy variables can be prohibitive in terms of computer time.
- The techniques used to generate CART and neural network models are particularly susceptible to the problem of over fitting. Having fewer predictor variables reduces the likelihood of over fitting and magnitude of its effects.

- Dummy variables significantly restrict the splitting that can occur for CART models, often resulting in significantly reduced predictive ability compared to using weight of evidence transformed variables.
- The misalignment issues associated with linear models, particularly when weight of evidence transformed variables are used, are reduced (but not necessarily eliminated) when non-linear modelling techniques, such as those that generate CART and neural network models, are applied. This is because the model structure is able to account for interaction effects without the need for explicit interaction terms.

6.5 Chapter summary

There are many types of data pre-processing that can be applied, but the two most popular approaches are:

1. Dummy variables. 1/0 indicator variables are used to represent each category of categorical and ordinal variables, and each coarse classed interval of an interval variable.
2. Weight of evidence transformed variables. The weight of evidence calculated from the univariate analysis report is substituted for the actual value of the predictor variable.

Both methods act to standardize the data, and create variables that display linear (or log linear) relationships with the dependent variable. When it comes to generating linear models, neither method can be said to be best and the decision as to which method to choose will depend on the problem in hand, the experience of the analyst building the model and the software available. For methods that generate CART and neural network models, dummy variables can be used, but weights of evidence transformed variables provide a number of advantages that means they generally lead to more predictive models that require considerably less computer time to generate.

To ensure that robust models are created, and to reduce the likelihood of over fitting, standard practice is to apply coarse classing during data pre-processing. Coarse classing is applied primarily to ensure that each transformed variable contains sufficient numbers of observations in each interval, but is also used as a method of smoothing trends in the data so that they confirm with business expectation as to what the relationships should be.

7
Model Construction (Parameter Estimation)

In this chapter, some of the ways of deriving the parameter coefficients of a model are discussed – a process I shall refer to as model construction, parameter estimation or modelling. Many different methods of model construction exist, and there are many theoretical arguments why one method is better than another, or why such and such a method is/is not appropriate in a given set of circumstances. However, for predictive modelling the method used to derive a model is arguably unimportant, as long as the final model is a good predictor of behaviour and satisfies any business requirements about the properties of the model. To some extent, the ends justify the means. There is no reason why you can't just make up a model's parameters based on your expert opinion, and in situations where data is scarce this is exactly what industry experts sometimes do. However, under normal conditions, where a good quality sample of data is available, modelling techniques that apply mechanical procedures (statistical or mathematical processes) nearly always generate models that are superior, in terms of predictive ability, than models created using more judgemental/subjective means.

There are literally dozens of modelling techniques that can be used to construct a model. However, while some methods may be more theoretically appropriate or more "of the moment" than others, most methods yield very similar levels of performance when applied to practical real world problems. It is interesting to note that in many textbooks and journals the primary focus of debate has, until relatively recently, been about the modelling technique that should be employed. Less emphasis has been placed on good project design, sampling strategies and the way in which data is collated, cleaned and pre-processed prior to modelling – topics that were covered in Chapters 2–6. Yet there is a growing consensus that such issues are many times more important in determining the value of a model than the choice of modelling technique.

As mentioned in the introductory chapter, this book is not about forecasting techniques. The goal in this chapter is to convey a high level understanding of several popular methods of model construction and the nature of the models they generated. Consequently, some terminology has been adapted in an attempt to make certain concepts more intuitive/understandable. For readers with the appropriate mathematical/statistical expertise, I apologize for adopting what may be considered a somewhat non-standard/ad-hoc approach to some of the material. However, reference is made to appropriate texts for those of you wishing to engage in more in-depth study of the modelling techniques discussed. Thomas et al. (2002), for example, covers all of the model construction techniques described in this chapter, with a focus on their application to credit scoring.

The main part of the chapter focuses on linear regression and logistic regression. These methods have been in use for decades and remain the most popular methods for generating forecasting models of consumer behaviour within the financial services industry. Despite many theoretical advances since their introduction, linear regression and logistic regression continue to generate models that are competitive with the most technically advanced methods available.

The latter part of the chapter discusses methods for generating CART and neural network models. Survival analysis is also introduced, albeit briefly, as a method of predicting when behavioural events are likely to occur, rather than if an event will/will not occur or the magnitude of that event.

These days there are many modelling packages that can be used to generate models. These include SAS, SPSS, Stata, MATLAB, R, S-PLUS and others. Personally, I am most familiar with SAS because this is what has been used by the organizations that I've worked for, and SAS is probably the most widely used package within the financial services industry. SAS also provides a comprehensive data processing language that facilitates data preparation, and is multi-platform. One can create data/code on a PC that can be ported to an IBM mainframe or a UNIX box and back again with relative ease. However, many other packages provide similar functionality. SPSS, in particular, is renowned for its ease of use and high quality output and is relatively affordable for organizations working on a tight budget (at this point I'd like to thank my former college, Dr Geoff Ellis, for his enthusiasm in bringing the benefits of SPSS to my attention).

7.1 Linear regression

Linear models are the most common form of model used to predict consumer behaviour. As discussed in Chapter 1, a linear model can be expressed in the form:

$$S = a + b_1x_1 + b_2x_2 +, ..., + b_kx_k$$

where:

- a is a constant. This can take any positive or negative value.
- $x_1 ... x_k$ are a set of k predictor variables. Following data pre-processing, these will be dummy variables taking 0/1 values, or weight of evidence transformed variables.
- $b_1 ... b_k$ are the parameter coefficients assigned to each predictor variable. Each parameter coefficient provides a measure of how much each predictor variable contributes, positively or negatively, to the model score.
- S is the score generated by the model. S is calculated by taking a and then adding the other terms of the model to it.

Linear regression was once a popular method for generating classification models. These days it has been superseded by logistic regression (see below). However, linear regression is still used very successfully by some practitioners. For regression problems linear regression remains the most popular method for generating predictive models of consumer behaviour.

7.1.1 Linear regression for regression

Consider a problem where the objective is to build a model to predict peoples credit card expenditure, based on their income. Figure 7.1 shows the relationship between income and credit card spend.

In Figure 7.1 it can clearly be seen that there is a linear relationship between income and credit card expenditure. Now, it would be a fairly simple task just to draw a straight line on the graph, representing the line you think gives the best fit to the data; that is, the line that best represents the relationship between income and card expenditure. This line could then be expressed in the form of a linear model: $S = a + b_1x_1$ where the score S is the estimated value of credit card expenditure based on someone's income. The dotted line in Figure 7.1 represents just such a case, where I have drawn the line on the basis of my "expert" opinion. The model constant, *a,* is the point where the line

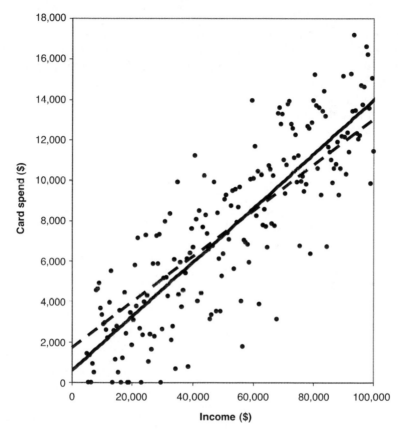

Figure 7.1 Relationship between income and card spend

crosses the Y axis and the single parameter coefficient of the model, b_1, is the gradient of the line. The model representing by the dotted line is: $S = 1{,}951 + 0.108 * Income$.

With linear regression a model's parameter coefficients are chosen to minimize the sum of the squared errors, where the error for each observation is the difference between the value of the dependent variable and the prediction generated by the model. To put it another way, the parameters are found that minimize:

$$\sum_{i=1}^{n} e_i^2$$

where n is number of observations in the sample used to construct the model and e_i is the error for the ith observation. In Figure 7.1, the model generated from minimizing the sum of squared errors is represented by the solid line. The equation of this line is: $S = 592 + 0.134 *$ *Income*. The sum of squared errors, rather than the sum of errors is minimized so that positive and negative errors don't cancel each other out. In theory, there is no reason why a linear model can't be constructed from minimizing the sum of absolute errors, or the sum of errors taken to the fourth, sixth or eighth power, but in all practical cases squared error is applied.

Figure 7.1 is an example of where there is only one predictor variable, and the model produced from using expert opinion is not that different from the model generated from minimizing the sum of squared errors. However, the principle of minimized squared errors is easily extended to problems containing many predictor variables, where it is impossible to visualize the data or to "draw a line" based on expert opinion. The parameter coefficients of the model that minimize the sum of squared error are found using calculus. Differentiating with respect to each of the predictor variables produces a set of simultaneous equations. Setting these to zero and solving the equations yields the parameters of the model.

7.1.2   Linear regression for classification

Technically, the process of deriving a model using linear regression is the same, regardless of whether the purpose is classification or regression. The linear regression process finds the parameter coefficients that minimize the sum of squared errors between the score and the value of the dependent variable. If the dependent variable has been defined as 0 (bad) and 1 (good) then the score can be interpreted as an estimated probability of an account being good. However, a major criticism that has been voiced about the use of linear regression for classification is that it is an inefficient estimator of probability. This is because the score generated by the model, can theoretically be outside the range of possible probability values (0–1), particularly if some of the predictor variables take extreme values. You may want to revisit the claim model (Model 1) introduced in the first chapter, and see what values of the predictor variables lead to the model generating values that are above 1 or below 0. However, for practical applications this is not usually of great concern when it comes to model usage, if the primary purpose is to rank accounts from best to worst, on the basis of the score that they receive – which is a common way that such models are used.

For binary classification problems it can be shown that linear regression is equivalent to Linear Discriminant Analysis (LDA). LDA is another popular method for generating linear classification models (Thomas et al. 2002, pp. 48–50), and was the first statistical approach used to construct models of repayment behaviour for the granting of loans (Durand 1941).

7.1.3 Stepwise linear regression

There are several flavours of linear regression. Standard linear regression applies the minimized squared error process to generate a parameter coefficient for every predictor variable included in the modelling process. This is regardless of whether or not there is a relationship with the dependent variable, and regardless of whether or not a predictor variable adds significantly to the predictive ability of the model. If standard linear regression is applied to problems with lots of predictor variables, many of which don't have a significant relationship with the dependent variable, then a large and unstable model may result and there is a risk of over-fitting. For this reason, standard linear regression is not widely used in consumer behaviour modelling. Instead, stepwise linear regression is more commonly applied.

Stepwise means a model is constructed in stages. Different predictor variables are added or removed at each stage, based on statistical tests that determine how much or how little each variable adds to the model – given the variables that are already in the model. The final model only contains predictor variables for which there is statistical evidence that they have a significant relationship with the dependent variable and their inclusion in the model adds significantly to the model. Consequently, if two variables are highly correlated, only one is likely to feature in the final model because the other is unlikely to add significantly to the model given that the first variable has already been included. There are three main types of stepwise procedure:

- Forward stepwise. Initially, there are no predictor variables within the model. Each variable is considered, and the one that has the highest degree of association with the dependent variable is chosen and used to construct a model. The remaining variables are then re-considered, taking into account the variable that is already in the model. The one that adds most significantly to the model is selected, and a new model constructed using both variables. The process continues until no further variables can be found that significantly improve the model.
- Backward stepwise. This can be considered the opposite of forward stepwise. The process begins by constructing a model containing all of the predictor variables. The least significant variable is removed

and the parameter coefficients for the remaining variables are recalculated. The process is repeated until all variables that remain in the model are statistically significant.

- Stepwise. This is the most popular and flexible of the three stepwise selection methods (Kvanli et al. 2003, p. 728) and the one I recommend. Model construction contains elements of both forward and stepwise procedures. To start, variables are added to the model one at a time, in an identical manner to forward stepwise. However, each time a new variable is added, the significance of the variables already in the model are re-evaluated and they are removed if they are no longer found to be significant. In theory, a variable may enter, leave and re-enter a model many times during stepwise regression.

In general, the predictive power of the resulting models are similar, regardless of which stepwise approach is adopted.

7.1.4   Model generation

To generate a model using stepwise linear regression, most software, such as SAS or SPSS will require the user to provide the following information:

1. The data set to be used for model construction. This is the development sample discussed previously.
2. The dependent variable. This represents the behaviour the model is going to predict. For a regression model the dependent variable will be a quantity. For classification, the dependent variable will take one of two values (typically 1/0) representing good/bad behaviour.
3. The list of predictor variables to consider for inclusion in the model. The development sample may contain some variables that you don't want to appear in the model. Therefore, most software packages allow a sub-set of predictor variables to be selected from those that are available.
4. Sub-population to use for modelling. If some observations within the sample have been classified as exclusions, indeterminates, not taken-up and so on, these cases should be excluded from the modelling process. Similarly, development and holdout samples may be contained in a single dataset, with a flag used to identify in which sample an observation belongs. Only observations in the development sample should be used for modelling.
5. Weighting. If a balanced sample has been created from an unbalanced population, then the user will need to identify the variable containing

the weights, if weighting is to be applied within the modelling process.

6. Entry/Exit criteria (significance levels). If forward or stepwise regression is employed, then the entry criteria sets the level of confidence that one must have that a variable provides a significant contribution to the model before it is included. Likewise, the exit criteria is the level of confidence below which variables are removed from the model for backward and stepwise regression.

7. Which statistics/metrics to produce. Some software automatically generate all available measures of how well the model fits the data. Others provide a range of reporting options, allowing the user to specify which metrics to calculate.

8. A holdout sample to apply the model to. Sometimes a user can specify a "score option" within the modelling software to automatically apply the model to another sample. In others, the user must apply additional operations after model construction is complete, in order to calculate scores for the holdout sample(s).

One major option which has not been discussed in previous chapters is option 6, the entry/exit criteria (the significance levels). For forward and stepwise regression the entry criteria for inclusion into the model is based on a statistical test called the partial F-test. The partial F-test statistic is calculated for each variable not currently in the model, and the one with the highest value is included, if the value of the test statistic provides a sufficient degree of certainty that adding the variable will improve the model. A 5 percent significance level can be interpreted as meaning that a predictor variable will only be included within the model if we are 95 percent certain that a genuine relationship exists between the predictor variable and the dependent variable.

The significance level chosen for model entry will be problem specific, but is often related to sample size. The argument being that if lots of data is available, then one should be very confident about the relationships being genuine before a variable is included in the model. For a model development sample containing many thousands of cases, it is common to set a relatively high threshold for model entry/exit. Perhaps a significance level somewhere between 0.1 percent and 1 percent. Where samples contain relatively few cases, perhaps 1,000 or less, then more relaxed significance levels are sometimes used, perhaps values of between 1 percent and 10 percent. If in doubt then one can always perform the stepwise procedure a number of times using different entry criteria and evaluate the different models that result.

The exit criteria is applied in a similar way to the entry criteria for stepwise and backward stepwise. If the value of the partial F-test for a variable is below the threshold of significance then the variable is removed from the model. Usually (although not always) the same significance level will be used for both model entry and exit.

7.1.5   Interpreting the output of the modelling process

Every software package produces output from the model construction process in its own way, but the information tends to be similar regardless of which package is applied. Consider a credit scoring project for a personal loan, where the objective is to construct a model to predict how likely someone is to be creditworthy over a period of 12 months. This is a classification problem where the good/bad flag (the dependent variable) has been defined as 1 for goods and 0 for bads. The set of predictor variables has been pre-processed as a set of dummy variables, as described in the previous chapter. Table 7.1 provides a (simplified)[1] example of the output that would be produced using a software package such as SAS or SPSS.

The top half of Table 7.1 shows details of the model that has been constructed by applying a stepwise procedure using a 1 percent criteria for model entry/exit. Columns A and B show the predictor variables in the model and the parameter coefficients of each one. To calculate the model score for this example, it is important to remember that the variables within the model refer to the dummy variables, created during pre-processing, to represent the attributes of the predictor variables. If you recall, a dummy variable takes a value of 1 if someone has that attribute and 0 otherwise. When using the model to calculate a score for someone, they will start with a score equal to the constant of 0.7636. If the person is aged 18–21 then 0.3939 is subtracted from the score (1 * –0.3939). If they are not aged 18–21 then the dummy variable for age 18–21 will have been assigned a value of zero. Therefore, nothing is subtracted (0 * –0.3939 = 0). If they are aged 22–25 then 0.0985 is subtracted, if their residential status = owner, 0.0653 is added and so on, for all of the variables that the feature within the model. If a dummy variable has not been included within the model, then this is the same as saying that the parameter coefficient for the attribute represented by that dummy variable is equal to zero. In this example, dummy variables were assigned for being aged 26–30, 31–40, 41–65 and 65+, but none of these where significant, and therefore, do not feature in the model. If weights of evidence transformations have been applied, then the interpretation of the parameter coefficients is a little different, and this covered in section 7.2 where a similar example is presented in relation to logistic regression.

Table 7.1 Linear regression output

A Predictor variable	B Parameter coefficient (weight)	C Standard error	D t-test statistic (t-value)	E p-value (Prob t>t)	F Variance inflation
Constant	0.7636	0.0039	195.795	<.0001	0.000
Age 18–21	-0.3939	0.0061	-64.574	<.0001	1.394
Age 22–25	-0.0985	0.0038	-25.921	<.0001	1.078
Residential status = Owner	0.0653	0.0023	28.391	<.0001	1.191
Residential status = LWP	0.1391	0.0036	38.639	<.0001	1.480
Mobile phone = yes	-0.1916	0.0064	-29.938	<.0001	1.240
Employment status = retired	0.1734	0.0039	44.462	<.0001	2.616
Income <$20,000	-0.1806	0.0063	-28.667	<.0001	1.035
Income >$175,000	0.0769	0.0297	2.589	0.0096	3.375
Number of credit cards >2	-0.2140	0.0057	-37.544	<.0001	1.982

Measure	Value	Derivation
Sum of Squared Errors (SSE)	8114.7857	$\sum_{1}^{n}(Y - S)^2$
Total Sum of Squares (TSS)	11280.4150	$\sum_{1}^{n}(Y - \bar{Y})^2$
R-squared (R^2)	0.2806	$1 - \dfrac{SSE}{TSS}$
Adjusted R-squared (A–R^2)	0.2805	$1 - \dfrac{(n-1)(1-R^2)}{n-k}$
Mean Absolute Error (MAE)	0.3023	$\sqrt{\dfrac{SSE}{n-k}}$

Y = value of the dependent variable
$\bar{Y}$ = mean value of the dependent variable
S = model score
n = number of observations used in the model construction process
k = number of predictor variables that feature within the model

Column C contains the standard error. This is the standard deviation of the parameter coefficient in column B. Column D contains the t-test statistic (calculated as column B/column C). The level of confidence associated with the test statistic (the "p value") is contained in column E. The p-value can be interpreted as the probability that the true parameter coefficient is equal to zero. To put it another way, although the variable has been selected by the regression process and a parameter coefficient has been generated, the variable is in reality, not a significant predictor of behaviour. This uncertainty about the parameter coefficient arises because one is only ever dealing with a finite sample – if a larger sample was available then more precise estimates about the value of the parameter coefficients could be made. Given that stepwise regression has been applied to select variables that are believed to have a significant relationship with the dependent variable, it is not surprising that all of the p-values are small. Most are significant beyond reasonable doubt, with a p-value of less than 0.0001. The only exception is the parameter coefficient for the dummy variable Income >£175,000, where the p-value is 0.0096. Given that the significance level set for entry into the model was 0.01, then there is enough confidence to say that it should be in the model, but only just. The final column in Table 7.1 is the variance inflation factor. Simplistically, this is a measure of correlation between each predictor variable and all of the other variables that feature in the model. The larger the variance inflation factor the greater the degree of correlation between the variables. How to use variance inflation factors is somewhat debatable, but one rule of thumb is that one should *consider* (so not an immutable rule) removing a predictor variable and rerunning the model if the variance inflation factor is greater than about 10. Alternatively, some model developers assess correlation using Pearson or Spearman rank correlation measures for all two way combinations of predictor variables that feature in the model. If any pair of variables displays a correlation factor greater than about 0.6–0.7, then one of the variables is removed[2] and the model rerun.

Note that Table 7.1 shows only the final model generated from the stepwise procedure. In practice, most software also provides details of all the intermediate models that were constructed at each stage of the stepwise process, as different predictor variables were added/removed from the model.

7.1.6   Measures of model fit

Once a model has been constructed, a key question is how well does it predict behaviour? The only certain way of determining how well any model performs is to test it using an independent holdout sample that was not used during model construction, and this is discussed in detail in the next chapter. However, a range of metrics are often used at the development stage to give an indication of how good the model is, which are often described in terms of how well the model *fits* the data used to construct the model. The bottom half of Table 7.1 contains examples of some of the most popular measures. The first row contains the Sum of Squared Error (SSE). This is the quantity the linear regression process has minimized when finding the parameter coefficients of the model. When comparing two models, all other things being equal, the model with the lowest sum of squared error is the one that provides the best fit to the data. The Total Sum of Squares (TSS) measures the sum of differences between the mean value of the dependent variable and the actual value of the dependent variable for each observation in the development sample. The TSS is not a measure of model fit in itself, but is used in conjunction with the sum of squared error to calculate R-squared. R-squared provides a standardized measure of the sum of squared error, calculated as one minus the Sum of Square Error divided by the Total Sum of Squares. R-squared therefore, takes values in the range 0–1.

The higher the R-squared value the better the model fits the data. However, a feature of linear regression (and other modelling techniques) is that every time an additional variable is added into the model the better the model fit becomes, regardless of whether or not adding the variable brings any additional benefit when the model is assessed using a holdout sample. Adding a new variable into a model always results in a lower value of SSE and a higher value of R-squared. In the extreme, it can be demonstrated that if there are n observations in the development sample and $n-1$ predictor variables, then a perfect fit will be obtained every time. The Sum of Squared Errors will be zero and R-squared will be 1. However, when it comes to applying the model to the holdout sample its predictive performance is likely to be much worse. This problem, which has been referred to before in several previous chapters, is called over-fitting. A good way to visualize over-fitting is to go back to Figure 7.1, which considered the relationship between income and credit card expenditure. If you pick any two points at random and apply linear regression to predict credit card expenditure using income as a predictor variable, then the result will be a model that can be represented by a straight line that contains the two points you selected. The Sum of Squared Errors, calculated using just the two points, will be zero and the R-squared will be 1. If you now apply this model to all the other data points in Figure 7.1, most, if not all, will lie some way away from the regression line, indicating that there are errors between what the model predicts and what actually occurs. Consequently, the R-squared value is very much less than 1. This is a very extreme example of over-fitting. As the number of observations becomes larger relative to the number of predictor variables, so the problem of over-fitting decreases. However, even when the ratio of observations to predictor variables is very large, a small degree of over-fitting can still occur.

One way that modellers attempt to get around the problem of over fitting is to derive penalized measures of model fit. The most popular of these "penalized measures" is the Adjusted R-squared value, the derivation of which is shown in the row immediately below R-squared in Table 7.1. When two alternative linear regression models are being compared, then all other things being equal, the one with the lowest adjusted R-squared is usually taken to be the better of the two.

When using a method such as stepwise regression, the Adjusted R-squared is often used to select the best model, from the set of models created during the stepwise procedure. The final model generated by the stepwise procedure will have been built up in stages with a different model constructed each time a variable was added or removed. It is important to realize that a variable can be statistically significant within a model, as measured by the partial F-test or t-test, but only provide a very small reduction in the sum of squared error compared to the model generated at the previous step. The net result is that as the increase in R-squared become smaller, a point is reached where the Adjusted R-squared begins to decline. What this means is that if one takes Adjusted R-squared to provide the best measure of model fit, then it becomes necessary to review all the models generated by the stepwise process and select the one with the highest Adjusted R-squared. This may be the last model generated by the stepwise regression process, but it may not. This is particularly likely to be the case if the entry/exit criteria used for the stepwise procedure were relatively lax, allowing a lot of additional variables to enter the model.

Adjusted R-squared is perhaps the most widely used measure of model fit, but there are many alternatives. These include, amongst others: the Akaike Information Criteria (AIC), the Corrected Akaike Information Criteria (CAIC), Mallows statistic (Cp), the Predicted Sum of Squares Statistic (PRESS) and the Bayesian Information Criteria (BIC). There are various arguments that can be put forward as to which of these measures is best, but most, like Adjusted R-squared, are derived from a function of the model errors, the number of observations in the development sample and the number of predictor variables within the model. Hence, most give similar (but not identical) results in terms of selecting the model that gives the best fit to the development data.

7.1.7 Are the assumptions for linear regression important?

Any training course that covers linear regression will place considerable emphasis on the model assumptions. The most important of these assumptions are:

- The errors (often referred to as residuals) generated by the model should be randomly distributed, and follow a normal (bell-shaped) distribution.
- The mean value of the errors should be zero.
- The spread (the variance) of the errors should be the same for any sub-set of observations within the sample.

So if one generates a scatter plot of the errors against the dependent variable, then there should be no discernible patterns and the errors should be randomly distributed around zero. If the model assumptions are violated then any inferences about the size of the parameter coefficients, the confidence one has that variables are significant within the model and confidence limits on predictions made by the model, can not be relied upon.

When applying linear regression to certain types of problem, one would be remiss if one did not carry out detailed residual analysis as a fundamental part of the model assessment process. However, when it comes to predictive modelling applied to large populations, the individual estimates generated by the model tend not to be very important. What people are more interested in are the properties of the score distribution of the population as a whole; that is, how many observations have particular scores and what the properties of the population are at those scores. When dealing with large numbers, individual estimates become relatively unimportant. What this means is, while it is important to have an appreciation of the assumptions underpinning linear regression (and other modelling techniques) it's not a big issue if the modelling assumptions are violated. In practice, the modelling assumptions are almost always violated, to a greater or lesser extent, when modelling consumer behaviour. For those interested in this discussion see Eisenbeis (1977, 1978).

7.1.8 Stakeholder expectations and business requirements

In some situations, models are required to conform to the expectations of senior management. Project stakeholders must be comfortable about which predictor variables feature within the model and the parameter coefficients that are assigned to each one. Likewise, no matter how good the model is statistically, it must meet the requirements of the business if it is to be usable. These issues have been discussed before in previous chapters, and most questions around the nature and form of the model, and the variables that feature within the model, should have been addressed well before one gets to the modelling stage. However, it is worth revisiting these issues before going further – otherwise one runs the risk of spending considerable time undertaking validation and producing performance metrics for the newly constructed model, only to be told by stakeholders that the model is unsuitable. Some common stakeholder expectations/business requirements of a model include:

- The parameter coefficients for each predictor variable should match the patterns seen within the univariate analysis reports. For example, if people who rent are observed to have a higher incidence of default on a loan than home owners, then one would expect the parameter coefficient for home owners to be higher than for renters, for a model constructed to predict good/bad repayment behaviour.
- The model should be simple. Simple models are generally more robust over time, and are easier to implement and monitor. Sometimes a model can be rejected simply because it contains too many variables. I recall one instance where stakeholders were presented with what I thought was a perfectly good model which contained 23 predictor variables. I was told categorically, this was too many and that the model should have no more than 20 variables! The model had to be rebuilt with this new constraint imposed upon it.
- The variables in the model must be available at the point where the model is going to be applied. If a model is going to be implemented within an organization's application processing system, then one must be absolutely certain that all the predictor variables are available in this system. If not, then there must be a plan to upgrade the system to make the data available.
- Legal compliance. In some countries and jurisdictions there are prohibitions on the use of certain predictor variables within some types of models. For example race, religion, gender, and so on.

7.2   Logistic regression

These days, logistic regression is probably the most widely used technique for producing classification models (Hosmer and Lemeshow 2000, p. 1; Crook et al. 2007). Like linear regression, logistic regression produces a linear model of the form $S = a + b_1x_1 + b_2x_2 +, ..., + b_kx_k$. Stepwise, forward and backward procedures are also available. These are applied in a similar manner to stepwise procedures for linear regression, with one variable added or removed at each stage depending upon how significantly it does or does not improve the model fit to the data.

With appropriate data pre-processing (dummy variables or weights of evidence) the performance of models constructed using logistic regression is generally very good, and it is widely acknowledged that logistic regression sets the standard against which other methods for constructing classification models should be compared. Therefore, if you are interested in developing classification models using techniques other than logistic regression, it's a good idea to also construct a model using logistic regression to act as a benchmark against which the competing method is evaluated (note that for regression problems, linear regression is recommended as the benchmark).

Logistic regression is specifically intended for classification problems, which in the context of this book means binary classification problems where the goal is to predict the probability that someone exhibits good or bad behaviour.[3] Logistic regression cannot be used to generate models for continuous objectives such as revenue, profit contribution or loss given default.

Logistic regression is based on the principle of maximum likelihood. The likelihood is calculated as:

$$\text{likelihood} = P_1{}^*P_2{}^*...^* P_G * (1 - P_{G+1})* (1 - P_{G+2}) *...* (1 - P_{G+B})$$

where:

G is the number of goods in the development sample.
B is the number of bads in the development sample.
$P_1, ..., P_G$ are the estimated probabilities of good, generated by the model, for each good in the sample.
$P_{G+1}, ..., P_{G+B}$ are the estimated probabilities of good for each bad in the sample. Therefore, $1 - P_{G+1}$ is the probability of bad for the first bad, $1 - P_{G+2}$ the probability of bad for the second bad and so on.

The parameters of the model are chosen so that the likelihood is maximized. Unlike linear regression, the model parameters that maximize the likelihood can not be found using standard calculus. Instead, parameter coefficients are found using algorithms that iterate towards an optimal solution. To start, parameter coefficients are set to zero or chosen arbitrarily. At each iteration of the algorithm the parameter coefficients are adjusted, based on the change in likelihood that is seen from one iteration to the next. The algorithm terminates when the change between iterations becomes so small as to be insignificant. The most common of these algorithms is the Newton-Raphson algorithm (Lee 1980) which is the default method applied within many popular software packages. For readers who are interested in the mechanics of logistic regression/ maximum likelihood then there are many good books on the subject. For a short, concise (and cheap) introduction to the application of logistic regression I recommend "Applied Logistic Regression Analysis" by Scott Menard (2002). See "Applied Logistic Regression" by David Hosmer and Stanley Lemeshow (2000) for a more in depth guide.

The score produced by a model constructed using logistic regression has a number of interesting properties. In particular, the score can be interpreted as the natural log of the good:bad odds.

$$S = a + b_1x_1 + b_2x_2 + ,..., + b_kx_k = Ln(Odds)$$

A score of 0 means the estimated good:bad odds are 1:1, which is the same as saying that for a score of 0, the estimated probability of good is 0.5, or that the bad rate is 50 percent. Likewise, a score of 1 equates to odds of e^1:1 (2.7183:1 or a bad rate of 26.9 percent), a score of 2 to odds of e^2:1 (7.389:1 or a bad rate of 11.9 percent) and so on.

The model as it stands can be used to generate scores for customers, and decision can be made based on the good:bad odds associated with a given score. For example, if the score predicts the likelihood of someone repaying a loan, and you feel it is only profitable to lend to customers where the good:bad odds are 25:1 or more, then this equates to a cut-off score of $Ln(25) = 3.219$. All loan applicants with a score below 3.219 should be rejected and all those scoring above 3.219 should be accepted. If you wish to convert the score into a probability of good, then the relationship can be rearranged, so as to provide a probability estimate:

$$P(Good) = \frac{e^s}{1 + e^s}$$

where

> $P(good)$ is the probability of a case being good and $1-P(good)$ is the bad rate.

S is the score generated by the model.
e takes a value of 2.7183.

If the model is biased and/or over-fitting has occurred, the score may be misaligned when assessed using a sample other than the model development sample. Therefore, it should not be taken for granted that the score will always be equal to *Ln(odds)* unless this relationship has been validated using an appropriate holdout sample. Validation is discussed in Chapter 8.

7.2.1   Producing the model

The modelling options that need to be selected when using logistic regression are very similar to those for linear regression, as detailed in section 7.1.4. The software will require the user to select the dependent variable, the predictor variables, which step-wise option to apply and so on.[4] The only additional option that the user must decide upon is which one of the two behaviours to select for the model to predict; that is, will the model predict the probability of good behaviour, or the probability of bad behaviour?

7.2.2   Interpreting the output

There are many analogies that can be made between linear and logistic regression, and consequently many of the model outputs generated by logistic regression are very similar to those generated from linear regression, despite the underlying mechanism for deriving the model parameters being different. Let us continue with the personal loan credit scoring example that was introduced in section 7.1.5. The same variables have been included within the modelling process, and the logistic regression process has been instructed to maximize the likelihood of individuals being good payers. However, for this example, assume the predictor variables have been pre-processed using weight of evidence transformations rather than dummy variables. The output of the model is shown in Table 7.2.

The top half of Table 7.2 provides details of the model. Columns A and B show the predictor variables that entered the model and their parameter coefficients. Remember that Weights of Evidence (WOE) transformed versions of the predictor variables have been used, hence the WOE suffix that has been added to the names of the predictor

Table 7.2 Logistic regression output

A	B	C	D	E	F
Predictor variable	Parameter coefficient (weight)	Standard error	Wald Chi-squared	p-value (Prob > Chi) squared)	Variance inflation
Constant	1.7272	0.0121	20,285.2487	<.0001	0.000
Age_WOE	0.3965	0.0283	196.4384	<.0001	3.221
Residential status_WOE	0.3109	0.0361	73.9907	<.0001	2.875
Mobile phone_WOE	0.4996	0.0375	177.5669	<.0001	1.197
Employment status_WOE	0.3547	0.0319	123.6172	<.0001	2.003
Income_WOE	0.2196	0.0799	7.5555	0.0060	4.556
Number of credit cards_WOE	0.6362	0.0466	186.4015	<.0001	1.288

Measure	Value	Derivation
-2 Log likelihood (L_m)	50,989.01	
-2 Log likelihood for model containing only a constant and no predictor variables (L_c)	74,864.59	
Model chi-squared statistic (χ^2)	23,875.58	$L_c - L_m$
Likelihood ratio	0.32	$\dfrac{(L_c - L_m)}{L_c}$
Pseudo R-Squared	0.30	$\dfrac{\chi^2}{(\chi^2 + n)}$
Akaike Information Criteria (AIC)	50,996.01	$2k + L_m$
Schwarz Information Criterion (SIC)	50972.48	$Ln(n) + L_m$
Somer's D concordance statistic	0.73	

n = number of observations used in the model construction process
k = number of predictor variables that feature within the model

variables. The parameter coefficient for the ith interval within a predictor variable is calculated as:

$$b'_i = WOE_i * b$$

where:

b'_i is the parameter coefficient of the model associated with the ith coarse classed interval for a given variable.
WOE_i is the weight of evidence for the ith coarse classed interval for a given variable.
b is the value of the parameter coefficient assigned to the weight of evidence transformed variable within the model (column B in Table 7.2).

So if the weight of evidence for the attribute "Age 18–21" is –0.9512 then the parameter coefficient for this interval will be –0.9512 * 0.3965 = –0.3772. Note that common parlance is to refer to the parameter coefficient b'_i as the "score" or "points" allocated to an attribute.

Column C in Table 7.2 is the standard error; that is, the standard deviation associated with the parameter coefficient in column B. Column D is the Wald chi-squared test statistic. This can be considered analogous to the t-test statistic for linear regression, and the p-value in Column E can be interpreted as the probability that the true value of the parameter coefficient is zero, given the value of the Wald chi-squared statistic. Column F contains variance inflation factors.[5]

The bottom half of Table 7.2 provides some standard measures of model fit. –2 Ln(likelihood) (L_m) is analogous to the sum of squared errors in linear regression. The smaller the value of L_m the better the model fits the data. Note that logistic regression maximizes the likelihood, but the natural log of the likelihood multiplied by –2 is usually quoted. This is for various practical reasons relating to the calculation of performance metrics and so on. Standard practice is for –2 Ln(likelihood) to also be calculated for a model that contains a constant but no predictor variables – we will term this L_c. The difference between (L_c) and (L_m) is referred to as the model chi-squared statistic.

The Likelihood Ratio is the nearest analogy to the R-squared statistic for linear regression. Similarly, Pseudo R-squared is analogous to the Adjusted R-squared value (Menard 2002, pp. 24–5). As with R-squared and Adjusted R-squared for linear regression, the Likelihood Ratio and

Pseudo R-squared take values in the range 0–1 with a higher value indicating a better fit.

When several models are being compared, such as when stepwise logistic regression has been applied, penalized measures of fit are used to select the best model. This is very similar to the process that was discussed in relation to selecting the best model for stepwise linear regression. Pseudo R-squared can be used, but various types of Information Criteria are most commonly applied. The Akaike Information Criteria (AIC) and Schwarz Information Criterion (SIC) are two of the most popular, but there are others.

The final measure in Table 7.2 is Somer's D concordance statistic. This provides a measure of separation between the two classes based on the model scores. In theory, values range from –1 to +1. A value of zero indicates a model whose scores provide no differentiation between observations of different classes. An absolute value of 1 indicates where the model scores provide perfect separation. Another way of thinking about this is, if the model has been constructed to predict good behaviour, then the more goods that get high scores and the more bads that get low scores the higher Somer's D will be. For two class problems of the type discussed here, Somer's D is equivalent to the GINI statistic. This is a very popular measure of group separation that is explained in Chapter 8.

7.3   Neural network models

Artificial Neural Networks (ANNs) evolved from research into Artificial Intelligence in the 1950s and 1960s (Rosenblatt 1958), but only came to prominence in the mid-1980s (Rumelhart et al. 1986). The main feature of neural networks is their ability to represent non-linear features of the data through the inclusion of two or more hidden nodes contained within the hidden layer of the network, as depicted in Figure 1.4 in Chapter 1. Without the hidden nodes a neural network model is, to all intents and purposes, just another form of linear model. In theory, a neural network model can have more than the one hidden layer. However, a network with enough neurons in a single hidden layer is, in theory, able to approximate any relationship between the predictor variables and the dependent variable to any desired level of accuracy. A network can also have more than one neuron in the output layer, but in practice, a single output neuron is almost always sufficient.

Unlike linear and logistic regression, stepwise procedures are not offered by many software packages that generate neural networks models (although various "stepwise like" procedures have been developed). However, even if such procedures are available, if one is using a large data set with many predictor variables it may not be practical in terms of computer time to apply them. Constructing networks in stages, adding or removing one predictor variable at a time can be very time consuming indeed. Instead, all variable selection is usually performed before model construction occurs and each retained variable provides one input to the input layer of the network.

One problem with neural networks is that there are so many different options that one can choose with regard to how the network is configured and the training algorithms that can be applied to find the parameter coefficients of the model. There is not one universally best set of options to choose and many different network configurations/ training algorithms will often yield very similar results. Therefore, in practical situations where there are deadlines to meet, the key is to allocate a fixed amount of time to experimenting with different options and then accept the best options found in the allotted time. In this section the main emphasis is on the options that are available when determining the structure of the network and the methods that can be applied to find the parameter coefficients of the model.

For a general, and not very mathematical, introduction to neural networks then I would recommend the book 'Introduction to Neural Networks' by Kevin Gurney (1997). For a more technical guide then books by Bishop (1995) and Haykin (2009) are recommended.

7.3.1 Number of neurons in the hidden layer

The general advice for neural networks is that the optimal number of neurons in the hidden layer is problem specific and much experimentation is required to find the best number to use. Having more neurons in the hidden layer increases the ability of the network to capture non-linear relationships within the data, but each additional neuron means the model has more parameters that require estimation. This increases the time to train the network and increases the chance of over-fitting occurring.

Most research into consumer behaviour modelling has concluded that the performance of linear models is as good, or almost as good (or sometimes even better) than neural networks in the majority of cases. This implies that most of the relationships that exist in samples of consumer data can be represented linearly if suitable data pre-processing has occurred and/or interaction effects have been considered. Any non-linear relationships in the data tend to be fairly minor, and provide only a marginal contribution to the predictive abilities of the model over and above the linear component. In my experience this translates into meaning that as a rule, you don't need very many neurons in the hidden layer. If you have the time to spare then do try different network configurations with anything from 2 to 2k neurons in the hidden layer, where k is the number of neurons in the input layer. A good strategy is to start with just 2 neurons and then examine models constructed with 4, 8, 16 neurons and so on. If the best performance is found with 8 neurons, then this implies the best performing model will be one that has between 4 and 16 neurons. Therefore, try 6 and 12 to narrow the search further and so on. If you are really pressed for time, then in my experience between $k/8$ and $k/4$ neurons will yield models that are very close to the optimum for most types of consumer behaviour modelling.

7.3.2 Objective function

Unlike linear or logistic regression, where the model is chosen to minimize least squares or maximize likelihood, a neural network can be trained to minimize/maximize any objective function for which a measure of error can be calculated. For regression problems minimized least squares is commonly used as the objective function and maximum likelihood is often used for classification, but others functions can be optimized if required.

7.3.3 Combination and activation function

There are many different combination and activations functions that can be applied to each of the neurons within a neural network. However, as mentioned in Chapter 1, a linear combination function of the inputs to the neuron is usually adequate.

When it comes to selecting an activation function, for binary classification problems the logistic or hyperbolic tangent function (both members of the sigmoid family of transformations) are good choices for all of the neurons in the hidden layer and the output layer. For regression problems, sigmoid functions can also be used in the hidden layer. However, for the output neuron, applying a sigmoid activation function is not recommended. This is because it limits the value of the output to a narrow range. Instead, the identity function should be applied. This is the same as saying that the raw value of the combination function is used as the model score.

7.3.4 Training algorithm

A number of different algorithms can be used to derive the parameter coefficients of a neural network model. Whatever algorithm is chosen, the general approach is to set the initial parameter coefficients of the model to random values. The error generated by the model is then calculated for the first observation, and this is used to inform the process of adjusting the parameter coefficients of the model. The process is then repeated for all observations in the data set. After all observations have been considered, the data set is randomly sorted and the whole process is repeated (each run through the data set is termed an epoch) until some stopping criteria is met. This may be that the reduction in errors from one epoch to the next falls below a predefined threshold, or when a given number of epochs have occurred.

The original training algorithm for neural networks was the back-propagation algorithm (Rumelhart et al. 1986) which is still widely used to generate good quality models. However, one of the drawbacks of the back-propagation algorithm is that it requires additional training parameters (the momentum and the learning rate), to be chosen to determine how quickly it iterates towards a solution. A second drawback is that it is slow. More modern algorithms such as Quasi-Newton and Levenberg-Marquardt are many times faster, and have the added benefit of not requiring additional training parameters to be chosen. Both of these techniques are recommended for the types of model discussed in this book.

One problem with all network training algorithms is they can find a local minima as opposed to a global minima. They iterative towards a good model, but not necessarily the best one. One way to reduce the chance of finding local minima is to generate a number of preliminary models (say at least 20), each starting with a different randomly selected set of parameter coefficients. The parameter coefficients for the best model found from these preliminary runs are then used as the starting point for the training proper.

Given that the choice of initial parameter coefficients is important in determining if a local or global minima is found, if one is undertaking many different experiments to determine the best configuration for the network (number of neurons in the hidden layer, the activation function and so on) then it is important that the same initial parameter coefficients are chosen each time. This is so that a fair comparison between models can be made. All good neural network software should provide this option as standard.

7.3.5 Stopping criteria and model selection

An important question is, when should network training finish? There are two standard approaches.

- Let the training algorithm run until the reduction in error from one epoch to the next falls below a predefined threshold (what this threshold is, will depend on what one is trying to predict).
- Let the model run for a fixed number of epochs. If one is using Quasi-Newton or Levenberg-Marquardt then in my experience rarely are more than about 200 epochs required before the reduction in errors becomes insignificant.

Neural network training algorithms are notorious for over-fitting the data. Over-fitting is far more of a problem for neural networks than for linear or logistic regression. There are many examples of people creating what they think is a fantastic neural network model, but which turns out to be extremely poor when assessed using an independent holdout sample. To get around this problem, standard practice is to segment the original development sample into two parts, which I will term the training sample and the validation sample (split 80/20 or 70/30 training/validation). The training algorithm adjusts the parameter coefficients of the model on basis of the error observed from the training sample. After each epoch, the error function is calculated for the validation sample and the parameter coefficients of the model at that point are recorded. When training has finished there will be X different models, where X is the number of epochs. The model that resulted in the lowest error for the validation sample is considered to be the best. The actual performance of the model is then evaluated using the holdout and/or out-of-time samples that have been taken.

7.4 Classification and regression trees (CART)

The Recursive Partitioning Algorithm, used to generate CART models, was initially developed by Breiman and Friedman in 1973 and became popular following the publication of their book *Classification and Regression Trees* (Breiman et al. 1984).

Many variants of the method proposed by Breiman and Friedman have been suggested since their original formulation, such as the popular C4.5 algorithm developed by Quinlan (1992) and its successor C5.0, but the basic principles remain the same. The development sample is segmented into two parts, based on the properties of the predictor variables and the relationship they display with the dependent variable. After segment-ation has occurred, the processes is repeated for each of the two "child" segments that resulted. With each round of segmentation, the new seg-ments contain observations that show increasingly divergent behav-iour from the parent population. For classification problems this means that if the good:bad odds in the parent group are X:1, one of the two segments will have odds greater than X:1 and the other less then X:1. The goal of the segmentation process is to find the split that maximizes the difference in odds between the two groups; taking into account the number of observations within each segment (one needs a measure that considers the number in each segment as well as odds, otherwise the seg-mentation algorithm would simply pull out one good or one bad each time a split occurred). Similarly for regression problems, the goal of the segmentation process is to maximize the difference in the average value of the dependent variable for observations in the two segments, again taking the number of cases in each segment into account. The segment-ation process halts when a given stopping criteria is met. For example, when all segments are >x% pure, or the number of observations in all segments is less than a specified minimum. A record of the segmentation process is then captured in the form of a classification and regression tree (CART) model, as illustrated in Figure 1.2 in Chapter 1.

The rules for creating each segment of the tree are determined by examining the domain of all possible splits and choosing the split that maximizes the discrimination between the two groups. There are many splitting rules that can be applied. For classification problems, the most popular splitting rules are very similar to those discussed in section 5.2, with regard to measures of association; that is, splits are chosen to maximize information value, chi-square, efficiency and so on.

A CART model does not generate a score as such, but the bad rate for observations in the leaf nodes of the tree can be considered as the model score for classification problems. For regression problems the score can be taken to be the average value of observations in each leaf node.

7.4.1   Growing and pruning the tree

Apart from deciding which splitting rule to apply, the other major decision is the stopping criteria. These days common practice is to grow a large tree, only stopping when each leaf node contains less than a given number of observations. For consumer behaviour prob-lems somewhere between five and 50 observations is usually a sensible number at which to stop the segmentation process.

As with neural networks over-fitting can be a big problem, even if the minimum size of the leaf nodes is set relatively high. To get around this problem pruning is applied after the segmentation process has completed. Pruning means that some of the leaf nodes in the tree are removed, thus reducing the size of the tree.

The best way to apply pruning is, like neural networks, to split the development sample into training and validation samples. The training sample is used to grow the tree to full size. Once this has been done, the model is assessed using the validation sample. Then a leaf node is removed and the performance of the model is assessed again using the validation sample. If model performance is better without the node, then this configuration becomes the benchmark. If performance deteriorates, then the leaf node is added back into the tree. Leaf nodes continue to be removed until no further improvement in performance is observed on the validation sample.

7.5   Survival analysis

Survival analysis covers a range of techniques for constructing models that generate estimates of the time until an event occurs, rather than the probability of an event occurring. Traditional applications of survival analysis have been by actuaries to determine how long someone is likely to live after retirement, by doctors to assess the time patients with a particular disease are likely to survive and by engineers to estimate the time to failure of machine components. However, the same principles can also be applied to consumer behaviour. From a marketing perspective, knowing the time between a communication being sent and the recipient responding can aid resource planning in customer contact centres, to ensure that just the right number of staff are available to deal with customer responses when they occur. From an insurance perspective, knowing the expected time to a claim can influence pricing decisions. Similarly, for retail credit, predicting the time to default can be an aid to cash flow, liquidity and capital requirements calculations.

Obviously, one can build a regression model to predict the time until the event of interest occurs using a method such as linear regression. The dependent variable in this case is the event time. However, the big attraction of survival analysis is the ability to predict events long beyond the length of the outcome window over which behaviour is observed. This makes it possible to construct models using data gathered over a short outcome period to predict the likelihood of events occurring over much longer timeframes. One could, for example, gather information about repayment behaviour on a loan product over a period of say 6–12 months, and then use this to construct a survival analysis model that predicts the likelihood of default over a much longer timeframe, say three or five years (Hand and Kelly 2001). Survival analysis is based on two key concepts:

1. The hazard function. This is the probability of an event happening at time t given that the event has not already occurred. Consider a personal loan where repayments are made on a monthly basis and one is interested in the probability of the customer defaulting on their repayments. The hazard function for default events would give the probability of loan default between months t and $t+1$, given that the customer had not previously defaulted before month t.
2. The survival function. This represents the probability of an event not having happened by a certain time. For the personal loan example discussed in (1), the survival function provides a measure of the probability of repayments being maintained until time t, or to put it another way, the probability that default does not occur before time t. This is obviously useful, because the number of payments that are made before default occurs will have a direct impact on the proportion of the loan that is written off.

The survival function and hazard function are related. For the personal loan example discussed above, where a customer can default in any month from 1…T. The probability of survival to time t $(t \leq T)$, is given by summing up the hazard function at month 0, month 1,…, month $t-1$ and subtracting this value from 1.

The major developments in survival analysis occurred in the 1960s and 1970s when regression methods were first applied to produce survival distributions for individuals within a population (Harris and Albert 1991). Of particular note was the introduction of proportional hazards methods for censored regression (Cox 1972). As described by Harris and Albert (1991) Cox's base model is:

$$h_i(t) = h_0(t)e^{(s_i)}$$

where:

$h_i(t)$ is the hazard rate at time t for the ith individual; that is, the probability of the event of occurring at time t, conditional on the event not occurring prior to time t.

$h_0(t)$ is the baseline hazard function. The baseline hazard function is unknown, but is assumed to have the same value for all individuals.

S_i is the score generated from a linear model of the form: $b_1x_1 + b_2x_2 + ,..., + b_kx_k$ (note no constant in the model). The score is sometimes referred to as the risk score or prognostic score.

Rearranging Cox's equation gives:

$$\frac{h_i(t)}{h_0(t)} = e^{(S_i)}$$

which is termed the relative hazard function. Taking natural logs gives:

$$Ln\frac{h_i(t)}{h_0(t)} = S_i$$

The model score can be interpreted as the natural log of the ratio of an individual's hazard function to the baseline hazard function. To find the parameters of the model Cox proposed representing the likelihood function (somewhat controversially at the time) in a form that removed the unknown base hazard $h_0(t)$ from the model. Therefore, it made it possible to calculate the hazard rate for an individual based on the score that they received.

The process of generating a survival analysis model is very similar to that for logistic regression, as discussed in section 7.2, as are the outputs generated. For more information about proportional hazards and other aspects of survival analysis see Hosmer et al. (2008).

7.6   Computation issues

These days, modern PCs provide immense computational resources compared to what was available just a few years ago. In 1993, when I built my first credit scoring model for a UK mail order catalogue company, the PC at my disposal had 4MB of RAM (that's megabytes not gigabytes) and a 40MB hard drive. The PC had a 486 processor running at 33MHz and was capable of about two million floating point operations per second. As I write less than 20 years later, my home PC has 4GB of Ram and more and 1,000GB of Hard Disk storage. The processor runs in excess of 3GHz and can perform billions of floating point operations a second.

Once consequence of the advances in computer hardware is that the time required to derive the parameters of a model has shrunk dramatically. For small samples containing a few thousand observations and a few dozen predictor variables, it can take just a fraction of a second to produce a model using linear or logistic regression. However, for very large problems, where the sample used to build the model contains hundreds of thousands of observations and thousands of predictor variables, it can still take a very considerable amount of time to find the parameters of the model. For the very largest problems, the time required to construct a complex model such as a neural network, could be many hours or days. In many cases this is impractical, particularly in situations where the model building processes is repeated many times as the results are evaluated, tweaks are made to the data-preparation/pre-processing and a new iteration of the model is constructed.

For many modelling techniques, the amount of computer time required to construct a model is linear in relation to the number of observations in the data set. Doubling the size of the development sample results in a doubling of the time required to construct the model. However, with the exception of CART (where the relationship is almost linear), computational requirements increase much more rapidly as the number of predictor variables increase. The resources required are (at the very least) proportional to the square of the number of predictor variables.

Linear regression is the least processor intensive method of model construction discussed in this book, followed by logistic regression and then recursive partitioning algorithms for CART models. If a stepwise procedure is being applied for linear or logistic regression, then it is important to remember that a separate model is constructed each time a variable is added or removed from the model. A model constructed in 50 steps will take about 50 times longer to generate than a model constructed using a non-stepwise procedure. Methods of training neural networks require the most computation resource by a considerable margin, and the choice of training algorithm also has a considerable impact on development times.

As a very rough guide, the modelling process generally starts to become unwieldy once the number of parameters (or splits for a CART model) that require estimation exceeds about 1,000. For neural networks it is important to remember that the number of parameters is equal to the number of input variables multiplied by the number of units in the hidden layer, so a network with 100 inputs and ten units in the hidden layer will meet this criteria. This is not to say larger numbers of variables/parameters can't be dealt with, but in situations where many iterations of modelling occur before a final model is arrived at, there begins to be a significant impact on the time/cost required. Personally, I have never come across a real world modelling project where it has not been possible to reduce the problem to a manageable subset. Therefore, if you do find yourself in a situation where the modelling process is taking far too long, then I would recommend revisiting preliminary variable selection to reduce the number of predictor variables and to be quite brutal about it. For neural networks you should ask yourself if you really need so many units in the hidden layer. Another option for neural networks is to use stepwise linear regression as a preliminary variable selection method. Stepwise linear regression is used to generate one or more preliminary models, and only variables that feature within the preliminary linear regression derived model(s) are carried forward for inclusion in the primary modelling process.

7.7 Calibration

Classification models are often calibrated to a specific score odds scale. Calibration does not affect the predictive power of a model or alter the ranking of observations within the population, but is undertaken for business/operational reasons. In particular, if an old model is being replaced there may be a requirement that the scores generated by the new model display the same score odds relationship as the model it replaces. Standard practice is to calibrate model scores such that:

- The good:bad odds are A:1 at a score of B.
- The odds double every C points.

Every organization has their own calibration scale, but the most widely used one in the credit industry is to calibrate scores such that the good:bad odds are 1:1 at score of 500 and the odds to double every 20 points ($A=1$, $B=500$, $C=20$). So at a score of 500 the odds will be 1:1, at 520 they will be 2:1, at 540 4:1 at 560 8:1, and so on.

The nature of the logistic regression process means that the score, S, should be equal to the natural log of the odds of the development sample. Therefore, for models produced using logistic regression a calibrated score can be calculated as:

$$S_{calibrated} = B - \frac{C * Ln(A)}{Ln(2)} + \frac{S * C}{Ln(2)}$$

As the original model is linear, this has the same effect as multiplying the model constant and each of the parameter coefficients by $C/Ln(2)$ and then adding $B-(Ln(A) *C/Ln(2))$ to the value of the intercept.

For methods that don't generate scores that can be interpreted directly as *Ln(odds)*, if the relationship between the score and *Ln(odds)* is approximately linear,[6] then a preliminary step can be undertaken to transform the score odds relationship so that the score is equal to *Ln(odds)*. Logistic regression is applied, to predict the dependent variable using the original score as the only predictor variable. This produces a model in the form:

$$S' = \alpha + bS$$

Where α nd *b* are the intercept and parameter coefficient of the logistic regression model. *S'* can then be used instead of *S* in the calibration formula to produce $S_{calibrated}$.

Following calibration, a common practice is to round parameter coefficients (and hence scores) to the nearest integer. There is no need to do this, but many people find integer representations of models easy to understand. Having simple models comprising integer coefficients helps non-technical managers understand the models that their analysts have developed. Using integers does result in a slight loss of precision, but as long as the calibration scale is sufficiently large, then the effect of rounding is trivial[7] for practical decision making purposes. For a typical application or behavioural credit scoring model, calibrated to odds of 1:1 at a score of 500 and a doubling of odds every 20 points, scores will typically range from around 450 to about 800; yielding about 350 possible scores that someone may receive.

The calibration process described above applies where the relationship between score and *Ln(odds)* is approximately linear. If the score odds relationship is non-linear, then the process of calibration is more complex. It may be possible to apply a non-linear transformation, or different calibrations may be applied to different sub-populations. Another, somewhat problematic, scenario is where the score odds relationship is partially linear – perhaps the score odds relationship is fine in the lower score regions, but not for higher scoring groups. These types of misalignment are often indicative of differences within the population that are not well represented by the model. One solution may be to introduce interaction terms into the model. Another is to construct distinct models for different segments of the population, but work will first be required to establish what the significant populations are – perhaps by examining patterns within the errors (residual analysis) or by applying a segmentation algorithm such as CART. It should be noted that replacing a single model with two or more new ones increases complexity and can result in considerable cost operationally. This is in terms of the cost of implementation and ongoing monitoring. Therefore, careful consideration should be given to the costs/benefit case of taking this option.

7.8   Presenting linear models as scorecards

It is important to remember that the calibrated parameter coefficients of the model refer to the transformed versions of the predictor variables, derived during pre-processing. For the model created using linear regression in section 7.1, the data was pre-processed as a set of dummy variables. For the model created using logistic regression in section 7.2, weight of evidence transformed variables were used.

If a model needs to be explicable, then the parameter coefficients need to be mapped to the actual values of the untransformed predictor variables following calibration. This mapping will often be presented in form of a "scorecard". An example of a credit scorecard, used to assess new loan applications, is shown in Figure 7.2.

Constant	+598		

Term of loan		Number of children	
≤ 12 months	+51	0	0
13–17 months	+28	1–2	+12
18–23 months	+9	3+	0
24–35 months	0		
36–47 months	−5		
48–71 months	−19		
72+ months	−36	Occupation status	
		Full-time employed	+7
		Part-time employed	−22
Accomodation status		Self-employed	−9
Owner	+32	Homemaker	−17
Renting	−17	Student	−47
Living at home	0	Unemployed	−84
		Retired	+2

Time at current address		Time in current employment	
< 1 year	−68	< 1 year	−59
1–2 years	−29	1–2 years	−23
3–5 years	−11	3–4 years	−14
6–10 years	0	5–7 years	0
11+ years	+33	6–12 years	0
		13–19 years	+6
		20+ years	+12
Gross annual income $		Not in employment	0
125,000+	+17		
90,000–124,999	+11	Number of previous good paid loans	
50,000–89,999	0	0	−12
30,000–39,999	−26	1	0
0–29,999	−49	2+	+17

Figure 7.2   A scorecard

For the scorecard in Figure 7.2, each applicant starts by being assigned the scorecard constant of 598. This is the value of the model constant, after calibration and rounding have been applied. Points are then added or subtracted on the basis of the attributes that apply to each individual. For example, 51 points are added if the loan term is 12 months or less, 17 points subtracted if the accommodation status is renting, and so on.

Although the calibrated model and the scorecard contain the same information, presenting a linear model in the form of a scorecard is attractive because it's so easy to explain and use. In particular, the score can be calculated using just addition to add up the relevant points that someone receives.

7.9   The prospects of further advances in model construction techniques

All the methods of model construction discussed in this chapter have been in use for more than 20 years. New modelling techniques and variations on existing methods are being developed all the time. This raises the question as to whether methods such as logistic regression, CART and neural networks, will become dated, and will eventually be replaced by techniques that generate significantly more predictive models (indeed, some people argue that this has already happened. For example, the type of neural network discussed in this book is considered somewhat old hat, compared to more modern forms of neural network such as radial basis function networks or related methods such as support vector machines).

One thing worth thinking about is the intense excitement that has accompanied new modelling techniques in the past. In the 1980s and early 1990s methods for generating various types of artificial neural networks were all the rage and received much attention both in academia and the media, as did other Artificial Intelligence (AI) techniques such as Genetic Algorithms (Holland 1975; Goldberg 1989) and Expert Systems (Ignizio 1990). In the 1990s and early 2000s support vector machines (Cortes and Vapnik 1995) and multi-classifier approaches such as boosting (Schapire 1990), bagging (Breiman 1996) and random forests (Breiman 2001) received similar attention. As I write at the start of the second decade of the twenty-first century, artificial ant colony optimization (Dorigo and Gambardella 1997) is one method that is currently in the limelight.

As I said in Chapter 1, in some circumstances a theoretical development in modelling techniques has been shown to provide marginal improvements over established methods, but in many situations they have not. It is also the case that in practical situations some techniques are considered too complex to develop and implement or lack transparency, or the bottom line business benefits are too small to justify when a full cost benefit analysis is undertaken. The performance of complex models also tends to be relatively unstable over time, with model performance deteriorating more rapidly than simpler alternatives (Hand 2006). This is not to say there are not some problems out there that have benefited from the application of cutting edge data mining/statistical techniques, but in my opinion they are few and far between when it comes to predicting consumer behaviour within the financial services industry. Many academics have come to similar conclusions, and are now turning their attention to other aspects of model construction. For example, better ways of aligning modelling objectives with business objectives, data quality issues, how data is pre-processed prior to model construction and how to select the sub-set of potential predictor variables to present to the chosen modelling technique. It is through improvements in these aspects of the modelling process where the greatest potential benefits are believed to lie.

Please do not take this to be an entirely pessimistic view. The overall message that I want to get across is that it is good to keep up with current developments and to look out for new and better ways of doing things, but don't be taken in by the hype that always accompanies new methodologies or the pitch made by vendors with a new solution to sell. If you do come across some new modelling/analytical technique that you think may be of benefit in your work, then make sure you undertake a proper evaluation of the method yourself, using your own data. This should include using development and holdout samples, and an out-of-time sample to test the robustness of the model over time. For the test to be really sound, ideally, one person will build the model by applying the new modelling technique to the development sample and someone else will independently carry out the evaluation using the holdout sample(s). If data is provided to a vendor to demonstrate their fantastic new model building methodology, then make sure that the holdout sample provided to them does not contain the dependent variable – only the predictor variables. This enables them to calculate scores for the holdout sample, but not to evaluate how good their model is. The sample is then returned to you so that you can evaluate the results yourself. Equally important is to undertake a business evaluation and a cost/benefit analysis of the process that takes into account things such as:

- Is there a requirement to buy specialist software/consultancy to construct/implement the model?
- How much additional time and effort will be required to implement the new solution within the operational environment?
- Is it important that the model is interpretable; i.e. do you need to be able to understand how individual scores are arrived at?
- Will it be easy to monitor the performance of the model on an ongoing basis?

For those of you who are interested in the debate about progress within the field of predictive modelling, please see the following two papers: 'Classifier Technology and the Illusion of Progress' (Hand 2006) and 'Forecasting and operational research: A review' (Fildes et al. 2008).

7.10   Chapter summary

There are many methods that can be used to construct models of consumer behaviour. For classification problems logistic regression is by far the most widely used method. Logistic regression has several desirable properties. These include:

- The model is linear, making it easy to understand how each predictor variable contributes to the model score, and can be presented in the form of a "scorecard" to aid explanation to a non-technical audience.
- Stepwise procedures can be employed within the modelling process to select the significant predictor variables to include in the model.
- The raw score generated by the model can be interpreted as the natural log of the good:bad odds, and therefore, transformed into a direct estimate of the probability of an event occurring.
- It is relatively easy and quick to apply logistic regression using popular statistical software such as SAS and SPSS.

For regression, linear regression is the most popular method of model construction. Like logistic regression, linear regression generates linear models that are easily interpretable, and variable selection can be incorporated within the modelling process using stepwise procedures. Linear regression can also be used to produce classification models, but is generally considered inferior to logistic regression for this purpose. However, in practical application the discriminatory properties of class-ification models constructed using linear regression are very similar to those generated from logistic regression.

Other popular modelling techniques involve the use of splitting rules to generate CART models, and gradient descent/optimization methods for finding the parameter coefficients of neural network models. CART is probably the next most popular type of model after linear models and also generates transparent models whose structure is easily interpretable. Neural networks do have some applications within financial services, but tend not to be widely used because of the difficulty in understanding the contribution individual predictor variables make towards the score that someone receives.

8
Validation, Model Performance and Cut-off Strategy

Once a model has been constructed, the only way it can be assessed accurately is by using an independent holdout sample. Where a model is going to be applied some time after the development and holdout samples were taken, then it is good practice to also assess the model using an out-of-time sample.

The first phase of the assessment process is validation. This involves comparing the properties of the scores generated by the model on the development and holdout samples. If the properties of the scores are consistent between the two samples, this indicates there has not been a significant degree of over-fitting. However, if the properties of the model scores are very different, then this suggests that over-fitting may have occurred and/or the model is biased. Consequently, it may be worthwhile revisiting the modelling process in order to try and generate an improved model.

Following validation, more in-depth analysis of model performance can be undertaken. Initial assessments of performance are often made using general statistical measures, but in practical situations, stakeholders are more concerned about the business impact that the model will have. This usually translates into questions about the financial consequences of using the model, the volume of customers scoring above/below different scores or a mixture of these two things. Sometimes statistical and business measures of model performance are well aligned (Finlay 2009), but this isn't necessarily the case (Finlay 2010).

This rest of this chapter is in five parts. The first two introduce score distribution reports and preliminary validation. The third part discusses generic measures of performance that are useful for providing an insight into a model's predictive abilities, but makes no reference to the business applications of the model. In the fourth part of the chapter, model performance is discussed in terms of cut-off strategies which deliver specific business objectives. The chapter concludes with a discussion about presenting models, performance measures and so on, to stakeholders. This is important because ultimately, the stakeholders are the ones who will judge whether or not the project has been a success. It is therefore, important that they understand the value of the model that has been developed.

Note that in this chapter the primary focus is on validation and assessment of classification models, but similar measures and principles also apply to regression models.

8.1   Preparing for validation

To assess model performance the model must be applied to the holdout sample. Specialist model development software, such as SAS, allows a model to be developed using one sample of data, that can then be applied to another sample. If a generic software package is used to develop the model, such as C++, JAVA or Visual Basic, then it may be necessary to write additional code to calculate the scores for the holdout sample. In this case, care should be taken to ensure that scores are calculated correctly.

Good practice is for no reference to be made to the holdout sample until all model construction is complete. In practice, a common error is to build preliminary models using the development sample, which are repeatedly tested using the holdout sample. Changes to the modelling methodology and/or data pre-processing are then made on the basis of the observed results. The problem with this approach is there is a danger of fitting the model to specific patterns that are present in the holdout sample. If the modelling/validation process is repeated only one or twice, then the risk of over-fitting is slight, but if many iterations occur then the chance of over-fitting the model to the holdout sample can be very significant indeed. The simplest way around this problem is to have two holdout samples (sometimes referred to as a development/validation/holdout methodology). One sample (the validation sample) is used for testing preliminary models, and the results from this sample are used to inform revisions to the modelling process. The other sample is the true holdout sample. This is put aside until all model construction has been completed.

Once scores have been calculated for a sample, it is possible to generate a score distribution report, as shown in Table 8.1.

Table 8.1 Score distribution report

		Marginal						Ascending cumulative						Descending cumulative					
Interval	Score range	Number of goods	Number of bads	Total number	% of total	Bad rate (%)	Odds	Number of goods	Number of bads	Total number	% of total	Bad rate (%)	Odds	Number of goods	Number of bads	Total number	% of total	Bad rate (%)	Odds
1	<=534	10,201	3,139	13,340	5.00	23.53	3.2	10,201	3,139	13,340	5.00	23.53	3.2	255,047	11,761	266,808	100.00	4.41	21.7
2	535–551	10,887	2,453	13,340	5.00	18.39	4.4	21,089	5,592	26,681	10.00	20.96	3.8	244,845	8,622	253,468	95.00	3.40	28.4
3	552–564	11,764	1,576	13,340	5.00	11.81	7.5	32,853	7,168	40,021	15.00	17.91	4.6	233,958	6,169	240,127	90.00	2.57	37.9
4	565–577	12,291	1,049	13,340	5.00	7.86	11.7	45,145	8,217	53,362	20.00	15.40	5.5	222,193	4,593	226,787	85.00	2.03	48.4
5	578–585	12,593	747	13,340	5.00	5.60	16.9	57,738	8,964	66,702	25.00	13.44	6.4	209,902	3,544	213,446	80.00	1.66	59.2
6	586–591	12,747	593	13,340	5.00	4.45	21.5	70,485	9,557	80,042	30.00	11.94	7.4	197,309	2,797	200,106	75.00	1.40	70.5
7	592–593	12,821	519	13,340	5.00	3.89	24.7	83,307	10,076	93,383	35.00	10.79	8.3	184,561	2,204	186,766	70.00	1.18	83.7
8	594–602	12,908	432	13,340	5.00	3.24	29.9	96,215	10,508	106,723	40.00	9.85	9.2	171,740	1,685	173,425	65.00	0.97	101.9
9	603–608	13,005	335	13,340	5.00	2.51	38.8	109,221	10,843	120,064	45.00	9.03	10.1	158,831	1,253	160,085	60.00	0.78	126.8
10	609–615	13,071	269	13,340	5.00	2.02	48.6	122,292	11,112	133,404	50.00	8.33	11.0	145,826	918	146,744	55.00	0.63	158.9
11	616–625	13,139	201	13,340	5.00	1.51	65.4	135,431	11,313	146,744	55.00	7.71	12.0	132,755	649	133,404	50.00	0.49	204.6
12	626–633	13,192	148	13,340	5.00	1.11	89.1	148,624	11,461	160,085	60.00	7.16	13.0	119,615	448	120,064	45.00	0.37	267.0
13	634–640	13,226	114	13,340	5.00	0.85	116.0	161,850	11,575	173,425	65.00	6.67	14.0	106,423	300	106,723	40.00	0.28	354.7
14	641–658	13,266	74	13,340	5.00	0.55	179.3	175,117	11,649	186,766	70.00	6.24	15.0	93,196	186	93,383	35.00	0.20	501.1
15	659–670	13,296	44	13,340	5.00	0.33	302.2	188,413	11,693	200,106	75.00	5.84	16.1	79,930	112	80,042	30.00	0.14	713.7
16	671–682	13,311	29	13,340	5.00	0.22	459.0	201,724	11,722	213,446	80.00	5.49	17.2	66,634	68	66,702	25.00	0.10	979.9
17	683–698	13,322	18	13,340	5.00	0.13	740.1	215,047	11,740	226,787	85.00	5.18	18.3	53,322	39	53,362	20.00	0.07	1,367.2
18	699–710	13,329	11	13,340	5.00	0.08	1,211.8	228,376	11,751	240,127	90.00	4.89	19.4	40,000	21	40,021	15.00	0.05	1,904.8
19	711–725	13,334	6	13,340	5.00	0.04	2,222.4	241,711	11,757	253,468	95.00	4.64	20.6	26,670	10	26,681	10.00	0.04	2,667.0
20	>725	13,336	4	13,340	5.00	0.03	3,334.0	255,047	11,761	266,808	100.00	4.41	21.7	13,336	4	13,340	5.00	0.03	3,334.0
	Total	255,047	11,761	266,808	100.00	4.41	21.7	255,047	11,761	266,808	100.00	4.41	21.7	255,047	11,761	266,808	100.00	4.41	21.7

The score distribution report provides all information required for validation and performance assessment. Table 8.1 is a "classed" version of a score distribution report for a sample of loan applications, where the model has been calibrated to odds of 1:1 at a score of 500 with a doubling of odds every 20 points. Scores have been segmented into 20 intervals, each containing 5 percent of the population. The totals row at the bottom tells us the sample contained 255,047 cases which exhibited good repayment behaviour and 11,761 which exhibited bad repayment behaviour. The overall bad rate is 4.41 percent which equates to good:bad odds of 21.7:1. The report has three sections. The marginal section contains information about each interval. For classification problems this will include the number of goods and bads in each interval, the good:bad odds and bad rate. For regression problems, columns will exist for the number of observations, the sum, the average and the standard deviation of the dependent variable.

The central section of Table 8.1 has the same columns as the marginal section, but shows cumulative ascending figures. The values in the ascending columns are calculated using all observations that are within or below each interval. Similarly, the cumulative descending section shows the sum of good, bads and so on, for all observations in an interval plus all observations in higher scoring intervals.

If desired, columns containing additional information can be included in a score distribution report. For example, for consumer credit it is very common to construct a classification model to predict good/bad repayment behaviour for a loan or credit card. The model is then used to make lending decisions. However, the average value of revenues received and the value of bad debts written-off are also of interest. The model has not been constructed to predict these quantities, but how they vary by score can influence how the model is used. Consequently, this information will be included within the score distribution report.

In practice, it is common to produce the score distribution report with very many more intervals than Table 8.1. Some organizations produce score distribution reports with 100 intervals, each containing 1 percent of the population. It is also common to generate a "raw" version of the report, where a separate interval exists for every score in the sample, resulting in a report containing hundreds or thousands of rows. In theory, the raw report should always be used to calculate performance metrics, such as the GINI coefficient and the KS-statistic, which are discussed later in the chapter. However, once there are more than about 20 intervals of approximately equal size, using a classed report will generate measures that are sufficiently accurate for decision making purposes. In addition, the classed report is often easier to work with and to explain. Even if you never have to manually calculate performance measures using a score distribution (most software will automatically calculate the measures required using an internal representation of the raw score distribution), presenting a classed score distribution report to stakeholders and including it within documentation is common practice. This allows people to see how the range of scores is distributed and how the marginal odds, bad rate and so on changes between intervals.

One issue with using the raw score distribution is, it is difficult to interpret the marginal values. This is because there will be very few observations associated with each score, making it impossible to calculate measures such as odds or bad rate with any precision. If there is only one observation with a given score, then the bad rate for that score can only ever be 0 percent or 100 percent. To get around this problem, measures such as marginal bad rate and marginal odds are calculated using additional observations with scores just above or below the score of interest. For example, for a score of 550, all observations scoring between 545 and 555 are used to calculate the marginal bad rate, for a score of 551 all observations between 546 and 556 are used and so on. As a rule, to generate stable values, the marginal odds and bad rate should be calculated using at least 100 observations and ideally several hundred.

Two versions of the score distribution report are required for validation. One for the development sample and one for the holdout sample. If classed reports are produced, then good practice is for the same score ranges to be used to define the intervals within both reports. This allows direct comparisons to be made between them.

8.2   Preliminary validation

Preliminary validation should be undertaken using the development and holdout samples. The purpose of the validation is threefold:

1. To check the distribution of the model scores. The same proportion of observations should fall above/below any given score for each of the two samples.
2. To check the alignment of the score odds relationship. The good:bad odds (or bad rate) associated with any given score should be the same for each sample.

3. To check that the score is unbiased for significant sub-groups with the population. The score:odds relationship for any sub-group should be the same as the population as a whole. If the model has been calibrated to odds of 1:1 at a score of 500, then the odds of people with say, an income of $90,000 and a score of 500, should also have odds of 1:1.

8.2.1   Comparison of development and holdout samples

One function of the validation process is to assess the effects of any over-fitting that has occurred. This is done by comparing performance metrics calculated using the development sample with the holdout sample. If performance of the model on the holdout sample is considerably worse than the development sample, then one concludes that over-fitting has occurred. A key assumption in this process is that the predictor variables within both samples are similarly distributed. If the sample distributions are different then the performance metrics will differ, and this may be incorrectly interpreted as a sign of over-fitting. Consider the variable residential status which has two attributes: home owner and renter. If the parameter coefficient associated with home owners is a large positive value and the parameter coefficient for renters is a large negative value, then if the proportion of home owners and renters in the two samples is different, the distribution of scores generated from each sample will also be different. If such situations exist, then consideration should be given to repeating the allocation of cases to the development and holdout samples and constructing a new model.

Now, one could examine the distributions for every predictor variable in the sample, but this is likely to be a time consuming process. Instead, a simpler solution is to carry out a single comparison of the distribution of the models scores, given that the score is a function of the predictor variables.

One test that can be applied to ascertain if the two samples have similar score distributions is the KS-test, which is calculated as follows:[1]

$$KS = D * \sqrt{\frac{n_1 n_2}{n_1 + n_2}}$$

where:

D is the absolute value of the maximum difference in the cumulative proportions of the two distributions across all model scores (D ranges from 0–1).

n_1 is the number of observations in the development sample.

n_2 is the number of observations in the holdout sample.

The starting hypothesis is that the two score distributions are the same. If the value of the KS-test is significantly large, then the initial hypothesis is rejected and it is assumed that the distributions are different. For a 5 percent degree of significance, then the hypothesis that the distributions are the same is rejected if the value of KS-statistic is greater than 1.36. For a 1 percent degree of significance (which I would tend to apply) the hypothesis is rejected if the KS value is greater than 1.63. Table 8.2 shows the application of the KS-test, using the ascending score distribution figures from Table 8.1, together with ascending figures for the holdout sample.

In Table 8.2, the maximum cumulative difference occurs for the interval 683–698. The corresponding value of D is 0.0569, giving a KS-test statistic of 12.00. The conclusion therefore, is that the hypothesis that the score distributions are the same should be rejected.

8.2.2 Score alignment

When it comes to making decisions about how to treat people on the basis of the scores they receive, it is important that the relationship between score and behaviour is as expected; otherwise incorrect conclusions will be made about the likely behaviour of some people. If the model displays bias, then the expected relationship may not be observed for the holdout sample. If this occurs, the score is described as being misaligned. Consider Figure 8.1.

Figure 8.1 has been produced using the development sample figures taken from Table 8.1, together with additional information from a separate holdout sample. The model was derived using logistic regression and calibrated to a target score odds relationship of odds of 1:1 at 500 and a doubling of odds every 20 points. *Ln(odds)* rather than odds or bad rate, is usually plotted for this type of graph for two reasons. First, the relationship between score and *Ln(odds)* is expected to be linear if linear/logistic regression has been used to construct the model. Second, the range of odds can be large, making it difficult to observe differences in the lower score ranges.

In theory, the target score odds relationship and the observed score odds relationship should be the same, although in practice there will always be some minor discrepancies. In Figure 8.1 the development sample is reasonably well aligned with the target score odds relationship. This is to be expected (although not guaranteed), given the model was constructed using this sample. However, the holdout sample odds are consistently lower than the development sample odds for any given

Table 8.2 KS-test

		Development sample				Holdout sample				
Interval	Score range	Number of goods	Number of bads	Total number	% of total	Number of goods	Number of bads	Total number	% of total	Difference (D)
1	<=460	10,201	3,139	13,340	5.00	2,000	625	2,625	4.92	0.08%
2	535–551	21,089	5,592	26,681	10.00	4,000	1,118	5,118	9.59	0.41%
3	552–564	32,853	7,168	40,021	15.00	8,000	1,434	9,434	17.68	2.68%
4	565–577	45,145	8,217	53,362	20.00	10,387	1,643	12,030	22.55	2.55%
5	578–585	57,738	8,964	66,702	25.00	12,734	1,793	14,527	27.22	2.22%
6	586–591	70,485	9,557	80,042	30.00	16,004	1,911	17,915	33.57	3.57%
7	592–593	83,307	10,076	93,383	35.00	17,985	2,015	20,000	37.48	2.48%
8	594–602	96,215	10,508	106,723	40.00	21,129	2,102	23,231	43.53	3.53%
9	603–608	109,221	10,843	120,064	45.00	22,879	2,169	25,048	46.94	1.94%
10	609–615	122,292	11,112	133,404	50.00	26,212	2,222	28,434	53.29	3.29%
11	616–625	135,431	11,313	146,744	55.00	29,052	2,263	31,315	58.68	3.68%
12	626–633	148,624	11,461	160,085	60.00	32,533	2,292	34,825	65.26	5.26%
13	634–640	161,850	11,575	173,425	65.00	34,022	2,315	36,337	68.10	3.10%
14	641–658	175,117	11,649	186,766	70.00	36,290	2,330	38,620	72.37	2.37%
15	659–670	188,413	11,693	200,106	75.00	39,390	2,339	41,729	78.20	3.20%
16	671–682	201,724	11,722	213,446	80.00	41,554	2,344	43,898	82.27	2.27%
17	683–698	215,047	11,740	226,787	85.00	46,045	2,348	48,393	90.69	5.69%
18	699–710	228,376	11,751	240,127	90.00	47,997	2,350	50,347	94.35	4.35%
19	711–725	241,711	11,757	253,468	95.00	49,012	2,351	51,363	96.26	1.26%
20	>=740	255,047	11,761	266,808	100.00	51,009	2,352	53,362	100.00	0.00%
Total		255,047	11,761	266,808	100.00	51,009	2,352	53,362	100.00	

Maximum difference (D)   0.0569
Number in development sample (n1)   266,808
Number in holdout sample (n2)   53,362
KS   12.00

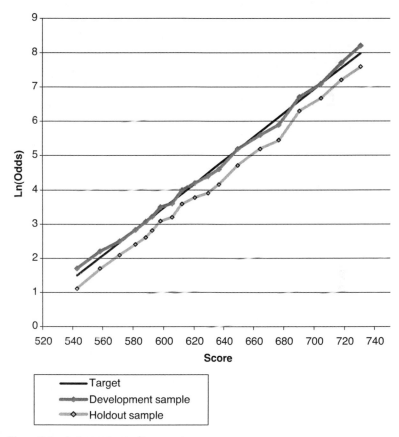

Figure 8.1 Intercept misalignment

score. This means the model is biased and is generating over optimistic estimates. For example, at a score of 633, the target *Ln(odds)* are 4.6 (odds of 100:1), but the actual *Ln(odds)* are only about 3.9 (odds of 50:1). Now consider Figure 8.2. Figure 8.2 illustrates a somewhat different situation. The gradients of the score odds relationships for the holdout and development samples are clearly different. This suggests that the model is biased and/or over-fitting has occurred.

Visual inspection of the score odds relationship is always a good idea and may be sufficient for validation purposes if the two score odds lines are seen to be closely aligned. However, statistical tests can also be performed to provide a more quantitative assessment of how well the

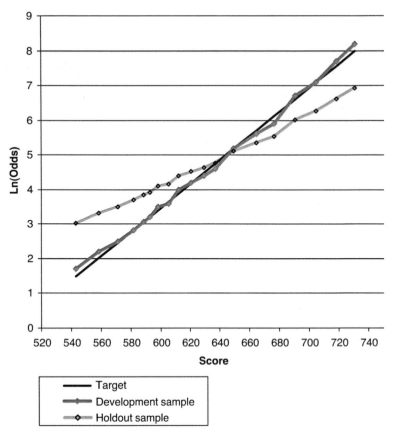

Figure 8.2   Gradient misalignment

score odds relationship for the holdout sample is aligned with the target score odds relationship. The chi-squared test is one such test, and was introduced in section 5.2.2. In relation to score misalignment, it is used to compare the difference between the observed number of bads (or goods) within each score range, against the number that is expected, given the scores that cases receive.[2] One hopes the value of the test statistic is sufficiently small so as to indicate there are no significant differences between the observed and expected numbers. A limitation of the chi-squared statistic is that if just one interval is strongly misaligned, this may not result in the test statistic being significant. Therefore, an alternative is to perform tests of population proportion (t-tests) for each interval, to see if actual and target bad rates are significantly different by interval.

8.2.3 Attribute alignment

If a model is aligned to a given score odds relationship, then all individuals with a given score should have the same probability of exhibiting the behaviour the model predicts. In practice however, this is not always the case. Sometimes groups of individuals with specific attributes display a higher or lower propensity to behave in a given way than their score indicates. In these cases the model is said to display misalignment for these attributes. The standard method for identifying attribute misalignment is to produce univariate (characteristic) misalignment reports for every variable that features within the model. These show if the parameter coefficients allocated to each of a variable's attributes are aligned with the scores received by the population as a whole. Table 8.3 provides an example of a univariate misalignment report for the variable "Ratio of loan amount requested to applicant's net annual income" which features within a credit scoring model used to assess the creditworthiness of personal loan applications.

This variable is often a strong predictor of creditworthiness for unsecured loans and features in many models of this type. The left most column in Table 8.3 shows the intervals in the model. So the first interval (>=1.00) displays information for people that are making loan applications for amounts that are equal to or greater than their net annual income. The left hand side of the table (columns one to seven) shows the behaviour that was observed using the holdout sample. Columns one through four show the total number of applications in each interval, the proportion of the total population in each interval, and the number of loans that subsequently displayed good or bad repayment behaviour. The next three columns (five to seven) show the bad rate, odds and natural log of the odds. The right hand side of the report (columns eight to twelve) shows the expected numbers of goods and bads, given the scores individuals received, together with the expected bad rate, expected odds and expected $Ln(odds)$. Each value in the expected columns has been calculated using the following steps:

1. Calculate the current score odds relationship for the entire sample. This can be achieved by applying logistic regression to produce a model: $S_2 = a + b_1 * S_1$, where S_1 is the score that has been calculated for each observation in the sample. Note that because logistic regression has been applied, S_2 should, in theory, be equal to $Ln(odds)$.
2. Use the model generated in step 1 to calculate S_2 for each observation in the holdout sample.

Table 8.3 Univariate misalignment report

		Ratio of loan amount requested to applicant's net annual income													
				Actual					Expected						
Column		1	2	3	4	5	6	7	8	9	10	11	12	13	14
Interval	Range	Total cases	% total	# Goods	# Bads	Bad rate	Odds	Ln (odds)	# Goods	# Bads	Bad rate	Odds	Ln (odds)	Delta score	Parameter coefficient
1	≥1.00	5,768	2.16	3,998	1,770	30.69%	2.26	0.81	3,693	2,075	35.97%	1.78	0.58	7	−55
2	0.93–0.99	9,334	3.50	7,072	2,262	24.23%	3.13	1.14	6,712	2,622	28.09%	2.56	0.94	6	−41
3	0.81–0.92	31,923	11.96	28,033	3,890	12.19%	7.21	1.97	27,700	4,223	13.23%	6.56	1.88	3	−22
4	0.69–0.80	41,866	15.69	40,666	1,200	2.87%	33.89	3.52	40,674	1,192	2.85%	34.11	3.53	0	−9
5	0.55–0.68	55,765	20.90	54,565	1,200	2.15%	45.47	3.82	54,579	1,186	2.13%	46.00	3.83	0	−5
6	0.42–0.54	29,887	11.20	29,215	672	2.25%	43.47	3.77	29,215	672	2.25%	43.47	3.77	0	0
7	0.35–0.42	27,133	10.17	26,809	324	1.19%	82.74	4.42	26,826	307	1.13%	87.36	4.47	−2	15
8	0.27–0.35	26,773	10.03	26,497	276	1.03%	96.00	4.56	26,520	253	0.95%	104.70	4.65	−3	25
9	0.10–0.26	28,805	10.80	28,678	127	0.44%	225.81	5.42	28,701	2,075	0.36%	277.20	5.62	−6	37
10	<0.10	9,554	3.58	9,514	40	0.42%	237.85	5.47	9,525	2,622	0.31%	325.98	5.79	−9	45
		266,808	100.00	255,047	11,761	4.41%	21.69	3.08	3,693	4,223	4.75%	254.145	12.663		

Adapted from (Finlay 2010)

3. Use the score from step 2 to calculate the expected odds and expected bad rate for each observation:

   Expected odds = e^{s_2}
   Expected bad rate = $1/(1 + e^{s_2})$

4. For each interval in the report, calculate the expected number of goods and bads. The expected number of bads is calculated by summing the expected bad rate for all observations within the interval. Likewise, summing (1 – bad rate) for all observations in the interval yields the expected number of goods.
5. Calculate the expected bad rate, expected good:bad odds and expected *Ln(odds)* using the expected figures from step 4.

In Table 8.3, the difference between actual and expected odds have been used to calculate a measure known as the "delta score" which is shown in Column 13. The delta score (δ) is calculated as:

$$\delta = C* \frac{Ln\left(odds_{actual}/odds_{expected}\right)}{Ln(2)}$$

where:

C is the number of points that double the odds for the expected score odds relationship.
$Odds_{actual}$ is calculated by dividing the actual goods by the actual bads (column three divided by column four in Table 8.3 to give column 6).

The delta score represents the difference between the parameter coefficient currently allocated to an attribute and the parameter coefficient that should be assigned to the attribute, for a model that is perfectly aligned with the expected score odds relationship. The larger the absolute value of the delta score the more misaligned the score is. If there is no correlation between variables within the model, then any misalignment can be corrected by simply adding the delta score to the parameter coefficient for the interval. For the first interval (>=1.00), the misalignment would be corrected by adding 7, so that going forward observations receive –48, instead of the –55 they currently receive. Note that misalignment reports and delta scores can also be calculated for variables that don't feature within the model, with the parameter coefficient assumed to be zero for all intervals of the variable. If a significant delta score is observed for any of the variable's attributes, this indicates the model could be improved by adding the variable into the model.

All models display some level of misalignment due to random fluctuations in the sample used to evaluate it. Therefore, one only tends to be concerned if the delta score for an interval exceeds acceptable tolerances. In practice, simple rules of thumb are often applied. These are based on the magnitude of the delta score for intervals that contain sufficient numbers of observations (say, more than 30 goods and more than 30 bads). An example of one such rule of thumb is:

$\lvert\delta\rvert < (0.125 * C)$	No significant misalignment.
$(0.125 * C) \leq \lvert\delta\rvert < (0.25 * C)$	Minor misalignment.
$(0.25 * C) \leq \lvert\delta\rvert < (0.5 * C)$	Moderate misalignment.
$(0.5 * C) \leq \lvert\delta\rvert$	Serious misalignment.

where C is the points that double the odds and $\lvert\delta\rvert$ means the absolute value of the delta score. In Table 8.3, where the expected score odds relationship of the model is for the odds to double every 20 points, then intervals 1, 2, 9 and 10 show moderate misalignment and intervals 3 and 8 minor misalignment. Statistical tests can also be performed. The chi-squared test is used to assess misalignment across all of the intervals and t-tests to assess the alignment for specific attributes.

If moderate or serious misalignment is observed, then corrective action may be deemed necessary. In practice, the predictor variables in consumer behaviour models are not highly correlated. Therefore, simple univariate adjustments (adding or subtracting delta scores) to individual parameter coefficients can be used successfully to realign a model and improve its predictive performance. However, if high levels of correlation exist between predictor variables, and/or many intervals are misaligned across several variables, then simple univariate adjustments may not be sufficient. Consequently, it may be necessary to rebuild the model.

Attribute misalignment is often more of an issue for models developed using weight of evidence transformed variables than dummy variable based models. This is due to the restricted nature of the weight of evidence transformation. One approach to attribute misalignment, when weights of evidence have been employed, is to rebuild the model with dummy variables included, in addition to weight of evidence transformed variables, for those attributes that are most significantly misaligned.

8.2.4   What if a model fails to validate?

Most models display a small amount bias or a slight degree of overfitting, and evidence of this may be seen during validation. The KS-test may fail, the score odds alignment for the holdout sample may differ from that of the development sample, and there may be some minor or moderate attribute misalignments. If this is the case, then it does not necessarily mean the model is completely useless and should be discarded. Instead, when a model fails to validate, there are four courses of action that can be taken.

1. To accept the model as it is. If a model fails to validate but still performs well based on relevant performance measures (discussed later in the chapter), then the pragmatic option may be to accept the model, even thought it may not be quite as good as it could be.
2. To make minor adjustments to the model. If the score odds relationship is misaligned then calibration can be applied to realign the model. If interval misalignments exist then simple changes to parameter coefficients based on delta scores can be surprisingly effective.
3. Rerun the modelling process using slightly different criteria within the modelling process. Perhaps different entry/exit criteria for stepwise regression, making minor changes to the coarse classing or including/excluding additional variables from the modelling process.
4. To rebuild the model from scratch. This may involve reallocation of observations to development and holdout samples, repeating preliminary variable selection and applying different coarse classing/data pre-processing. If development and holdout distributions are very different indeed, or the levels of misalignment within the model are very severe, then this may be the best course of action to take.

In most cases options 1, 2 or 3 usually suffice. Option 4 is not usually required, unless the degree of misalignment is particularly high and the model's performance is very poor.

8.3 Generic measures of performance

Ultimately, model performance should be based on how well the model predicts behaviour within the context of an organization's objectives. However, before getting to this stage, model performance is usually assessed using a range of generic measures. It is also the case that in some situations the business objectives of the model are unknown when it is constructed. This situation is faced by developers of models that are used by different institutions, each of which has its own business objectives. Perhaps the best known examples of this type of model are those used to generate FICO scores in the US and Delphi scores the UK. These models, developed by FICO (formally Fair Issacs) and Experian, are credit scoring models that predict an individual's creditworthiness and other behaviours. FICO and Delphi scores are used by very many credit granting institutions in the US, UK and other countries. FICO and Experian don't know themselves what each individual lender's business strategy is when they build their models. Even if they did know what their clients' objectives were, each organization uses the model scores they are supplied with to meet their own specific goals, and therefore, it would be impossible to have a single "business objective" upon which the performance of a model could be assessed. In these situations model developers are forced to relay on more general measures of model performance.

The most popular measures used to assess the performance of binary classification models are the percentage correctly classified (PCC), the GINI coefficient and the KS-statistic. Measures such as GINI coefficient and KS-statistic are also widely applied during model development to provide a standardized benchmark of model performance as different versions of a model are developed. So when several competing models are being evaluated, the one with the best KS or GINI statistic is deemed to be the best.

8.3.1 Percentage correctly classified (PCC)

The most straightforward method for assessing how well a model predicts good/bad behaviour is the percentage correctly classified (PCC). One begins by selecting a point in the score distribution. One may, for example, choose the mid-point score, where 50% of cases score at or below the score and 50 percent score above the score. All cases scoring at or below the cut-off are assumed to be bad and all those above the cut-off are assumed to be good. The ascending and cumulative columns in the score distribution report are then used to produce a classification table (also called a confusion matrix) showing how many goods and bads were correctly classified using this score, as shown in Table 8.4.

Table 8.4   A classification table

		Actual class	
		Good	**Bad**
Predicted class	**Goods (above score)**	A	B
	Bads (at or below score)	C	D

Total population = A + B + C + D
Total correctly classified = A + D

The classification table is then used to calculate the PCC:

$$PCC = 100\% * \frac{A + D}{A + B + C + D}$$

So for Table 8.1, the score at the mid-point of the distribution is 615. The value of the PCC at a score of 615 is:

$$PCC = 100\% * \frac{132,755 + 11,112}{132,755 + 649 + 122,292 + 11,112} = 53.92\%$$

If two competing scores are being compared, such as where a new model has been developed to replace the incumbent one, or where two different models have been constructed using different techniques, then the one with the highest percentage correctly classified is considered to be the best.

One thing to note is that the PCC is only 53.92 percent and even if the score generated perfect predictions then the PCC would not be much higher. The reason for this is there are so many more goods than bads. Therefore, using the mid-point score is bound to result in a large proportion of the goods having lower scores than this and being incorrectly classified as bad. To take the imbalance between goods and bads into account, a better option is to calculate the PCC using the score that would generate a PCC of 100 percent for a perfect model. This is the score at which the proportion of accounts falling at or below the score is equal to the bad rate. For the score distribution report in Table 8.1 the bad rate is 4.41 percent. The score at which 4.41 percent of the population score at that score or below is 529 and this results in a PCC of 94.27 percent (Note that this cannot be explicitly calculated from Table 8.1 because there is no interval boundary at a score of 529. In practice one would use the raw version of the score distribution to make the calculation).

Often, when comparing competing models the PCC will be considered at several different points in the distribution. For example one might be interested in how well the model predicts at the low end, mid-point and high end of the distribution. Therefore, the PCC is compared using the scores that define the lowest scoring 10 percent, 50 percent and 90 percent of the population respectively.

8.3.2 ROC curves and the GINI coefficient

The Lorentz diagram or ROC (Receiver Operator Curve) is a way of representing how well a model discriminates between goods and

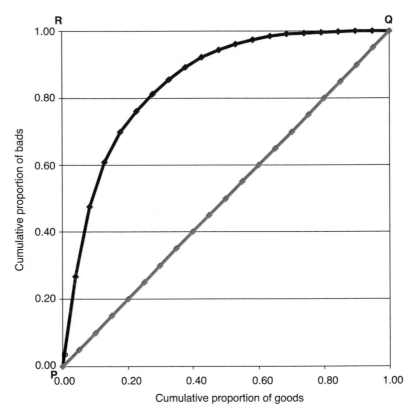

Figure 8.3   A ROC curve

bads over the range of model scores. An example of a ROC curve is shown in Figure 8.3.

In Figure 8.3 the ROC curve has been produced by using the cumulative ascending part of the score distribution report. The cumulative proportion of goods at each score are plotted against the cumulative proportion of bads. If a model has no predictive ability; that is, the scores it generates make no distinction between goods and bads, then the cumulative proportion of goods and bads at any given score will be the same. This is represented by the line PQ. If the model scores do provide some level of discrimination between the goods and bads, then one would expect there to be a higher proportion of bads with low scores. This is represented by the curved line. The more pronounced the curve, the better the model is at discriminating between the two classes.

The GINI coefficient is a quantitative measure of how well the model score discriminates between goods and bads. Graphically, the GINI statistic can be expressed as the ratio of the following two areas of Figure 8.3:

1. The area between the ROC curve (represented by the curve in Figure 8.3) and line PQ.
2. The region defined by triangle PQR. This is the ROC curve generated by a perfect model; that is, a model for which there is a score where all bads score at or below the score, and all goods score above the score.

The higher the GINI coefficient the better the model. For a model that provides perfect discrimination (where the area C is equal to the area PQR) the GINI coefficient is equal to 1. For a model that provides no discrimination the GINI coefficient will be zero (note that negative values are also possible). The GINI coefficient can be calculated using the Brown formula (also known as the trapezium rule):

$$\text{GINI} = 1 - \sum_{i=2}^{n} [G(i) + G(i-1)][B(i) - B(i-1)]$$

where:

n is the number of observations in the sample.
$G(i)$ is the cumulative proportion of goods up to and including the ith observation in the sample.
$B(i)$ is the cumulative proportion of bads up to and including the ith observation in the sample.

If a classed version of the score distribution report is used, then n is the number of intervals in the report, and $G(i)$ and $B(i)$ are the cumulative proportion of goods and bads in the ith interval. An example of the calculation of the GINI coefficient, calculated using the Brown formula applied to the figures from Table 8.1 is shown in Table 8.5. This yields a GINI coefficient of 0.6947.

What can be classified as a "Good" GINI coefficient depends on the type of behaviour being forecast and how the good/bad definition has been defined. It is therefore, not appropriate to say that a model constructed to predict one type of behaviour is better or worse than a model used to predict a different behaviour on the basis of the GINI coefficient. Models should only be compared using the GINI coefficient if they have been applied to the same population and have the same dependent variable. Similarly, it is often possible to generate models with very high GINI coefficients if the definition of good and bad are very different, and/or there is a large category of indeterminates between goods and bads. However, this does not necessarily mean the model is a good one. For some problems a GINI coefficient of 0.4 or less might be considered good, while for others a GINI coefficient of 0.8 or more may be achievable.

Note that the Brown formula is just one method for calculating the GINI coefficient. An alternative expression of the GINI coefficient is as the area under the curve generated from plotting specificity Vs 1-sensitivity.[3] For binary classification problems, the GINI coefficient is also equivalent to Somer's D concordance statistic.

8.3.3 KS-statistic

The KS-statistic was introduced earlier in the chapter. It was derived using the maximum cumulative difference (D) between two cumulative distributions. If one distribution is the cumulative proportion of goods and the other is the cumulative proportion of bads, then the value of D can be used on its own as a measure of how well a model discriminates between good and bad behaviour.[4] The larger the value of D the better the model is deemed to be. As with the GINI coefficient, what constitutes a "good" value for the KS-statistic is problem specific, but values between 0.3 and 0.7 are common. The KS-statistic for the score distributions of Table 8.5 is 0.5362 (81.26% – 27.64%), occurring at the score range 586–591.

8.3.4 Out-of-time sample validation

If a model validates using the holdout sample, this indicates the model is unbiased and the score is well aligned. However, models are often constructed using samples taken from 1–2 years or more in the past, and if the underlying relationships in the data have changed since this time, then the model will not perform as expected. To try and gauge what changes have occurred, a more recent (out-of-time) sample of data is used to repeat the validation process and the assessment of model performance.

Given that population changes are expected to occur over time, and models only have a finite lifespan before redevelopment is required, then one should not be overly surprised if a model fails to validate using the out-of-time sample. As with the holdout sample, failure to validate doesn't mean that the model isn't fit for purpose. As long as one is

Table 8.5 Calculation of GINI coefficient using the Brown formula

Interval (i)	Score range	Number of goods	Number of bads	% goods	% bads	Cumulative goods: G(i)	Cumulative bads: B(i)	G(i) + G(i-1)	B(i) - B(i-1)	[G(i) + G(i-1)] * [B(i) - B(i-1)]
0	N/A	0	0	0.00%	0.00%	0.00%	0.00%	0.0000	0.0000	
1	<=534	10,201	3,139	4.00%	26.69%	4.00%	26.69%	0.0400	0.2669	0.0107
2	535–551	10,887	2,453	4.27%	20.86%	8.27%	47.55%	0.1227	0.2086	0.0256
3	552–564	11,764	1,576	4.61%	13.40%	12.88%	60.95%	0.2115	0.1340	0.0283
4	565–577	12,291	1,049	4.82%	8.92%	17.70%	69.87%	0.3058	0.0892	0.0273
5	578–585	12,593	747	4.94%	6.35%	22.64%	76.22%	0.4034	0.0635	0.0256
6	586–591	12,747	593	5.00%	5.04%	27.64%	81.26%	0.5027	0.0504	0.0253
7	592–593	12,821	519	5.03%	4.41%	32.66%	85.67%	0.6030	0.0441	0.0266
8	594–602	12,908	432	5.06%	3.67%	37.72%	89.35%	0.7039	0.0367	0.0259
9	603–608	13,005	335	5.10%	2.85%	42.82%	92.19%	0.8055	0.0285	0.0229
10	609–615	13,071	269	5.13%	2.29%	47.95%	94.48%	0.9077	0.0229	0.0208
11	616–625	13,139	201	5.15%	1.71%	53.10%	96.19%	1.0105	0.0171	0.0173
12	626–633	13,192	148	5.17%	1.26%	58.27%	97.45%	1.1137	0.0126	0.0140
13	634–640	13,226	114	5.19%	0.97%	63.46%	98.42%	1.2173	0.0097	0.0118
14	641–658	13,266	74	5.20%	0.63%	68.66%	99.05%	1.3212	0.0063	0.0083
15	659–670	13,296	44	5.21%	0.37%	73.87%	99.42%	1.4253	0.0037	0.0053
16	671–682	13,311	29	5.22%	0.25%	79.09%	99.67%	1.5297	0.0025	0.0038
17	683–698	13,322	18	5.22%	0.15%	84.32%	99.82%	1.6341	0.0015	0.0025
18	699–710	13,329	11	5.23%	0.09%	89.54%	99.91%	1.7386	0.0009	0.0016
19	711–725	13,334	6	5.23%	0.05%	94.77%	99.97%	1.8431	0.0005	0.0009
20	>=740	13,336	4	5.23%	0.03%	100.00%	100.00%	1.9477	0.0003	0.0007
Total		255,047	11,761	100.00%	100.00%	100.00%	100.00%			0.3053

GINI = 0.6947

confident the new model provides better predictions of consumer behaviour than the incumbent system, then the model will provide some benefit. What one does need to be careful about is ensuring the decision rules that are applied on the basis of the model score are aligned to the patterns of behaviour observed on the out-of-time sample. If the odds associated with a given score are much lower for the out-of-time sample than for the holdout sample, then the scores used to define the decision rules about how to treat individuals need to be raised accordingly. It is also common to see some deterioration in the model performance on the out-of-time sample compared to the holdout sample. Therefore, don't make the mistake of telling everyone that the GINI coefficient of 0.8, calculated from the holdout sample is representative of how well the model will discriminate between goods and bads, only to then discover that the GINI coefficient is only 0.75 when measured using the out-of-time sample.

If model performance measured on the holdout sample is very good, but very poor indeed using the out-of-time sample, the nuclear option is to conclude that the sampling process was inappropriate because the relationships captured by the model no longer provide good predictions of behaviour. Consequently, the entire modelling process will need to be revised. Thankfully, this is a relatively rare event if good quality project planning has occurred, resulting in a representative development sample being taken from an appropriate sample window.

8.4   Business measures of performance

Measures such as the percentage correctly classified, GINI coefficient and KS-statistic are very useful for providing a general indication of how good a model is at predicting behaviour. What these measures do not provide is guidance about how the model should be used, or what the business benefits of using the model will be. Being able to say the new model has a GINI coefficient that is 10 percent higher than the old model it replaces is of interest, but it does not translate into a dollar value of the benefit that the new model will bring.

The normal way models are used is to define a cut-off score. Individuals who score above the cut-off are treated in one way, those who score at or below the cut-off are treated in another way. Different financial outcomes then result on the basis of the treatment people receive. For example, for a credit scoring model to predict good/bad repayment behaviour on a loan, an accept/reject cut-off score will be set. Those scoring above the cut-off have their loan applications accepted. These cases then go on to generate a loss if they default (are bad) or a contribution towards profit if they do not (are good). Those with lower scores are rejected and hence make no contribution to profit or loss. For a response model used to target customers with promotional offers or a model to predict insurance claims, similar outcomes result. In a practical context this means two things. First, the cut-off score(s) that are going to be applied need to be chosen. Second, model performance needs to be assessed using the selected cut-off(s) scores.

8.4.1 Marginal odds based cut-off with average revenue/loss figures

Imagine that the organization which constructed the model used to produce the score distribution report in Table 8.1, has carried out some analysis of its existing loan customers. It found that, on average, a good paying customer who keeps to the terms of their loan agreement generated a \$100 profit contribution and a bad customer who defaulted resulted in a \$2,000 loss due to the debt being written-off. Using these figures it is easy to work out that in order to make a profit from a group of customers, there must be more than 20 good paying loans for each one that defaults. To put it another way, the good:bad odds must be greater than 20:1 (bad rate of less than 4.8%). In general, if the average revenue generated by a good is R and the average loss generated by a bad is L then the marginal good:bad odds at which loans should be accepted is equal to L/R.

From the marginal section of Table 8.1 it can be seen that the odds of people in intervals 1 to 5 who score 585 or less, are below 20:1. Likewise, for intervals 6 to 20, containing cases that score more than 585, the odds are above 20:1. Therefore, a suitable cut-off strategy to maximize profit contribution would be to reject all those scoring 585 or less and accept the rest.

Having established what the cut-off strategy should be, it is possible to estimate the financial properties of the accepted population scoring above the cut-off. Assume that in the organization's marketing plan it has been estimated that 250,000 new loan applications will be received next year. The cumulative descending part of the score distribution report (interval 6) tells us that using a cut-off of 585 will result in 75 percent of applications being accepted – a total of 187,500 new customers. The overall bad rate of these customers is estimated to be 1.40 percent (Descending cumulative bad rate for interval 6). Given that each good customer makes an average \$100 contribution and each bad a $2,000 loss, this allows the total annual contribution from using the model to be calculated:

Contribution from goods = 187,500 * 98.60% * $100 = $18,487,500
Loss from bads   = 187,500 * 1.40% * $2,000 = $5,250,000
Total contribution   = $13,237,500

Often a new model is replacing an existing one. The expectation is that the new model will perform better than the one it replaces. Therefore, what is of interest is the increase in contribution that the new model provides over and above the old model. As long as the scores for the old model are present within the sample, then the contribution calculation can be repeated using the score distribution report generated using the old score. The difference in contribution from using each score is taken to be the improvement that the new model provides. Assume that for the purpose of this example, the estimated contribution from using the old model is $11,500,000. This suggests that the benefit of implementing the new model will be $13,237,500 – $11,500,000 = $1,737,500 per annum.

8.4.2 Constraint based cut-offs

Often, constraints are placed upon organizations. This means it may not be possible to apply a pure marginal odds based cut-off strategy. Instead, the cut-off needs to be adjusted to take the constraints into account. Some examples of the constraints that commonly exist are:

- A minimum number of cases must have a certain decision made about them. If an organization is committed to acquiring say, 80,000, new customers in a year, then a cut-off must be chosen that meets this objective, even if this means accepting some customers who score below the marginal cut-off score.
- Limited budget. An organization may identify that it could profitably target three million consumers with a product offering, but only has budget to target two million of these. Therefore, the cut-off is set so that only the highest scoring two million are targeted.
- Limited capital. Banking organizations and insurers must maintain sufficient capital to cover potential write-offs and claims respectively. If a bank only has a limited amount of capital available then this will act to restrict the amount it can lend to borrowers.
- Operational capacity. An organization may have limited capacity for dealing with consumers, requiring the cut-off to be set so as not to overwhelm the resources available. For example, a customer contact

centre may only be able to process the paperwork associated with a maximum of 5,000 new mortgages each month. Therefore, the cut-off for accepting new mortgage customers must result in no more than 5,000 mortgages being accepted.

8.4.3 What-if analysis

Sometimes an organization wants to explore different cut-off scenarios before making a decision about which cut-off to use. In particular, stakeholders will often want to explore a scenario in the context of how much benefit the new model provides over and above the benefit provided by the incumbent model (or other forecasting method) that the new model is replacing. Some examples of the scenarios that are commonly considered are:

1. Maintain the same population proportions. The cut-off for the new model is chosen so that the proportion of cases scoring above/below the cut-off is the same as for the old model. One would hope that this scenario will result in fewer bads above the cut-off, and corresponding increase in the number of goods above the cut-off.
2. Maintain the same proportion of goods. The cut-off for the new model is chosen so that the proportion of goods scoring above the cut-off is the same as for the old model. One would hope that with this scenario, the proportion of bads scoring above the cut-off will reduce.
3. Maintain the same proportion of bads. As for (2) but the cut is chosen so that the same proportion of bads score above the cut-off.
4. Maintain the same quality. The cut-off is chosen so that the bad rate for cases above the cut-off is the same for the old and new models. One would hope that with this scenario, the total number of cases scoring above the cut-off will increase.

All of these scenarios (and any that lie in between) can be evaluated using score distribution reports produced using the old score and the new score respectively. This is conditional on the old score being present on the holdout sample and knowing what cut-off score was applied to the old model.[5] One begins by finding the relevant numbers from the old score distribution, and then mapping these to the appropriate score in the new score distribution. For example, imagine that we are dealing with a portfolio of credit cards, where accounts that score above the cut-off have their credit limits raised. If the customer is subsequently a good payer, then the credit limit increase, on average, results in an additional $20 profit. However, if a customer subsequently defaults, then on average a $1,000 additional loss is incurred. If one is interested in scenario 2, for example, then one would use the descending cumulative part of the score distribution report for the old score to find the number of goods and bads that scored above the old cut-off score. One would then use the descending part of the new score distribution to identify the cut-off score at which the same number of goods score above the cut-off[6] as for the old model. The number of bads scoring above the cut-off for the new model can then be determined. The benefit from using the new score is calculated by multiplying the difference in the number of bads above each cut-off by $1,000. Calculation of the benefits of the new model using the other three scenarios is undertaken in a similar manner.

8.4.4 Swap set analysis

When a new model is replacing an existing one, a swap set will exist. A swap set is the group that would have been treated one way using the existing decision making system, but will have a different decision made about them using the new system. To put it another way, some people who would previously have scored above the cut-off on the old model will score below the cut-off when assessed using the new model. Likewise, some cases that scored below the cut-off will now score above it.

The swap set does not have any impact on a model's predictive ability, but analysis of the swap set is often important from an operational perspective. Consider a scenario where a retail bank is replacing its old credit scoring model, used to assess new applications for credit cards. Imagine the marketing department has traditionally targeted people aged 25–34. If the new credit scoring model allocates significantly lower scores (higher probability of being a bad credit risk) to those aged 25–34 than the old model, then the marketing department is unlikely to be very happy about it. This is because all other things being equal, when the new model is implemented the conversion rates for its target market will fall significantly. In situations like this, good practice is to undertake swap set analysis well before the model is implemented. Key groups within the population are identified. The impact of the new cut-off strategy for each group is then evaluated, and compared with the outcomes that would have resulted from using the incumbent decision making system. Where significant differences exist, these are communicated to relevant stakeholders for discussion and to give them time to make any changes that may be necessary to their day-to-day operational activities.

8.5   Presenting models to stakeholders

Once a final model has been produced and its performance has been assessed, the results need to be presented to stakeholders. For a large scale modelling project that is going to be implemented within an operational decision making system, then this will invariably involve a meeting/ presentation to stakeholders, supported by relevant project document-ation. The meeting will often be held at the end of the model develop-ment process, but prior to model implementation so that the relevant person(s) can take stock and decide whether or not the finished model can be signed off and put to use. Decisions may also be made about the precise strategy to be employed; that is, when several alternative cut-off strategies are available, which one is to be applied. The primary goal at this point is not to provide every detail of the project in minute detail, but to demonstrate to those in authority that the project has delivered what was intended and present the options for implementation. Another perspective is that as a member of a project team that has put a lot of time and effort into delivering a model, I want to convince senior man-agement that I have done a good job and that my achievement is recog-nized when it comes time for me to have my annual appraisal and pay review. Therefore, I need to be attuned to their objectives in order to achieve my own.

There is much advice that can be given about presentation style and format and I don't claim to be an expert on the subject, but most things that lead to a good presentation are based on common sense principles. Perhaps the most important thing to bear in mind is: what do the people in the audience want to hear? Put yourself in their shoes. Focus on the key points that you want to get across and avoid digress-ing into minor technical details or irrelevant subject matter that result in a loss of audience attention. Another suggestion is to follow a KISS (Keep It Simple Stupid) Philosophy. If you are dealing with people with different backgrounds and experience, then identify who is important and tailor your material to their objectives and level of understanding. If you don't know someone's background, then it is generally a good thing to err on the side of caution and pitch to the intelligent (but naïve) layperson – don't assume any technical knowledge, but don't talk down to them either. Unless dealing with an exclusively technical audience leave formulas, equations and acronyms out of the discus-sion. However, do have at your disposal more detailed technical mater-ial that you can call upon if necessary. Bear in mind that someone is unlikely to judge something a success if they don't understand what's been achieved or whether or not their objectives have been met. I have been in more than one presentation where an analyst presenting the results of a modelling project has begun with an opening along the lines of: "We have applied radial basis function networks with equal heights and unequal widths to generate a model that maximises..." when addressing senior managers with no background in model development. Remember, the goal isn't to show off the technical expertise of the model developer, but to convey an understanding of what has been achieved in terms that the audience understands and are interested in. If, as more often than not, the primary goal of the project is to reduce costs, increase profits and/or increase the size of the customer base, then this is what the primary focus should be. My own preferred method of proceeding in such situations is to have three levels to the material I present. To begin, I present a short (2–3 minute) summary, using a single slide/sheet of paper. This contains only the most important information about the project and what has been achieved. For a credit scoring project to develop a model to assess the creditworthiness of new loan applications, the summary may be presented as a few bullet points stating the benefits implementation of the model will deliver. For example:

- Implementation of the new model will deliver the following benefits:
  - An annual increase in net profit of $4.5m per annum.
  - An annual reduction in bad debt write-off of $0.9m per annum.
  - No change to the volume of new loans granted.
  - A 20 percent reduction in underwriter referrals.

After the summary I cover off other things that are important from a business perspective. For example, what the model looks like (the calibrated scorecard for a linear classification model or the tree structure for a CART model) and when the new model can be expected to be implemented. Risks and issues around implementation and the schedule for monitoring the model once it goes live may also be covered, as will impacts to the operational areas of the business. Finally, I'll have a technical appendix included with the slide deck or as an attached document covering some of the more specialist aspects of the project in detail. Usually this won't be presented in full, but will be used to address any technical questions about the project that are raised.

8.6   Chapter summary

Models developed using the development sample may not perform optimally for a number of reasons. The model may have been over-fitted or the world may have changed, meaning the relationships that are observed in the population today, are very different from those observed during the sample window from which the model development sample was taken. To establish just how well a model performs in practice, validation is undertaken following model development using an independent hold-out sample and/or an out-of-time sample. The predictive properties of the model on the holdout sample(s) are then assessed to provide a more accurate picture of how well the model performs.

There are often two stages to the validation process. The first stage is to assess the score distributions generated by the model, to see if the model is misaligned at a global or attribute level. Following this, measures of performance are calculated such as the percentage correctly classified, the KS-statistic and the GINI coefficient. Finally, the model can be assessed in terms of business benefit. Typically, this will involve deciding upon a cut-off score, and then examining the properties of the population above and below the cut-off. If financial information is available, then this can be incorporated into the analysis.

Very often a new model is developed to replace an existing one. Therefore, it is common practice to produce much of the analysis for both the old and new scores, allowing comparisons to be made between them, and ideally, to generate a dollar value for the benefit that the new model will deliver over and above the one it replaces.

9
Sample Bias and Reject Inference

Credit scoring models that predict the likelihood of someone repaying the credit they have applied for suffer from a problem known as sample bias.[1] Consider the flow through a typical credit application process, as shown in Figure 9.1.

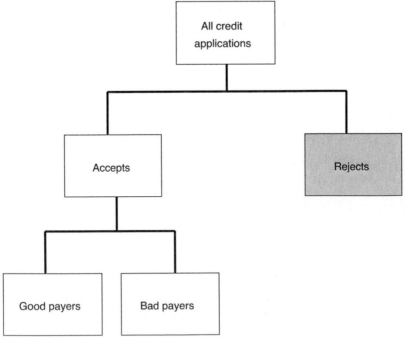

Figure 9.1   Population flow

As Figure 9.1 illustrates, good/bad repayment behaviour is only known for people who had their credit applications accepted and were subsequently granted credit. When it is time to develop a new model, a sample of cases will be taken from the accepted population and a modelling process applied to determine the parameter coefficients of the model. For rejects, no information about repayment behaviour is available. Therefore, rejected cases cannot be used for model construction. Figure 9.2 illustrates what happens when the new model is applied.

Using the new model, some people who would have had their credit application accepted under the old system are now declined. Likewise, some that would have been rejected by the old system are now considered creditworthy and accepted. There is said to be a swap set between the old and new systems. If there isn't a swap set, then using the new

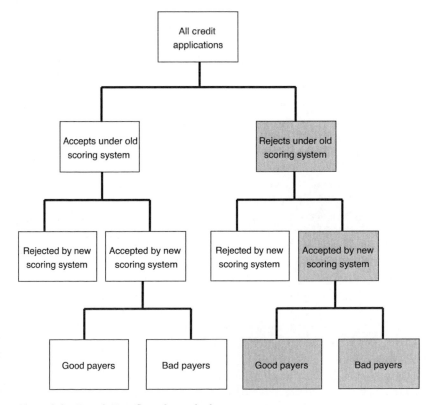

Figure 9.2   Population flow through the new system

model will result in the same decisions as made previously. In which case, there is little justification for the new model that has been developed.[2]

The consequence of having a swap set is that the new model is developed on one group of people (previous accepts) but is also used to make decisions about another group of people (previous rejects), which were not included in the model building process. To put it another way, the new model captures the significant relationships between the accept population and good/bad repayment behaviour, but not the relationships between the reject population and good/bad repayment behaviour. The model is said to display bias toward the accepts. Is this a problem? If the previous decision making system made decisions more or less at random then the answer is no. This is because the properties of the accepts and rejects will be more or less the same. Therefore, the population used to build the model will contain a representative sample of all credit applications. However, this is very unlikely to be the case because even the worst credit rating systems are able to provide some discrimination between good and bad payers, resulting in the least creditworthy credit applications being rejected.

The effect of sample bias is that models tend to be over-optimistic about the behaviour of less creditworthy applicants. Table 9.1 provides an example of why this occurs.

Table 9.1 shows a univariate analysis report for the variable time since bankruptcy. There appears to be no relationship between the time since bankruptcy and good/bad behaviour. The odds, bad rate and weight of evidence are more or less the same across all of the variable's attributes and the information value is zero. However, an experienced credit professional will know there is always a strong relationship between bankruptcy and creditworthiness. People who have been declared bankrupt in the past are nearly always less creditworthy then those that have not. In addition, the more recent the bankruptcy, the worse credit risk people represent. So why is no evidence of this relationship seen in Table 9.1? The answer is given by the reject rates in the right most column of the report. The reject rate for the population as a whole is 46.7 percent – less than half of all credit applications are rejected. However, the reject rate for people who have been declared bankrupt within the last five months, for example, is very much higher. In this group only 1 in a 100 had their credit application accepted – a reject rate of 99 percent. What this is telling us is that within the population of recent bankrupts, those that were accepted are a-typical. They represent a very small minority of individuals who are actually quite creditworthy despite their recent bankruptcy. If all those declared bankrupt were actually given credit (so they all have

Table 9.1 Effect of sample bias

		Univariate analysis report for time since bankruptcy					
	Number of goods	Number of bads	Total accepts	Bad rate	Good:bad odds	Weight of evidence	Number of rejects	Reject rate
No bankruptcy	238,048	12,933	250,981	5.15%	18.41	0.00	207,097	45.2%
0–5 months	17	1	18	5.56%	17.00	−0.08	1,618	99.0%
6–11 months	56	3	59	5.08%	18.67	0.01	1,975	97.1%
12–23 months	167	9	176	5.11%	18.56	0.01	2,055	92.1%
24–35 months	260	14	274	5.11%	18.57	0.01	2,181	88.8%
36–47 months	378	20	398	5.03%	18.90	0.03	2,190	84.6%
48–59 months	833	45	878	5.13%	18.51	0.01	2,483	73.9%
60+ months	1,329	72	1,401	5.14%	18.46	0.00	3,038	68.4%
Total	241,088	13,097	254,185	5.15%	18.41	0	222,638	46.7%

Information value: 0.00

Table 9.2 Through the door population

				Univariate analysis report for time since bankruptcy		
	Number of goods	Number of bads	Total (accepts + rejects)	Bad rate	Good:bad odds	Weight of evidence
No bankruptcy	411,531	46,547	458,078	10.16%	8.84	0.07
0–5 months	642	994	1,636	60.74%	0.65	-2.55
6–11 months	1,088	946	2,034	46.50%	1.15	-1.97
12–23 months	1,374	857	2,231	38.42%	1.60	-1.64
24–35 months	1,812	643	2,455	26.19%	2.82	-1.07
36–47 months	2,097	491	2,588	18.97%	4.27	-0.66
48–59 months	2,848	513	3,361	15.26%	5.55	-0.39
60+ months	3,828	611	4,439	13.76%	6.27	-0.27
Total	425,221	51,602	476,823	10.82%	8.24	0

Information value: 0.1166

repayment behaviour and can be classified as good or bad), then a very different story would emerge. The univariate analysis report for the entire "through the door" population would be as shown in Table 9.2.

In Table 9.2 a clear trend in bad rate can be seen. Of course, in real life situations this information isn't readily available. Therefore, what model developers do is modify the data used to build the model to correct for the bias that exists, so that the sample is more representative of the "through the door" population.

Within the financial services industry the process of modifying a sample to counter the effects of sample bias is termed "reject inference". There are many different approaches to reject inference. However, these can broadly be classified into two types:

1. Data methods. These seek to obtain additional information about the behaviour of rejects. This can then be used within the modelling process, along with the information that is already known about the accepts.
2. Inference methods. These begin by examining the differences between the accepted and rejected populations. The results are then used to adjust the sample used to build the model.

We shall begin by looking at data methods followed by inference methods.

9.1 Data methods

9.1.1 Reject acceptance

The best way to address sample bias is to accept some applications that should be rejected. The repayment behaviour of these "accepted rejects" can then be observed and included within the model development process (Rosenberg and Gleit 1994). As discussed in Chapter 3, to allow a robust model to be constructed around 1,500–2,000 goods and bads are required. A similar number of rejects should also be included in the sample to allow reliable reject inference to be performed.

Reject acceptance is the best method for producing unbiased models. However, it is not popular for two reasons. The first is that considerable forward planning is required. If the good/bad payer classification is based on 12 months of repayment behaviour, then it is necessary to start accepting some cases that should be rejected at least 12 months before the model development sample is taken. The second reason is cost. The primary reason for declining a credit application is because the applicant is uncreditworthy, meaning the likelihood of them generating a loss due to non-payment of their debt is unacceptably high. The cost of bad debts is not trivial. Consider a sample of 2,000 accepted rejects. 1,500 go on to be good payers, who make an average $200 contribution towards profits. The other 500 go on to be bad payers, generating an average $2,000 write-off. Overall that's a $700,000 loss (1,500 * $200–500 * $2,000). Therefore, for this example, any improvement in model performance resulting from using a sample of rejects, must translate into at least $700,000 worth of better decision making for it to be worthwhile. An additional consideration is that this is an up front cost, incurred well before any benefits from the new model are realized. However, it is possible to mitigate against these costs to some extent. One way is to grant accepted rejects lower credit limits/lines than standard customers. Another way is to only accept marginal rejects that were only just deemed uncreditworthy. This works because the swap set that occurs when a new credit scoring model is implemented comes from marginal cases around the cut-off. Those that are particularly uncreditworthy will still be declined and not form part of the swap set.[3] On this basis my recommendation would be that accepted rejects only need to be taken from the region where the good:bad odds are greater than one quarter of the cut-off odds. If the existing credit scoring system has a cut-off rule that accepts all cases where the good:bad odds are greater than 8:1, then a sample of rejects only needs to be taken from the region where the odds are between 2:1 and 8:1.

For some consumer credit portfolios the cut-off rule to accept or decline applications is not based on marginal profitability at the cut-off. If the funds available to lend are limited, then loans will only be granted to the most creditworthy. This means there is a region below the cut-off where it would be profitable to lend, but there are insufficient funds available to do so. This was a significant feature of the credit crunch of 2008–9. The main reason lending reduced in this period was because of a lack of funds, not because of a deterioration in the creditworthiness of applicants.[4] Therefore, accepting some cases from this region will not result in any loss. For example, a cut-off score may be set at good:bad odds of 50:1 to deliver a specific volume of new lending. However, the odds at which loans can be granted profitably is 10:1. Anyone with odds of between 10:1 and 50:1 is creditworthy. Therefore, it would be reasonable to grant credit to a small sample of such cases to allow their behaviour to be observed.

9.1.2 Data surrogacy

Someone who applies for credit with one organization and is rejected, may have other accounts with the same lender, and/or credit agreements with other lenders. Information about how these accounts performed can be used as a surrogate for the application that was rejected (McNab and Wynn 2003, p. 58). If credit cards are predominantly provided to existing personal loan customers, then for someone who applies for a credit card and is rejected, information about their loan repayments could be used as a surrogate for their credit card behaviour. The key assumption is that if they defaulted on their loan over the forecast horizon, then they would also have defaulted on their credit card, had one been granted.

The other (and most common) source of surrogate data is a credit reference agency, which can provide information about peoples' repayment behaviour with other lenders. The data supplied by the credit reference agency is used to classify rejects as good or bad payers for modelling purposes.

There a number of issues that need addressing when using surrogate data. The first problem is that the data may not be in exactly the same format as the lender's own data. For example, what a credit reference agency defines as being in 1, 2, 3,... months in arrears may differ from the definition used by the lender. Some organizations define three months in arrears as 90 days past due, while others define it as three calendar months past due (89–93 days past due depending on the time of year). A few even use a four week (28 day) month, meaning three months in arrears is defined as just 84 days past due. A second issue is when a credit reference agency reports that an individual has multiple credit agreements. In this case, a decision needs to be made about which accounts to use as a surrogate. Another question is what to do in cases where the credit reference agency returns no data because an individual does not have any other credit accounts. This can be expected to occur in anything from 5–25 percent of cases, depending on the nature of the portfolio for which reject inference is required. One option is to treat these cases as indeterminate, effectively excluding them from the model development process. The other option is to apply one of the inference methods to this group, as described in section 9.2.

Given the differences between an organization's own data and data provided by the credit reference agency, a mapping exercise will be required to match the definition of good/bad payer based on the organization's own data to the definition of good/bad payer based on data supplied by the credit reference agency. If the two definitions are not well aligned then the modelling process will effectively be trying to model two different behaviours, and this will result in a sub-optimal model. Therefore, it is important to validate that the two good/bad definitions are well aligned. The easiest way to do this is to obtain surrogate data for the

Table 9.3   Data surrogacy mapping exercise

Good/bad definition based on lender's data	Good/bad definition based on data supplied by credit reference agency			
	Good	Indeterminate	Bad	Total
Good	25,550 (99.3%)	147 (0.6%)	23 (0.1%)	25,720 (100%)
Indeterminate	76 (7.1%)	988 (91.7%)	14 (1.3%)	1,078 (100%)
Bad	11 (0.5%)	37 (1.6%)	2,215 (97.9%)	2,263 (100%)
Total	25,637	1,172	2,252	29,061

Bad rate for accepts based on lender's data: 8.09%
Bad rate for accepts based on credit reference data: 8.07%

accepts as well as the rejects. A cross tabulation of the two good/bad definitions can then be produced for the accepts and the bad rates for the two good/bad definitions compared. Table 9.3 provides an example of a model development sample containing 29,061 accepts, where the lender's original good/bad definition has been cross tabulated with the good/bad definition based on credit reference data.

In Table 9.3 the two definitions of good, indeterminate and bad agree in 99.3 percent, 91.7 percent and 97.9 percent of cases respectively. This isn't perfect, but given the differences in the data it is very unlikely there will be a 100 percent match between the two good/bad definitions. In my experience, if the two definitions agree in more than about 95 percent of cases for the goods and bads, then this is acceptable. So on this basis, the results of the mapping exercise in Table 9.3 are quite good, and it can be concluded that the two definitions are well aligned. This is supported by the bad rates which are almost identical. If the level of agreement between the two good/bad definitions is lower than about 95 percent then this suggests the mapping exercise between the two good/bad definitions is inappropriate and should be revised.

A more in-depth approach to validating the mapping is to develop two preliminary models, just using the accepts. One model is constructed using the lender based good/bad definition and the other using the surrogate definition. If the two models and their resulting score distributions are very similar, then this suggests that the good/bad definitions are well aligned.

Overall, data surrogacy works well if there is good alignment between the two good/bad definitions. There will however, be some additional costs/time implications for the project if credit reference (or other externally sourced) data is required.

9.2 Inference methods

9.2.1 Augmentation

Augmentation is reported to be the most widely used reject inference method (Banasik et al. 2003). Augmentation works on the assumption that marginal accepts (cases that were just deemed to be creditworthy) are very similar to marginal rejects (cases that were just deemed to be uncreditworthy). Given that the swap set will predominantly come from cases around the margin, then if a model is constructed using a sample that is heavily weighted towards marginal accepts, then the bias within the population will be reduced.

The first stage of the augmentation process is to determine how close the accepts are to the margin. There are several ways this can be done, but the most common method is to construct an "accept/reject model" to predict the probability that applications were accepted. Constructing an accept/reject model follows exactly the same principles that are used to construct any other type of classification model. All previous accepts (goods, bads, indeterminates etc.) are treated as one class (the dependent variable is assigned a value of 1) and all rejects are treated as the other class (the dependent variable is assigned a value of 0). The predictor variables such as age, residential status, income and so on are then pre-processed in exactly the same way as described in Chapter 6. Next, a modelling technique, such as logistic regression, is applied to construct the accept/reject model. Finally, a second model is constructed that predicts good/bad behaviour. This model is constructed using only the goods and bads from the accepted population. Within the modelling process, each observation is assigned a weight equal to 1 minus the probability of accept, generated by the accept/reject model. The net result is that observations that are most marginal have the greatest weights, and therefore, the greatest influence in determining the structure of the model.

Augmentation is attractive, but the downside is that by focusing on the margin, the bias displayed for the population that lies well above the margin will increase. The model becomes less accurate the further from the margin you go. In many situations the accuracy of the model is not that important, as long as the estimate is such that an applicant falls on the correct side of the decision rule employed. Consider a bank that sets a score cut-off such that loan applications are accepted if the probability of being a good payer is 0.8 or more. If the true likelihood of an applicant being a good payer is say, 0.98, but the model estimates the probability to be 0.85, then the correct decision will still be made. However, if the model is also used to assign different lending strategies to different population segments on the basis of the probability estimate that the model generates (a practice known as pricing for risk), then this can be a problem and the performance of the model derived from the augmentation process may be inferior when compared to a model constructed using just the accepts (goods and bads).

9.2.2   Extrapolation

Another popular inference technique is extrapolation. This is similar to the more general bi-variate probit approach to dealing with truncated data, as described by Heckman (1976). The basic assumption underpinning extrapolation is that the bias increases as one moves away from the margin. To put it another way, the bias that exists for rejects that were only just deemed uncreditworthy is much smaller than for rejects that were considered very uncreditworthy indeed.

With augmentation, the properties of the accept population are modified so that more emphasis is placed on cases near that margin. With extrapolation a different approach is adopted. The weighting of the accepts is left unchanged. Instead, each reject is used to create two new observations, one good and one bad. These are referred to as "inferred goods" and "inferred bads" respectively. Each new observation is assigned a weight, reflecting an estimated probability of them being a good or bad payer. A final model is then produced using a combination of the known and inferred populations; that is, known goods and inferred goods form one class, known bads and inferred bads the other.

The extrapolation process to create the inferred goods and bads, and their associated weights is as follows:

1. An accept/reject model is constructed. This is identical to the accept/ reject model used for augmentation, as described in section 9.2.1.
2. A good/bad model is constructed to predict the probability of good repayment behaviour. This model is constructed using just the goods and bads within the accept population.
3. The accept/reject and good/bad models are applied to the entire population (accepts and rejects), so that all observations have a probability of accept and a probability of good assigned to them.
4. The population is sorted in ascending order of probability of accept.

5. The population is classed into a number of equally sized groups. Around 20–30 groups is usually adequate, but anything up to 50 or more groups can be assigned if the model development sample is large enough. Each group should contain at least 100 observations and ideally several hundred.
6. The average probability of accept and the average probability of good is calculated for each group.
7. An extrapolation graph is produced, as illustrated in Figure 9.3.

In Figure 9.3, the accepts are clustered towards the top right hand side of the graph. As the probability of good decreases, there is a corresponding decrease in the probability of accept. For rejects with a high probability of

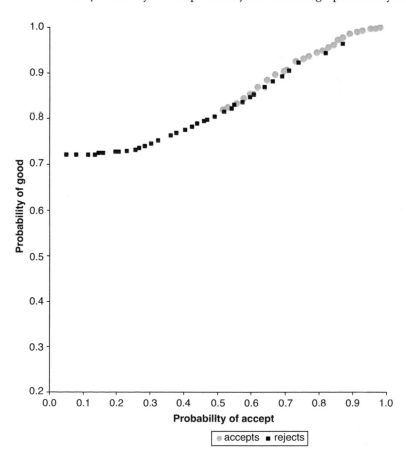

Figure 9.3   Extrapolation graph

acceptance, their probability of good is similar to the accepts (indicating they are marginal cases that were only just deemed uncreditworthy by the old system). The interesting part is the pattern of behaviour seen in the rejects as the probability of acceptance falls. The probability of good initially declines along a similar trend line to that displayed by the accepts, but then flattens off. This is counter intuitive. What one would expect to see is the rejects continuing to follow the trend line displayed by the accepts, suggesting that the flattening off is an effect of the bias generated by the good/bad model, constructed using only the accepts.

To correct for the bias, the trend seen in the accept population is extrapolated into the region dominated by the rejects, as illustrated in Figure 9.4.

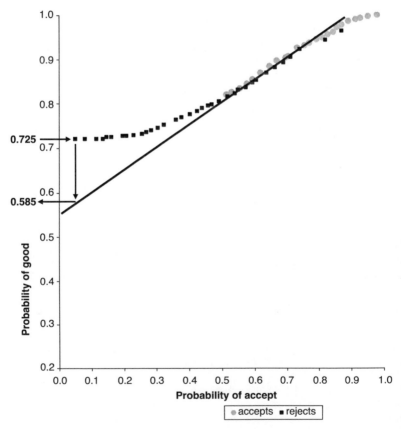

Figure 9.4   Extrapolated trend

Once the trend line has been extrapolated, the probability of good that has been calculated for the rejects is adjusted to fit the trend line. For the leftmost point in Figure 9.4, the average probability of good for rejects is 0.725. The corresponding point on the trend line is 0.585. Therefore, the probability of good for the rejects represented by this point is reduced by a factor of 0.585/0.725 = 0.807.

Determining the trend line is something of a mixture of a science and an art. The simplest way is to fit a linear trend line (a straight line) to marginal accepts, and this is what has been done to produce the trend line in Figure 9.4. However, some modellers adopt a more conservative approach, fitting a non-linear trend line that bends away towards the 0,0 point on the graph. Alternatively, the whole trend line may be shifted downwards by a fixed amount. A conservative view of reject performance is often taken because the impact of overestimating the performance of rejects is much greater than the impact of underestimating them.[5] However, if the trend line is too steep or lies too far below the accepts, then there will be no swap set, if the probabilities assigned to better performing rejects are below the cut-off that is used to make lending decisions. My general advice would be that if you are performing extrapolation for the first time, then if at all possible, take the advice of a more experienced model developer who has undertaken reject inference a number of times. If such advice is not available, then my recommendation would be to stick with a simple linear trend line, fitted to the marginal accepts (the lowest scoring 50 percent).

The final step is to create inferred goods and bads; a process sometimes referred to as "Parcelling". Each reject is replaced by two new observations. One is assigned to be good (so a value of 1 is set for the dependent variable for modelling purposes) and the other is assigned to be bad (a value of 0 for modelling purposes). The good case is assigned a weight equal to the adjusted probability of good, the bad a weight of 1 – (adjusted probability of good).

Before a final model is produced, the model development sample, containing known performance of the accepts and the inferred performance of rejects, will need to be pre-processed again. It will be necessary to reproduce fine/coarse classed univariate analysis reports, and create new dummy variables/weight of evidence variables using the total known plus inferred population.

A good question to ask at this point is, how do you know if the extrapolation process has been performed correctly? In particular, has the correct trend line been chosen to fit the rejects to? The simple answer is: you don't! It is impossible to tell how good the inference is until after the model has gone live and it's performance monitored using real data. However, there are some sense checks that have been recommended by industry experts. One commonly quoted rule of thumb is that the overall performance of rejects should be somewhere between one half and one eighth of the accepts. So if the average good:bad odds for the accepts is 16:1, then you would expect the average good:bad odds for the inferred rejects to be in the range 2:1 to 8:1, and you certainly wouldn't expect the performance of rejects to be equal or better than the accepts. Continuing with the previous example, if the average odds of the inferred rejects is less than 2:1, this would suggest that the trend line is too steep and a more moderate trend line should be applied. Similar logic also applies to individual attributes within univariate analysis reports. The good:bad odds for inferred rejects with a given attribute should not be higher than the good bad odds for accepts with the same attribute. The trend in bad rates for inferred rejects should also mirror the reject rate. The bad rates for highly rejected groups should be greater than for groups with lower reject rates.

9.2.3   Iterative reclassification

A third inference method is iterative reclassification, as described by Joanes (1993):

1. Construct a good/bad model using just the accepts for who good/ bad behaviour is known.
2. Apply the good/bad model from step 1 to the rejects, so that all rejects have a probability of good assigned to them.
3. On the basis of the probability estimate that has been assigned, allocate each reject as either good or bad.
4. Construct a new good/bad model, this time using the accepts and the rejects.[6]
5. Reassign rejects as good or bad, on the basis of the probability estimate that are generated by the new model.
6. Repeat steps 2–5 until the difference between subsequent iterations is sufficiently small; that is, the model from the latest iteration assigns rejects the same good/bad classification as the model from the previous iteration. In practice, sometimes only two or three iterations are required, and rarely more than ten.

To perform iterative reclassification a decision needs to be taken about the probability of good to use, to assign rejects as good or bad respectively. This is something that is often based on a mixture of expert opinion and trial and error. A simplistic view is to use a probability of

0.5. However, for anything except the most sub-prime of credit portfolio's this tends to result in a vast overestimate of the number of goods. Better results are usually obtained by using a probability that mirrors the lender's cut-off strategy. For example, if a lender rejects credit applications where the probability of good is less than 0.9, then a probability of 0.9 is applied within the iterative reclassification process.

A limitation of augmentation and extrapolation is that they deal purely in terms of goods and bads. This can lead to an overestimate of the total number of goods and bads within the population because no cases are assigned to be indeterminate. An attractive feature of iterative reclassification is that it can be adapted to include an indeterminate class for rejects. The algorithm in step 5 is modified to assign rejects to one of three classes instead of two.

9.3 Does reject inference work?

When discussing the worth of reject inference there are several questions that need to be considered, especially given that reject inference can add significantly to the time/cost required to complete a modelling project.[7] The first question is: what is the scope for reject inference? By this, I mean is there any evidence that having information about the repayment behaviour of rejects enables significantly better models to be constructed? The conclusions drawn from academic research into reject inference and anecdotal evidence from industry experts is that yes, having information about rejects does improve the quality of the resulting models by a reasonable amount (Banasik and Crook 2003; Crook and Banasik 2004; Banasik and Crook 2005; Verstraeten and Van den Poel 2005; Banasik and Crook 2007). Consequently, data based methods such as reject acceptance and data surrogacy tend to work well, and I would recommend using these methods if possible. Some of the same research also found the potential benefits of reject inference to be greater the higher the reject rate. Again, this concurs with my personal experience and that of other industry experts.

The benefit provided by reject inference is only likely to be significant for portfolios where the reject rates are significantly high. For portfolios with rejects rates in the region of 10–20 percent the benefits start to become questionable, and it is probably not worth considering reject inference at all if the reject rate is below about 5 percent.

If it is not possible to accept some cases that should have been rejected, or to apply data surrogacy, then a model developer must decide whether or not to apply one of the true inference methods such as augmentation, extrapolation or iterative reclassification. These methods are widely applied within the credit industry, and if you find yourself working on a modelling project you may be expected by your peers/line manager to apply them. However, the evidence supporting the use of such methods is dubious at best. One of the most comprehensive and highly cited academic papers about reject inference came to the conclusion that it is impossible to reliably predict what a rejected credit applicant's behaviour would have been, using only information about the repayment behaviour of those that were accepted (Hand and Henley 1993); that is, methods such as augmentation, extrapolation and iterative reclassification will not generate any useful information about how rejects would have behaved. More recent empirical Research by Crook and Banasik (2004) and Banasik and Crook (2007) came to more or less the same conclusion, and in particular, that augmentation is more or less useless.[8]

What is particularly interesting, is Crook and Banasik also surmised that in some cases inference methods could actually result in worse models. Why? Because if a model developer applies reject inference incorrectly, then the bias within the population will be made worse not better. This naturally leads on to the other major argument against inference methods. They cannot be validated at the time the inference is applied. It is impossible to know whether the performance of rejects has been estimated correctly because there is no data to check the inference against. To try and get round this problem various rules of thumb, such as those discussed in section 9.2.2, are applied by practitioners in an attempt to check the quality of the inference that has been applied, but there is little or no evidence that these provide any real benefits. Another partial (and somewhat unsatisfactory) solution to the problem of validation is to monitor the quality of the decisions made by the model once it has been put live and is making real lending decisions. Credit applicants that would have been declined under the previous decision making system, but are accepted using the new model are identified[9] and the quality of the decisions that the new model made about these cases is examined. However, in all my years working within the credit industry, I have not come across a single organization that does this.[10]

9.4   Chapter summary

There is general agreement that credit scoring models constructed using only previously accepted credit applications suffer from sample bias. Reject inference is the name given to the family of techniques that are applied to correct the bias that exists.

The reject inference methods applied within the credit industry fall into two categories; data methods and inference methods. Data methods seek to obtain additional data about rejected cases that is then used within the modelling process. Ideally, a sample of credit applications that should have been rejected will actually be given credit to see how they perform, but this requires considerable forward planning and may (but not necessarily) be costly due to the additional bad debt that can result. If this is not feasible, then the next best option is to seek surrogate data about an individual's repayment behaviour when using other credit products. Typically, the source of this data will be a credit reference agency, or possibly an organization's own internal files containing details about customers' other product holdings. The repayment behaviour that is observed on these other credit products is then assumed to be representative of how the individual would have behaved, if their credit application had been accepted.

Data methods generally work well, and should be the first choice for a model developer. If it is not feasible to follow a data based method of reject inference, then a true inference method can be applied to make an educated guess about how rejects would have behaved, had they been granted credit. Common inference methods include augmentation, extrapolation and iterative reclassification. Of these, augmentation is the most popular. However, the evidence supporting the use of inference methods, and in particular augmentation, is weak, and several questions can be raised over the appropriateness of such methods. In particular, it is almost impossible to validate the quality of the reject inference that has been applied at the time a model is constructed, and therefore, it is not possible to know if the resulting models are better or worse than would result if no inference had been applied. However, such methods are widely applied by practitioners and most organizations would expect such a process to be applied as part of a model development project.

10
Implementation and Monitoring

One question which should have been addressed during project planning is the mechanism that will be used to calculate model scores and apply decision rules based on the scores people receive. If a model has been constructed as a "proof of concept" or as a standalone research project, this may be a trivial question because nothing needs to be done. A second scenario is when a model is used to generate scores within an off-line environment. Within a target marketing context, for example, a model may have been developed to predict the likelihood of people responding to a marketing communication. The model will be used, perhaps just once, to produce a list of prospects to target. The list is then handed to the organization's marketing team who upload it to a telephone dialler, e-mail generator or some other contact system. In this type of scenario the model, while important, is not "business critical". If the production of the list is delayed by a few days, or the model is not quite as good as it could be, then the impact on the business will be relatively small.

The third scenario is where the model forms part of a business critical system. The model is used on an ongoing basis, perhaps for many years, as part of a wider decision making/account management system. Examples include insurance quotation systems, systems for processing personal loan applications and credit card account management systems. In these cases, the finished model will need to be integrated into the wider IT infrastructure used by the organization to carry out its day-to-day operations. Incorrect implementation of the model may result in the loss of many millions of dollars over the life of the model.

In the remainder of this chapter the focus is predominantly on the third scenario; that is, business critical systems in which the model is just one component. In the first part of the chapter implementation issues are discussed. In particular, the testing that needs to be undertaken to ensure that model scores are calculated correctly. The second part of the chapter discusses monitoring within the context of classification models (although similar principles are applicable to regression models). Monitoring is the process of carrying out ongoing evaluation of a model to determine if it continues to provide good quality predictions in line with expectation, and to ensure that the best decisions are being made on the basis of the scores generated by the model.

10.1   Implementation

10.1.1   Implementation platform

When scoring models first began to be used within operational decision making systems in the 1960s and 1970s, standard practice was to treat model implementation as an IT project. A work request would be raised, an IT project manager, business analyst and programmer allocated to do the work, and code written to implement the model using COBOL, FORTRAN, C or whatever computer language was prevalent within the organization at the time. What soon became apparent was that model implementation was a long winded and costly affair that took many months or even years to accomplish, often taking many times longer than the actual model build itself. Part of the problem was that the IT people who became involved didn't understand how a model worked or what it was used for, and therefore, wrapped a layer of additional require-ments and risk management protocols around the project. Likewise, after a model had been implemented, if the team responsible for maintaining the model wanted to change something, such as increasing the cut-off score used to decide which loan customers to accept or decline, it would be treated by the IT department just like any other work request. The work would be prioritized and wait in the IT work queue until resource was available to make the change.

To get around the IT bottleneck, these days many organizations employ a decision engine as a means of implementing and updating their models. A decision engine is based on the idea that all the scores and rules required to make lending decisions can be captured as a set of para-meters maintained by the people responsible for model development. A typical decision engine has two parts. The "front end" is a user friendly piece of PC software that allows an analyst to type in model parameters, set cut-off scores, define policy rules and so on. The better ones also pro-vide testing functionality. This allows data to be run through the system to check that scores and decision rules have been applied correctly. The second part of the decision engine is an "implementation module". This sits on the relevant IT platform and has an interface with the systems responsible for processing customer information. To implement a model and associated decision rules, the person responsible for the model simply chooses a menu option within the PC front end to upload the model to the implementation module. This circumvents any requirement for IT involvement. What this means in practice is that many organizations operate very dynamic consumer management policies that they fine-tune on a regular (sometimes daily) basis.

Not all organizations use decision engines, and some models are still implemented as IT projects. However, any organization that takes this approach will be at a competitive disadvantage, being unable to react as quickly as competitors that do have decision engine capability embedded within their systems. Some organizations use decision engines they have developed in-house, but most use decision engines developed by third party suppliers, such as FICO or Experian, whose decision engine technology has been evolving since the early 1990s, based on their experience of working with dozens of different financial services organizations. These systems provide a more flexible and robust platform, at a far cheaper price, than most organizations could develop themselves.

Some decision engines can only implement linear models; that is, models in the form $\alpha + b_{1x}x_1 + b_1x_1 + ,..., + b_kx_k$. Some can also implement other model forms such as neural networks and CART models, but some do not. Therefore, if a decision engine is to be employed, it is imperative that its capabilities are taken into account during project planning, when the form of model is being considered. There is no point developing a model using a cutting edge statistical technique if it can't be implemented using the organization's implementation mechanism.

Another area that should have been considered at the project planning phase is the interface between the decision engine and the host system. An assessment should have been made as to which predictor variables are or will be available, and can therefore, be used to construct the model. If the model introduces new variables that are not currently available within the decision engine, then the resources required to implement the new data items should have been considered long before model construction was undertaken.

10.1.2 Scoring (coding) instructions

Often the person responsible for implementing a model won't be the person who developed it. Although the structure of the model may seem obvious to the developer, the interpretation of how the model should be implemented may be ambiguous to anyone else. One reason for this may be because the format of the data used to construct the model is different from the format of the data within the host system that will be used to calculate model scores. A model developer might have constructed a model that contains the predictor variable "Time living at current address". In the model development sample this was held in MMMM format. For example, someone who had lived at their address for 8 years and 6 months had the value 0102 (8*12 + 6). However, within the operational system, time living at current address is held in YYMM format. 8 years and 6 months is represented as 0806.

The person implementing the model may have no knowledge of model development, and therefore, have no idea what the numbers mean. If the model developer produces documentation that says, "the parameter coefficient for someone who has a time at current address of 0102 is +50 points", then within the operational system this will mean that anyone who has lived at their address for 1 year and 2 months will be incorrectly allocated 50 points.

Another issue is precision. A model developer may describe a variable such as outstanding balance as an integer number of dollars, but within the operational system it is held as a real number. In the mind of the model developer, people with an outstanding credit card balance of between $5,000 and $10,000 are assigned one score, those with a balance of $10,001–$15,000 are assigned another and so on. But what about an account with a balance of $10,000.25? These cases, although few, will be scored incorrectly if this issue is not dealt with appropriately.

To reduce the likelihood of such errors occurring, good practice is for the model developer to produce "scoring instructions". This is documentation that contains an unambiguous explanation of the structure of the model, in terms of the variables formats that exist within the operational system.

10.1.3 Test plan

Once an implementation route has been established, the model and associated decision rules need to be tested before they are put live. This is to ensure scores are calculated correctly and the right decisions are made on the basis of the score. It is surprising how often errors are introduced during model implementation, particularly from simple typing errors. For example, coding a parameter coefficient as positive rather than negative or adding an extra zero. To avoid such pitfalls, a comprehensive testing facility should exist that enables a significant volume of test cases to be processed within the live system. The test system should also facilitate dual scoring. By this, I mean it should be possible to compare the scores generated by the test system with model scores that have been independently calculated using a different system. If both sets of scores are identical then this supports the case for the model being coded correctly.

It should be noted that having a large database of test cases is not in itself sufficient to guarantee the model has been implemented correctly. Often it is exception cases or those with extreme values that are scored incorrectly. The test database should also contain cases that lie on interval boundaries to ensure intervals are correctly defined.

10.1.4   Post implementation checks

After a model has been implemented and is being used to make decisions, a monitoring regime should be instigated, as discussed later in the chapter. However, it may be several weeks or months before monitoring begins. Therefore, it is prudent to undertake some preliminary checks of the scoring process in the hours and days immediately following implementation. This involves taking a sample of a hundred or so accounts, and once again recalculating the scores independently, to ensure they are calculated correctly. The distribution of model scores should also be checked against the holdout and/or out-of-time samples. This is to ensure the expected numbers of people score above/below the decision rules that have been implemented. Checks should also be made to ensure policy rules, which override the score in certain situations, have also been applied correctly.

10.2   Monitoring

Following implementation, model performance should be monitored on a regular basis. Monitoring is required because model performance has a tendency to deteriorate over time. There are lots of reasons why this occurs. Sometimes the whole economy shifts, resulting in the entire population behaving differently. Alternatively, if an organization changes its marketing strategy, the people who end up being scored may have a very different profile to those used to develop the model. Consequently, the model won't be as good at predicting the behaviour of these people. Similarly, the nature of the relationships between predictor variables and the dependent variable can change as the economy and society evolves over time. Within credit and insurance markets, a typical model has a lifespan of anywhere between one and five years before its performance has degraded to the point where it is worthwhile replacing it.

For credit scoring models monitoring is usually carried out on a monthly (or sometimes quarterly) basis.[1] For each reporting period a set of reports is produced to identify if the following has occurred:

- Score misalignment: A very common phenomena is for a model to continue to rank cases correctly, but for the relationship between score and behaviour to change. If there is an economic downturn, for example, write-off rates will rise across the board. All other things being equal, loan applicants continue to receive the same scores, but the probability of default associated with each score increases.
- Score degradation: This is when the relationships between the independent variables and the predicted behaviour change, resulting in attributes within the model becoming misaligned. As changes accumulate over time, so the ability of a model to discriminate between good and bad behaviour deteriorates further.

The effect of score misalignment is that the decision rules associated with given scores will no longer be optimal. If score misalignment is observed then it is a relatively easy process to recalibrate the model, as discussed in Chapter 7, so that the desired score:odds relationship is restored. Alternatively, the model can be left unchanged, but the decision rules that use the score are amended so that they are aligned with the current score:odds relationship.

Score degradation is potentially a more serious issue. If a small reduction in model performance is observed, then minor adjustments can sometimes be made to one or more of the model's parameters to improve its performance. This can be done by using measures such as the delta score, as discussed in Chapter 8, to inform the process of making adjustments to the parameter coefficients of the model. However, if more major changes are observed, the usual course of action is to construct a completely new model to replace the incumbent one.

10.2.1 Model performance

To determine how well a model is performing, measures are calculated each reporting period as part of the standard monitoring pack. These measures are typically the same ones that were used to assess the model's performance when it was originally constructed. For example, the KS-statistic, GINI coefficient and/or the percentage correctly classified for a given cut-off score.

If the monitored population has been censored, then it is important to take the degree of censoring into account; that is, the proportion of the population for which behaviour is missing. If a model is very good at discriminating between goods and bads, then the worse the model will appear to be, using measures such as the GINI coefficient or the KS-statistic. This is because most potential bads will have been subject to censoring (declined), leaving a relatively homogenous pool of accepted (mostly good) cases upon which monitoring is undertaken. Another issue is the effect on performance measures when an organization tightens it's decision making criteria. For example, if a bank finds itself with constraints on the amount of capital it has available, it may respond by raising the cut-off scores for loan applications to restrict the volume of lending. Following the cut-off change, the model will appear to show less discrimination than before, even if the model is still performing optimally. The easiest way to get around this problem (although not an ideal solution) is to measure performance using only the highest scoring *x* percent of cases, where *x* percent or more of the population are accepted at all times. For example, an organization may see reject rates vary between 20 and 50 percent over a number of years. Therefore, it measures the discrimination of its model by calculating the GINI coefficient using only the highest scoring 50 percent of cases.

As a rule of thumb, if model performance has decreased by more than about 5–10 percent since the model was deployed, then there will be a financial case for fully redeveloping the model. If the drop in performance is of a lower order, then it may be possible to "fine-tune" the model by making minor changes to one or more of the parameter coefficients within the model on the basis of the delta scores for misaligned attributes. The process for calculating delta scores was covered in section 8.2.3.

10.2.2 Policy rules and override analysis

The monitoring of a model should also include analysis of any other decision making criteria applied in addition to score based decisions. Principally, this includes:

- Policy override rules. These are rules that take preference over a score based decision. A mortgage provider may have a rule to accept all mortgage applications from members of staff, regardless of the score they receive. Similarly, a provider of motor insurance may refuse to provide insurance quotations for drivers under the age of 21.
- Manual overrides. In consumer credit markets in particular, it is common for some credit applications to be referred for manual review, regardless of the credit score they receive. For example, credit applications which only just fail the cut-off score may be reviewed by a

trained underwriter, who can overturn a score based decision if they believe the application is creditworthy. Similarly, a loan or mortgage application may be referred for manual review if the credit score indicates they are creditworthy, but they have requested to borrow more than their income suggests they can afford.

One effect of policy override rules and manual decision making is it "corrupts" the observed behaviour of the model. Consider a mortgage application model where the lender has a policy of declining anyone with a score of less than 633 (equating to odds of 100:1). Now assume the lender takes the view that anyone scoring 633–653 (odds of between 100:1 and 200:1) is a "marginal accept". These cases must be reviewed by an underwriter, who makes the final decision as to whether or not the application should be accepted. The underwriter makes a subjective judgement about the creditworthiness of applicants, based on what is known about them. They may even contact the applicant directly to obtain additional information, if they think this will aid their decision making. Let us assume that the bank has undertaken some analysis of previous underwriting decisions. This shows that the use of underwriters, while adding considerably to the cost of processing each case, does provide some added benefit, over and above that provided by the credit score alone.[2] Consequently, some additional bad cases are rejected that would otherwise have been accepted. When it comes to monitoring, the model scores will appear to be positively misaligned between 633 and 653 because of the additional bads that have been removed by the underwriters. To get around this problem, cases that have been subject to override decisions or policy rules should be removed from analysis of the model, and reported upon separately. Analysis of overrides is usually undertaken for the following two groups:

- Low score overrides. These are cases that score below the cut-off, indicating that an individual is likely to exhibit bad behaviour. Therefore, they should have their application for a product or service declined. However, they subsequently have their application accepted.
- High score overrides. These are cases where individuals score above the cut-off, indicating they should have their application accepted. However, they are declined due to a policy override rule or manual decision making.

For low score overrides, score misalignment reports can be produced to confirm if the override rules are having the desired effect. One would hope that the average odds for the overrides will be above the odds at the cut-off. Monitoring high score overrides is more difficult. Having been declined, there is no behaviour to subsequently monitor. Therefore, reporting on these cases often just involves examining the numbers of cases and the distribution of the scores they receive.

10.2.3 Monitoring cases that would previously have been rejected

As discussed in Chapter 9, with many forms of reject inference it is not possible to confirm that it has been applied correctly at the time a model is constructed. Therefore, when monitoring models developed using reject inference, separate monitoring should be performed on the portion of the population that would have been rejected under the previous decision making system. However, in practice this is rarely, if ever, undertaken.

If the reject inference process has been over-pessimistic, resulting in cases that would have been rejected under the old system receiving lower scores than they should, this will manifest itself within the monitoring suite with cases around the cut-off having better odds (lower bad rates) than the score suggests; that is, they will appear to be positively misaligned. Similarly, if the reject inference has been over-optimistic about performance, the score may appear negatively misaligned around the cut-off region.

10.2.4 Portfolio monitoring

It is worth being aware that where operational models are employed to assess credit applications, insurance quotations and the like, then in addition to scorecard monitoring organizations also undertake portfolio monitoring. Although outside the scope of this book, portfolio monitoring is often included as part of an organization's regular monitoring process. Some aspects of portfolio monitoring are linked to model performance, but portfolio monitoring is primarily concerned with how the profile of customers changes over time, in terms of their geo-demographics, and how different cohorts of customers (customers acquired at different points in time) behave as their relationship with an organization matures. Sometimes changes to the profile of a portfolio are indicative of scorecard misalignment or scorecard degradation, but this is not necessarily the case. A provider of home insurance may see a very large shift in the age profile of people asking for quotations, but the relationship between age and claim behaviour, as captured in the model, continues to hold true. If being young is indicative of a high likelihood of making a claim, the net result of more young people taking out insurance will be a dramatic rise in the number of claims, even if the model continues to perform optimally.

10.3   Chapter summary

If a model is to be implemented as part of a business critical system then it is important that detailed testing of the model is undertaken before and after it goes live. This includes testing that scores are calculated correctly and that associated decision rules are applied correctly on the basis of the scores that people receive.

Once a model is live it needs to be monitored on a regular basis. Monitoring is required for two reasons. The first is to ensure that the model continues to generate accurate forecasts of consumer behaviour. Models have a tendency to deteriorate over time, and if model performance falls significantly then it is prudent to develop a new model to replace the incumbent one. The second reason for monitoring is to assess the alignment of the model. Often a model will continue to discriminate, but the score odds relationship changes significantly. As a consequence, decision rules based on the model score are no longer appropriate. To resolve the problem of misalignment there are two approaches. One is to recalibrate the model so the desired score odds relationship is restored. The other is to leave the model unchanged, but to adjust the decision rules to accommodate the score odds relationship that is observed.

11
Further Topics

The information provided in Chapters 1 through 10 should be sufficient to provide an understanding of the processes involved in the construction and application of predictive models of consumer behaviour. In this chapter three further topics are discussed. The first considers model construction and validation when only small samples are available. The second topic looks at alternative methods of assessing model performance, which are particularly useful when two competing models are being compared. The third and final topic examines multi-model systems, sometimes referred to as ensembles or fusion systems. A multi-model system is when several different models are constructed to predict a single behaviour. The predictions made by each model are then combined together in some way to deliver a better overall prediction than that generated by any single model on its own.

11.1   Model development and evaluation with small samples

If a model development sample contains relatively few observations (below about 1,000 cases of each class for classification problems) then a number of issues come to the fore:

1. The chance of over-fitting increases significantly as sample size reduces.
2. Assigning a significant proportion of cases to the holdout sample can result in a noticeable reduction in model performance compared to using the entire sample for model construction.
3. The holdout sample may be too small for precise measurements of performance to be calculated, or robust score distributions to be produced.

11.1.1 Leave-one-out cross validation

One method for reducing the problems associated with small samples is leave-one-out cross validation. Assume the development sample contains N observations. N models are constructed, with a different observation left out of the modelling process each time. Each model is then used to calculate a score for the observation that was excluded. After all N models have been constructed, a holdout score exists for every observation. These scores can then be used for calculating performance metrics such as the percentage correctly classified, GINI coefficient, KS-statistic and so on, which means there is no requirement for a separate holdout sample.

For practical applications, one wants a single model at the end of the day. This is achieved by constructing a final model using all N observations. The assumption is that the model constructed using N observations will not be significantly different from any of the N models that were constructed using $N - 1$ observations. An alternative approach, that yields very similar results, is to calculate the average value for each of the parameter coefficients from across the N models. The assumption in this case is that all of the models contain the same predictor variables and have been subject to the same data pre-processing. Therefore, the parameter coefficients within each model are similar.

At one time, leave-one-out cross validation would have required far to much computer time to be of practical use. These days, for modelling techniques such as linear/logistic regression, it is possible to perform leave-one-out cross validation with up to 10,000 observations and 30 predictor variables in an hour or two using a modern PC and efficient software. With the SAS Base/Stat software modules, for example, it is relatively easy to write a sub-routine (macro) that automatically generates all of the models. This includes calculating the score for the left out observations and the average value of each parameter coefficient. The trick to enable the procedure to be performed quickly is to use a non-stepwise procedure. All variable selection is performed before the leave-one-out process is undertaken. The most expedient way to achieve this is to run an initial stepwise regression using all N observations, and then only include those variables that featured within the preliminary model within the leave-one-out procedure.

11.1.2 Bootstrapping

Bootstrapping (Efron 1979) is based on the idea of resampling. Assume the development sample contains N observations. A bootstrap sample, also containing N observations, is created by randomly sampling from the original sample, with replacement. It can be shown that the bootstrap sample will, on average, contain 0.632 * N unique observations, which in turn means on average (1–0.632) * N observations are not included in the sample. A model is constructed using the bootstrap sample, which is then evaluated using the remaining, unsampled, cases. The bootstrap process is repeated a number of times, each time using a different randomly selected sample. At the end of the process there will exist performance metrics for each of the bootstraps. The mean and variance of these can be calculated, allowing confidence limits to be calculated for the model's performance. The final model is then constructed using all N observations.

Bootstrapping is less computationally expensive than leave-one-out cross validation if the number of bootstraps is less than N. As few as 50 bootstraps can be sufficient, although it is not uncommon for 100–200 or more bootstraps to be performed.

The major criticism of bootstrapping applied to small samples is that by using only about 2/3 of the data for each model, the performance of the bootstrapped models can be expected to be significantly lower than for a single model constructed using the full sample.

Another option is to combine bootstrapping with leave-one-out cross validation. Model construction is undertaken using leave-one-out cross validation. Bootstrap sampling is then applied to generate samples from the holdout sample, which are used to calculate the model's performance and associated confidence limits.

11.2   Multi-sample evaluation procedures for large populations

It is easy to conclude that one model is better than another, based on how well each model performs using a single holdout sample. However, what you can't always tell from a single sample is the degree of variation in the results. This makes it difficult to come to a firm conclusion as to whether there is a genuine difference in performance, or if the difference is just due to random variations that arise from the sampling process. To put it another way, if a different holdout sample was taken, then the results might be different. This problem is particularly acute when small holdout samples are used, but can still be an issue when relatively large samples are employed.

11.2.1   *k*-fold cross validation

Bootstrapping, as discussed in the previous section, can be used to generate confidence limits for the mean performance of a model, but can be time consuming when large samples are employed. A popular alternative to bootstrapping is k-fold cross validation. The development sample is randomly segmented into k equally sized segments (folds). For classification problems stratified random sampling should be applied to ensure each fold contains the same proportion of goods and bads. Popular value for k are 5 and 10, but if large samples are available then a higher value of k can be chosen.

k models are then constructed. For each model k–1 folds are used as the development sample, with a different fold assigned as the holdout sample for each model. By the time all k models have been constructed, the entire sample has been used as the holdout sample. Average performance can then be calculated across each of the holdout folds and confidence limits assigned. For practical applications, a final model is constructed using all observations.

11.2.2   *kj*-fold cross validation

If your objective is to evaluate two competing methods of model construction then, if large samples are available, an alternative to leave-one-out cross validation, bootstrapping or k-fold cross validation, is a method I refer to as *kj*-fold cross validation (Finlay 2008). With *kj*-fold cross validation, the first part of the process is identical to k-fold validation. The population is segmented into k equally sized folds. k models are then constructed with a different fold assigned as the holdout sample for each model. The holdout fold is then segmented into j sub-folds for which performance metrics are calculated. The process is repeated, k times, generating a population of k*j performance measures. The performance of two competing models can then be compared using a paired t-test.

One desirable feature of *kj*-fold cross validation is it requires less resources than other multi-sample procedures. k=2 and j=25 is often sufficient, meaning only two models need be constructed. Another feature of *kj*-fold cross validation is that for the special case where k=2, each model is constructed and validated using independent data sets. This overcomes the problem of non-independence of the training data associated with standard k-fold validation (k>2) which can lead to inflated values of test statistics when applying paired t-tests (Dietterich 1998).

11.3   Multi-model (fusion) systems

As discussed in previous chapters, different models, taking different forms and constructed using different techniques, tend to display very similar performance when used to predict a wide range of consumer behaviours. However, sometimes better forecasts can be achieved by constructing a suite of models and then combining the forecasts from each model to produce a final estimate of consumer behaviour.

Broadly speaking, there are three approaches to the construction of multi-model systems, each of which is discussed in the following sections.

11.3.1   Static parallel systems

The first, and probably the most popular type of multi-model system, are static parallel approaches. A static parallel approach is where two or more models are developed independently of each other. The scores generated by each model are then combined in some way to deliver a final model score (Zhu et al. 2001). For binary classification problems a common combination strategy is simple majority vote. A decision about whether an individual should be classified as "good" or "bad" is made independently using each model. The classification decision that is made most often is taken as the final classification decision. An advance on simple majority vote is weighted majority vote. Each model is again used to make a classification decision, but this time each model contributes a different amount to the overall decision. Perhaps the contribution that each model makes to the final score is based on a relative measure model of performance, such as the GINI coefficient or the percentage correctly classified.

Another method for combining model scores, which can also be used for regression models, is for the scores generated by each model to be used as the predictor variables within a second stage model (Kuncheva 2002). So if one has a CART, neural network and a linear regression derived model, the scores generated by these models could be used as predictor variables within a logistic regression model. Decisions about how to treat people are then based on the score generated by the second stage model.

Some static parallel approaches use identical representations of the data. All models are constructed using the same development sample and the same data pre-processing. Different methods of model construction are then applied to create models of different forms, such as linear models, neural networks and CART models. Model scores are then combined before a final decision about how to treat someone is made. Other static parallel approaches utilize a single method for classifier construction, but use different representations of the data to produce each classifier. Two popular examples are cross validation and bagging (Bootstrap aggregation). With cross validation data is segmented into *k* folds (usually somewhere between 10 and 100) in a manner similar to k-fold validation discussed earlier. k models are then constructed with a different fold excluded for each model. With bagging (Breiman 1996), classifiers are constructed from different sub-sets of the data randomly sampled with replacement (as with bootstrapping), with anything from 25 to 200 "bags" being undertaken for a typical exercise. Breiman developed bagging further with random forests (Breiman 2001), where additional random elements are entered into the procedure. For example, randomly selecting sub-sets of the predictor variables to use in each model and randomly selecting the order in which predictor variables are added into each model.

11.3.2 Multi-stage models

The second type of multi-model systems are multi-stage ones. Multi-stage models are constructed iteratively. At each iteration the process for determining the parameters of the model are dependent upon the properties of the model(s) from previous stages. Some multi-stage approaches generate models that are combined using the same combination rules used for static parallel methods. For example, most forms of boosting (Schapire 1990) generate a set of "weak" models that are combined using majority (or weighted majority) vote to create a better one. The most well known boosting algorithm for classification problems is AdaBoost (Freund and Schapire 1997). At each iteration of the AdaBoost algorithm the model scores from the previous iteration are used to adjust the weights assigned to each observation before the next stage model is constructed. Observations for which the score makes good predictions have their weights reduced, and observations for which the model does not predict so well have their weights increased. As the algorithm progresses, greater and greater weights are assigned to observations for which behaviour is difficult to predict. Many variants of AdaBoost have subsequently appeared such as Arc-x4 (Breiman 1998), BrownBoost (Freund 2001) and LogitBoost (Friedman et al. 2000). The discrete AdaBoost algorithm is as follows:

1. Initialise $t = 0$
2. Initialise a probability distribution $D_0(i) = 1/n_0$ for all $i \in (1 \dots n_0)$
3. DO While $t < T$
4. Construct classification model C_t from M_0 using weights D_t

5. Calculate weighted error as: $E_t = 1 - \sum_{i=1}^{n^0} D_t(i)|C_t(x_i) - y_i|$

6. IF $E_t \leq 0$ OR $E_t \geq 0.5$ then STOP

7. Calculate $\alpha_t = 0.5\ln\left(\dfrac{1 - E_t}{E_t}\right)$

8. Create distribution $D_{t+1}(i) = \dfrac{D_i(i)\exp(-\alpha_t y_i C_t(x_i))}{Z_t}$

9. $t = t+1$

10. END While loop

11. Assign final classification decision as $C^* = \sum\limits_{t=0}^{T-1} (\alpha_t C_t(x))$

The development sample M_0 contains n_0 observations. The set of predictor variables are represented by x and the dependent variably by y. We use $(x_1, y_1)...(x_{n0}, y_{n0})$ to represent the individual values of the predictor variables and the dependent variable within the sample. The dependent variable takes values of -1 for bads and $+1$ for goods (or vice-versa). Initially (Step 2 of the algorithm), all observations are assigned a weight equal to $1/n_0$. T models are then constructed. At each iteration of AdaBoost a classification model is constructed using the weighted population (Step 4). A sum of errors measure is then calculated for the tth model (E_t in Step 5) and used to calculate α_t (Step 6). α_t is then used to adjust the weights for observation in the development sample (Step 8). The result is that the weight assigned to correctly classified cases is diminished, while the weight for incorrectly classified cases is increased. Z_t in Step 8 is a normalizing constant, chosen such that the sum of weights at each iteration are equal to one. The final classification decision (C^*) is then made using a weighted majority vote (Step 11), with the value of a_t providing the weight assigned to each model. The choice of T is problem specific, but values ranging from 25 to 100 are widely used.

My own favourite boosting algorithm is Error Trimmed Boosting or ET Boost for short (Finlay 2008), which can be considered to be a boosted variant of the trimmed least squares regression approach proposed by Ruppert and Carroll (1980).

1. Initialize $t = 0$
2. DO while $t<T$
3. Construct model C_t from M_t
4. $e_{ti} = f(y_i, C_t(x_i))$, $x_i \in M_0, i = 1 ... n_0$
5. sort elements of M_0 in descending order of e_{ti}

6. $n_{t+1} = INT(n_t * \lambda)$
7. Create set M_{t+1} containing first n_{t+1} elements of M_0
8. $t = t+1$
9. END while
10. Assign final model score as $C^* = \phi(C_0 ... C_{T-1})$

ET Boost applies a trimming strategy which successively removes well predicted cases from the training set. At the tth iteration the error, e_{ti}, is calculated for all n_0 observations using model C_t (Step 4). Then, $INT(n_t * \lambda)$, $(0 < \lambda < 1)$ observations with the largest error are selected for construction of the $t+1^{th}$ model (Steps 5–7). λ is a control parameter that determines the rate at which the size of the development sample decreases between subsequent iterations, and values of between 0.95 and 0.975 generally give reasonable results. A key feature of ET Boost is that at each iteration all observations are reconsidered for inclusion in model construction. There is no weighting of observations. Thus observations excluded from model construction in one iteration may be included in the next iteration if the relative error of an observation increases between subsequent iterations. Any type of combination function can be chosen in Step 10. For classification problems I would recommend weighted majority vote. Stepwise logistic regression is used to derive the parameter coefficients for each of the T models. The scores generated from each model act as the predictor variables within this second stage model. For regression problems stepwise linear regression is recommended.

With ET Boost the value of T needs to be chosen with care. The performance of the algorithm peaks and then deteriorates rapidly. Therefore, an evaluation run needs to be performed to establish the best value of T to use. Usually, good values of T lie between 10 and 100, but the choice of T is also dependent to some extent upon the choice of the decay rate, λ.

ET Boost is a very simple yet flexible boosting algorithm. This is because it can cater for many different error functions and many different combination functions (Step 10). It can also be applied to any type of classifier/regression methodology, regardless of whether or not it generates likelihood estimates. It can therefore, be applied to problems with multi-category or continuous outcomes. In practice the error function I tend to use is absolute error: $|y_i - C_t(x_i)|$.

Other multi-stage methods produce a separate model at each stage. A decision about some individuals is then made and these are then removed from the development sample for the next stage model. A variation on this theme is to make the final decision for all observations using a single model from one stage with all other models being discarded (Myers and Forgy 1963). This approach also has a practical advantage in that it results in a single model. This makes it more attractive in operational environments than multi-stage methods such as boosting because it is much simpler to implement and monitor a single model than multiple models with serial dependencies.

11.3.3 Dynamic model selection

The third type of multi-model system is dynamic model selection (subpopulation selection). Different models are developed or applied to different segments of the population. One model may be best overall, but it may not dominate all other models entirely. Weaker competitors will sometimes outperform the overall best in some regions (Kittler et al. 1997). With dynamic model selection an important issue is identifying the best regions to develop and apply each model too. In some situations regions are defined using purely mechanical means. For example, the method described by Kuncheva (2002) is to apply a clustering algorithm. Another is to develop a CART model, and then build a separate model for observations within each leaf node of the tree. As noted by Thomas et al. (2002), mechanical means of segmenting a problem domain may be employed, such as applying a CART model. However, segmentation is often driven by political decisions, the availability of data, product segmentation (e.g. cards and loans) or other business rules.

11.4 Chapter summary

If one only has a small sample available for model construction, then it may not be practical to assign a proportion of cases to an independent holdout sample. In such cases a leave-one-out cross validation methodology and/or a bootstrap procedure can be applied, allowing all observations in the sample to be used for both model development and validation.

If large samples are available then using a single holdout sample can still lead to ambiguity when measuring model performance, particularly when two competing models are being compared. A bootstrap approach can be applied in this situation, but alternative methods of evaluation include k-fold and kj-fold cross validation.

Sometimes, combining the predictions made by several different models can lead to better predictions than any single model would make on its own. There are very many different types of multi-model systems that can be developed. These include:

- Static parallel systems. Each component model is developed independently and in parallel. The outputs from each model are then combined in some way.
- Multi-stage models. The model development process at each stage is driven by the properties of the model developed at the previous stage.
- Dynamic selection. Each model is developed and/or applied to a different sub-sets of the population.

Notes

Chapter 1   Introduction

1   Sometimes the model scores (such as those generated by models developed using logistic regression) need to be subjected to a transformation before they can be interpreted directly as probability estimates. In other situations the scores may be subjected to transformations for operational reasons. For example, some systems can only implement integer scores. Therefore, the score will be multiplied by a suitable factor (often 1,000) and rounded to the nearest whole number. These issues are covered in more detail in later chapters.

2   In statistics $\hat{Y}$ or $E(Y)$ is more commonly used to describe the model output and is referred to as the "predicted value" or the estimate of the dependant variable Y, where Y is the value that one is trying to predict. However, for some types of model, the model output can not be interpreted directly as an estimate of the dependent variable, but only as a measure of rank; that is, a relative position of an observation within a distribution, rather than an estimate of likelihood or value. Therefore, to retain generality the S notation is used to represent the value generated by the model.

3   In some texts the weights are referred to as parameter coefficients. In this book both terms are used interchangeably.

4   Also commonly referred to as terminal nodes or end nodes.

5   Although the combination function is nearly always of this form, it is possible to use other types of combination function.

6   The constant, a, is termed "the bias" in neural network terminology.

7   Also called a transfer function.

8   The hyperbolic tangent function is another popular activation function. Both the logistic function and the hyperbolic tangent function can be used for neurons in the hidden layer for classification or regression problems. For classification problems, they can also be applied to the neuron in the output layer. However, for regression problems an activation function is required that does not result in the output being bounded, so that it is representative of the quantity one is trying to predict. For regression problems it is common to use the identity function, which in practical terms means that the score generated by the output neuron is taken to be the value of the combination function, with no activation function applied.

9   The reason for this is that the strength of neural networks (and other non-linear methods such as support vector machines) is their ability to deal with non-linearities in the data. In the academic literature many theoretical examples of such problems are presented and networks from these studies are sometimes shown to perform much better than linear models. In practice however, most problems found within the financial services environment are essentially linear in nature. Therefore, they do not benefit from the added flexibility that neural networks provide.

10 Difficult, but not impossible. Various rule extraction techniques can be applied to gain a reasonably good understanding of how a network makes it decisions (Baesens et al. 2003b).

11 Although this is generally true, there are cases where the objective is to predict a current but unknown behaviour. For example, with application fraud detection in credit or insurance, the attempted fraud is happening in the present, not the future.

12 This type of agreement is common in retailing because stores do not want to alienate large numbers of customers by declining them for credit. Therefore, they demand that the lender with whom they have an agreement accepts a minimum proportion of those that apply. This means lenders are sometimes forced to accept people who are uncreditworthy to comply with their contractual obligations.

Chapter 2   Project Planning

1 Often a project manager will need to interpret the objectives so that they are clearly understood by the project team. The project manger may also facilitate the definition of the project's objectives and scope in conjunction with the key decision makers and the project sponsor, but this is not the same as setting the objectives.

2 Prior to 2001, it was common in the UK to use information about other family members when calculating someone's credit score. This was deemed illegal under the Data Protection Act 1998. Organizations were given a three year grace period to allow them to make their systems compliant with the Act. Today in the UK, information about other individuals can only be used to calculate someone's credit score if there is a proven financial association between them. For example, they share a mortgage or have previously taken out a loan in joint names.

3 Describing credit risks in terms of "Good" and "Bad" behaviour is common parlance within the consumer credit industry. Good refers to those that display satisfactory repayment behaviour, and bad to describe those that do not. However, in other areas of financial services different terminology is applied. For example, marketing professionals tend to talk about response and non-response rather than "good" and "bad" for response models. Likewise, insurers talk about claim propensity. However, I use good and bad so as to present common terminology throughout the book.

4 Sometimes one may also be interested in the good rate – which is simply defined as: Good Rate = (1 – Bad Rate).

5 If the proportion of indeterminates is somewhere between 5 percent and 25 percent then in my experience the models that are built still perform reasonably well, although perhaps not quite as well as models developed using a lower proportion of indeterminates. If there is a good business reason for having more indeterminates than this, it should not prevent model development from proceeding, but the model developer should be aware of the potential impact on the performance of the resulting model.

6 For consumer lending, readers should be careful not to confuse good/bad definitions used for constructing credit scoring models of repayment behaviour that

are used for decision making purposes, with BASEL II definitions of default used to calculate capital requirements. For BASEL II default (Bad) definitions are usually based on accounts reaching a more severe delinquency status – often 180 days (six months) past due. If a model is being developed for both decision making purposes and BASEL II, then a mapping exercise will be undertaken to translate predictions of bad, based on 90 or so days delinquent, into predictions of default based on 180 days delinquent.

7 At the time, it was claimed that the resignation was nothing to do with the termination of customers' credit agreements.

8 Net present value is a way of thinking about how much future income is worth in today's terms, taking into account things like inflation, the cost of funds and lost investment potential. Put simply, the value of a sum of money in today's terms is worth less the further into the future you have to go before you get it. The general formula for calculating net present value is:

$$NPV = A/(1 + P)^N,$$

A is the amount, P is the interest rate per unit time and N is the number of time periods in the future for which the net present value is calculated. For instance, the net present value of $2,000 in three years time, based on an annual interest rate of 7 percent is calculated as:

$$NPV = \$2,000/(1 + 0.07)^3 = \$1,632.60$$

9 Although a 12 month forecast horizon is common, longer forecast horizons may also be of interest. Some insurers will model claim likelihood over 2–3 years. They then discount the price of insurance for the first 12 months to attract new customers, on the assumption that they will be able to retain the customer and charge a higher premium in future years.

10 There is no reason why a good rate curve could not be produced instead because it contains the same information. However, bad rate curves are the norm in the consumer credit industry.

11 This pattern is common – but I have come across situations where the bad rate just keeps on rising, which is a problem! For example, when the bad rate curve covers a period during which economic conditions worsen. In such situations, one approach is to accept that the bad rates used in the model development sample are not representative of long term behaviour. Therefore, a weighting factor is applied to bads in the sample to make the sample more representative.

12 In the US and a number of other countries legislation about how personal data is used, starts from the position that personal data is a freely accessible commodity that can be used for any desired commercial purpose. Specific laws are then drafted to prevent specific abuses of personal data.

Chapter 3   Sample Selection

1 This figure includes both development and holdout samples.

2 The organization that supplied the data has requested that its identity remains anonymous.

3 As a very rough guide, for a classification problem where the sample population represents less than about 5 percent of the parent population and the sample

contains less than about 2,000 cases of each class, I would expect adaptive sampling, using clustering, to provide an uplift in performance of the order of 1–2 percent. This is compared to using a single stratified random sampling strategy by good/bad status.

4   A classic case of thick/thin data relates to consumer credit applications. When a credit application is made a lender will request a credit report from a credit reference agency. In around 5–10 percent of cases it can be expected that an individual will have no previous credit history – they have what is termed a "thin credit file". Constructing two separate models, one for those with some credit history and one for those with a thin credit file generally results in better forecasts of customer repayment behaviour than a single model.

5   In many regions, legislation gives consumers a short "cooling off period" after a credit agreement is signed to change their mind and cancel the agreement. As long as the borrower returns the funds then no further charges can be made. This type of behaviour is interesting because there are valid arguments for classing it as good, bad and indeterminate. One could argue these cases are "good" because no default occurred. However, one could argue the case for classifying them as bad because the loan provider certainly would have lost money due to the administrative costs incurred. Others might argue that these cases more naturally fall into the indeterminate category because although a loss was incurred, the customer acted in good faith and did not take advantage of the money that was made available to them.

Chapter 4   Gathering and Preparing Data

1   Most organizations also have a number of operational systems containing consumer data that is used to manage relationships on a day-to-day basis. For example, call centre work flow systems, application processing systems, account management systems and so on. On a regular basis (usually daily or monthly) relevant data will be transferred to the data warehouse where it is maintained for analytical and reporting purposes.

2   Via a left join procedure, to retain all cases on the Policy table, regardless of whether or not a claim exists on the Claim table.

3   Gathering this type of behavioural data will often be required during the project design phase for tasks such as producing bad rate (emergence) curves or calculating how many goods and bads exist within different sample windows. Therefore, it often makes sense to add relevant data to this sample rather than starting a fresh data gathering exercise.

4   Council tax bands are used in the UK to determine the local tax residents must pay. Houses are assigned to bands from A to H, with the lowest value properties assigned to band A and paying the lowest tax.

5   It is not uncommon for numeric (interval) data to be stored as a character string. Therefore, a conversion process may be required to convert it into a numeric type that is recognized by the software used to process the data.

6   Statisticians often discuss missing values in terms of one of three types. Missing Completely At Random (MCAR) is where there is no pattern to the missing data. Missing At Random (MAR) is where the missing values depend to some extent on the properties of other predictor variables. Not missing at

random (NMAR) is where the reason why data is missing is directly related to the value of the missing data.

7   For example, taking the square root or natural log of a variable.

8   The ratio for observation 2 might appear to be invalid because the ratio is negative. However, negative values are valid for this variable. This is because a negative card balance represents an account that is in credit; i.e. the customer has overpaid, or has had a refund or charge-back credited to their account.

9   Some texts suggest that two standard deviations should be used to identify outliers. However, for data mining problems where large data samples are employed and there are many predictor variables, using two standard deviations is likely to lead to a very significant proportion of the population being excluded. I would not recommend using anything less than three standard deviations for this purpose and ideally at least four.

10   If the out-of-time sample is taken towards the end of the project then this may not be possible.

11   The prospects database is a central repository of data used by marketing functions to maintain information about prospective customers.

Chapter 5   Understanding Relationships in Data

1   This may seem quite old, but one must remember that card holders must be at least 18. This acts to place the average age of card holders above that of the population at large.

2   This is often referred to as "fine classing" in contrast to "coarse classing" that occurs during data pre-processing.

3   An assumption when using the Z-statistic is that the samples are 'large' meaning it can be assumed that the population follows a normal distribution. For tests of population proportion "large" is usually taken to mean where $p * n > 5$ and $(1 - p) * n > 5$. p is the bad rate and n is the number of observations in the interval. For small samples, the t-statistic should be used instead of the Z-statistic. However, as we are only using the Z-statistic to give an indication of the strength of a relationship, rather than performing a strict test of significance, a somewhat laissez faire approach can be adopted to the calculation at this stage of model development.

4   The significance will determine if the variable enters the final model or not, but just because a variable features in a model does not necessarily mean that it adds to the predictive power of the model. Very often a technique such as stepwise logistic regression will result in several predictor variables entering the model which are statistically significant, but add only marginally (or sometimes not at all) to the model's predictive ability.

5   The sample standard deviation is a measure of the range of values within a sample. It is calculated as:

$$s = \sqrt{\frac{\sum_{1}^{n}(x_i - \bar{x})^2}{n - 1}}$$

x_i is the value of the ith observation in the sample. n is the total number of observations in the sample. $\bar{x}$ is the mean value of observations in the sample.

6 Other popular measures of association include Pearson's correlation coefficient (which assumes the relationship between the two variables is linear) and Kendall's tau rank coefficient (which does not require an assumption of linearity).

7 My own experience is that as long as a reasonable number of intervals are defined (say 20–25), then the benefits of such approaches, over and above defining a number of equally sized intervals, are marginal.

8 I would tend to look at variance inflation factors, which are discussed in more detail in Chapter 7.

9 The other main family of variable selection methods are called "filter" methods. Using measures such as information value, the coefficient of correlation or the application of expert opinion to select variables, are all examples of filter methods.

10 More than about 1,000 variables for logistic regression, for example.

Chapter 6 Data Pre-processing

1 One option is to excluded the dummy variable containing the largest number of observations. Another strategy is to exclude the dummy variable for which the average value of the dependent variable (average odds or bad rate for a classification problem) is most similar to the population average.

2 These are unweighted figures. A common mistake is to create a balanced sample for model development, and then apply a weighting factor to define intervals and produce univariate analysis reports. So if for the goods a weighting of say, 30, has been applied, then if a report contains 270 goods within an interval then this figure will be based on nine unweighted goods. This is far too few to facilitate the production of robust parameter estimates and may lead to over fitting.

3 It is quite difficult to say precisely what a "manageable number" of variables is, but for a development sample containing, say 100,000 observations, logistic regression will take a significant amount of time to generate a model once the number of predictor variables exceeds about 1,000. For neural networks, what is critical is the total number of weights in the network requiring estimation (calculated by multiplying the number of predictor variables by the number of units in the hidden layer, and then adding one). Typically, once you have more than about 1,000 weights then processing time becomes very significant indeed. Linear regression requires less resource than other methods. It should therefore, be possible to include 5,000+ variables within the modelling process before processing time becomes an issue.

Chapter 7 Model Construction (Parameter Estimation)

1 For a software package such as SAS, a great deal of additional output is produced. Table 7.1 shows the t-tests that are performed after model construction is complete. For stepwise procedures, the software will usually generate a summary of the F-tests that have been performed at each stage of the stepwise procedure. Therefore, the total output can run to hundreds of pages for a project with hundreds of predictor variables available. For expediency, only the post model construction t-tests are displayed. Note that for SAS users, the VIF

option would need to be selected within the stepwise selection procedure to generate t-tests and VIF figures.

2 If two variables are correlated, then a good question is which one should be removed? One answer is to remove the variable that has the lowest information value (or other measure of association). Another is to consider the correlations across all of the variables in the model and remove the one that has the highest variance inflation factor.

3 Logistic regression can be applied to multi-class problems where there are more than two behaviours of interest – but this is beyond the scope of the text.

4 Although many of the basic modelling options for linear and logistic regression are the same, there are also many subsidiary options that can be chosen, and these differ markedly for each approach.

5 The calculation of variance inflation is independent of the method of model construction and involves only the predictor variables. Therefore, if two models are constructed using different techniques, but the models contain the same set of predictor variables and have been developed using the same development sample, then the variance inflation factors should be identical.

6 One way to do this is to rank observations by score, divide the population into about 20 intervals and calculate the *Ln (odds)* for each interval and the mean score in each interval. The odds of each interval are then plotted against the average score. If the observed relationship appears to be roughly a straight line, then this is usually adequate.

7 For any scorecard where the points that double the odds is more than about ten, the loss of precision will usually have little impact on the quality of the decisions made on the basis of the model score.

Chapter 8   Validation, Model Performance and Cut-off Strategy

1 This formulation is an approximation of the test, that is valid for large samples (n_1 and $n_2 > 100$)

2 So one uses the target score odds relationship to determine the expected odds and hence bad rate for an observation, given the score that they receive. Observations are then grouped by score range (as in the classed score distribution report) and the expected number of bads in the interval is calculated by summing up the expected bad rate for all cases within the interval. The chi-squared test is then applied to the differences between the expected and observed number of bads in each interval.

3 Sensitivity is proportion of goods scoring above the cut-off. Specificity is proportion of bads scoring below the cut-off.

4 Note that in many texts the value of D is referred to as the KS-statistic.

5 Sometimes there may not be an existing score available for observations in the holdout sample. This will certainly be the case if the new model has been constructed to replace a manual decision making system. However, if the holdout sample contains a suitable indicator, that corresponds to the decisions that were made about individuals (such as whether they were accepted or declined for a credit card) then the indicator can then be used to identify the proportion of cases that had that decision made about them.

This proportion can then be applied to the score distribution for the new score, to find the cut-off score that would yield the sample proportions for the new model. This allows a comparison between the new model and the existing decision making system to be made.

6   It is assumed in this example that the two score distribution reports have been produced using the same sample of accounts, and therefore, using the same number of accounts is equivalent to using the same proportion.

Chapter 9   Sample Bias and Reject Inference

1   The problem of sample bias primarily relates to credit scoring problems dealing with predictions about the behaviour of new credit applications. It is not generally a problem for response models or insurance.

2   The exception to this is when a new model is constructed because some of the variables in the existing model will not be available in the future. For example, legislation is introduced which prohibits the use of some data. In this case, the primary objective is to produce a model that complies with the new legislation, not to produce a more predictive one.

3   Technically, the model will still display some bias, with the most uncreditworthy cases receiving higher scores than they should, but these scores will not be sufficient for them to pass the cut-off.

4   The overall creditworthiness of the population did decline during this period, but this had a much more minor impact on the volume of lending than the lack of available funds.

5   This is because the cost of accepting a bad payer usually far outweighs the lost opportunity cost of rejecting a good payer. Therefore, it's better to be over-pessimistic about how rejects will behave rather than being over-optimistic.

6   Note that if the data has been pre-processed using weights of evidence, then the weights of evidence will need to be recalculated for each iteration as the numbers of goods and bads change. Ideally, the fine/coarse classing should also be reviewed for each iteration, but this can be very time consuming. Therefore, it is not recommended that you do this unless large shifts within the population are suspected to have occurred. A compromise position is to review the fine/course classing after the first and final iterations, but not for intermediate iterations.

7   Typically this will be anything from a couple of days to several weeks, depending upon the size of the project, the software employed and the experience of the analyst.

8   However, in some of their earlier research they did report modest improvements when using the bi-variate probit method which shares some of the characteristics of extrapolation. Similar results were also reported by Kim and Sohn.

9   For example, by applying the old model and associated decision rules to identify which applications would have been rejected by the old system, but are now accepted by the new one.

10   I would like to think that I am wrong to say this or have missed something that has been published in other texts. If the reader knows of any such cases then I would be very interested to hear about it!

Chapter 10   Implementation and Monitoring

1 For binary classification models, the frequency of monitoring is often driven
   by the rate at which bad events emerge. As a general rule, several hundred
   events are required to produce a reliable set of monitoring reports.
2 As discussed in Chapter 1, models derived using mechanical means generally
   provide better predictions than those made by human assessors. However, there
   are often benefits from combining mechanically derived models with human
   judgement, to provide a solution that is better than either method on its own.
   In practice, cost and time considerations generally prevent it being cost effective to enhance quantitative models with judgemental opinions in all but a
   small minority of cases.

Bibliography

Anderson, R. (2007). *The Credit Scoring Toolkit. Theory and Practice for Retail Credit Risk Management and Decision Automation*, 1st edn. Oxford: Oxford University Press.

Arminger, G., Enache, D. and Bonne, T. (1997). 'Analyzing credit risk data: A comparison of logistic discrimination, classification tree analysis, and feed-forward networks'. *Computational Statistics* 12(2): 293–310.

Baesens, B., Gestel, T. V., Viaene, S., Stepanova, M., Suykens, J. and Vanthienen, J. (2003a). 'Benchmarking state-of-the-art classification algorithms for credit scoring'. *Journal of the Operational Research Society* 54(5): 627–35.

Baesens, B., Setiono, R., Mues, C. and Vanthienen, J. (2003b). 'Using neural network rule extraction and decision tables for credit-risk evaluation'. *Management Science* 49(3): 312–29.

Baesens, B., Viaene, S., Van den Poel, D., Vanthienen, J. and Dedene, G. (2002). 'Bayesian neural network learning for repeat purchase modelling in direct marketing'. *European Journal of Operational Research* 138(1): 191–211.

Banasik, J. and Crook, J. (2003). 'Lean models and reject inference'. *Credit Scoring & Credit Control VIII*, Edinburgh.

Banasik, J. and Crook, J. (2005). 'Credit scoring, augmentation and lean models'. *Journal of the Operational Research Society* 56(9): 1072–81.

Banasik, J. and Crook, J. (2007). 'Reject inference, augmentation, and sample selection'. *European Journal of Operational Research* 183(3): 1582–94.

Banasik, J., Crook, J. N. and Thomas, L. C. (1996). 'Does scoring a sub-population make a difference?'. *International Review of Retail Distribution and Consumer Research* 6(2): 180–95.

Banasik, J., Crook, J. N. and Thomas, L. C. (2003). 'Sample selection bias in credit scoring models'. *Journal of the Operational Research Society* 54(8): 822–32.

Bishop, C. M. (1995). *Neural Networks for Pattern Recognition*, 1st edn. Oxford: Clarendon Press.

Breiman, L., Friedman, J., Stone, C. J. and Olshen, R. A. (1984). *Classification and Regression Trees*. London: Chapman and Hall.

Breiman, L. (1996). 'Bagging predictors'. *Machine Learning* 24: 123–40.

Breiman, L. (1998). 'Arcing classifiers'. *The Annals of Statistics* 28(3): 801–49.

Breiman, L. (2001). 'Random forests'. *Machine Learning* 45: 5–32.

Cohn, D., Atlas, L. and Ladner, R. (1994). 'Improving generalization with active learning'. *Machine Learning* 15(2): 201–21.

Cortes, C. and Vapnik, V. (1995). 'Support vector networks'. *Machine Learning* 20(3): 273–97.

Cox, D. R. (1972). 'Regression models and life tables'. *Journal of the Royal Statistical Society Series B* 34(3): 187–202.

Crook, J. and Banasik, J. (2004). 'Does reject inference really improve the performance of application scoring models?'. *Journal of Banking & Finance* 28(4): 857–74.

Crook, J. N., Edelman, D. B. and Thomas, Lyn C. (2007). 'Recent developments in consumer credit risk assessment'. *European Journal of Operational Research* 183(3): 1447–65.

Dietterich, T. G. (1998). 'Approximate statistical tests for comparing supervised classification learning algorithms'. *Neural Computation* **10**(7): 1895–1923.

Dorigo, M. and Gambardella, L. M. (1997). 'Ant colonies for the travelling salesman problem'. *Biosystems* **43**(2): 73–81.

Durand, D. (1941). *Risk Elements in Consumer Instatement Financing*, 1st edn. New York: National Bureau of Economic Research.

Efron, B. (1979). 'Bootstrap methods: Another look at the jackknife'. *The Annals of Statistics* **7**(1): 1–26.

Eisenbeis, R. A. (1977). 'Pitfalls in the application of discriminant analysis in business, finance and economics'. *The Journal of Finance* **32**(3): 875–900.

Eisenbeis, R. A. (1978). 'Problems in applying discriminant analysis in credit scoring models'. *Journal of Banking & Finance* **2**(3): 205–19.

Farrell, S. (2008). 'Man who culled egg borrowers resigns'. *The Independent* 12/03/2008.

Fildes, R., Nikolopoulos, K., Crone, S. F. and Syntetos, A. A. (2008). 'Forecasting and operational research: A review'. *Journal of the Operational Research Society* **59**(9): 1150–72.

Financial Services Authority (2009). *The Turner Review. A Regulatory Response to the Global Banking Crisis*. The Financial Services Authority.

Finlay, S. (2008) 'Multiple classifier architectures and their application to credit risk assessment'. Lancaster University Management School Working Paper 2008/012. http://www.lums.lancs.ac.uk/publications/viewpdf/005620/

Finlay, S. (2009) 'Are we modelling the right thing? The impact of incorrect problem specification in credit scoring'. *Expert Systems with Applications* **36**(5): 9065–71.

Finlay, S. (2010). 'Credit scoring for profitability objectives'. *The European Journal of Operational Research* **202**(2): 528–37.

Finn, M. C. (2003). *The Character of Credit. Personal Debt in English Culture, 1740–1914*, 1st edn. Cambridge: Cambridge University Press.

Freund, Y. (2001). 'An adaptive version of the boost by majority algorithm'. *Machine Learning* **43**(3): 293–318.

Freund, Y. and Schapire, R. E. (1997). 'A decision-theoretic generalization of on-line learning and an application to boosting'. *Journal of Computer and System Sciences* **55**(1): 119–39.

Friedman, J. H., Hastie, T. and Tibshirani, R. (2000). 'Additive logistic regression: A statistical view of boosting'. *The Annals of Statistics* **28**: 337–74.

Gurney, K. (1997). *Introduction to Neural Networks*, 1st edn. Boca Raton, Florida: Routledge.

Guyon, I. and Elisseeff, A. (2003). 'An introduction to variable and feature selection'. *Journal of Machine Learning* **3**: 1157–82.

Goldberg, D. E. (1989). *Genetic Algorithms in Search Optimization & Machine Learning*, 1st edn. Reading, Massachusetts: Addison-Wesley.

Hand, D. J. (2006). 'Classifier technology and the illusion of progress'. *Statistical Science* **21**(1): 1–15.

Hand, D. J. (2001). 'Modelling consumer credit risk'. *IMA Journal of Management Mathematics* **12**: 139–55.

Hand, D. J. and Adams, N. M. (2000). 'Defining attributes for scorecard construction in credit scoring'. *Journal of Applied Statistics* **27**(5): 527–40.

Hand, D. J. and Kelly, M.G. (2001). 'Lookahead scorecards for new fixed term credit products'. *Journal of the Operational Research Society* **52**(9): 989–96.

Hand, D. J. and Jacka, S. D. (eds) (1998). *Statistics in Finance*, 1st edn. London: Edward Arnold.

Hand, D. J. and Henley, W. E. (1993). 'Can reject inference ever work?'. *IMA Journal of Mathematics Applied in Business and Industry* 5(1): 45–55.

Harrell, F. E. Jr, Lee, K. L. and Mark, D. B. (1996). 'Multivariable prognostic models: Issues in developing models, evaluating assumptions and adequacy, and measuring and reducing errors'. *Statistics in Medicine* 15(4): 361–87.

Harris, E. H. and Albert, A. (1991). *Survivorship Analysis for Clinical Studies*. New York: Marcel Dekker.

Haykin, S. (2009). *Neural Networks and Learning Machines: International Version: A Comprehensive Foundation*, 3rd edn. Pearson Education.

Heckman, J. (1976). 'The common structure of statistical models of truncation, sample selection and limited dependent variables and a simple estimator for such models'. *Annals of Economic and Social Measures* 5(4): 475–92.

Holland, J. H. (1975). *Adaptation in Natural and Artificial Systems*, 1st edn. Michigan, The University of Michigan Press, Ann Arbor.

Hosmer, D. W., Lemeshow, S. and May, S. (2008). *Applied Survival Analysis: Regression Modeling of Time to Event Data*, 2nd edn. New York: Wiley Blackwell.

Hosmer, D. W. and Lemeshow, S. (2000) *Applied Logistic Regression*, 2nd edn. New York: John Wiley & Sons.

Ignizio, J. P. (1990). *Introduction to Expert Systems*, 1st edn. New York, McGraw-Hill.

Joanes, D. N. (1993). 'Reject inference applied to logistic regression for credit scoring'. *IMA Journal of Mathematics Applied in Business and Industry* 5(1): 3–17.

Kang, J., Ryu1, K. and Kwon, H. (2004). 'Using cluster-based sampling to select initial training set for active learning in text classification'. In: *Advances in Knowledge Discovery and Data Mining 3056/2004*. Springer.

Kim, Y., Street, W. N., Russell, G. J. and Menczer, F. (2005). 'Customer targeting: A neural network approach guided by genetic algorithms'. *Management Science* 51(2): 264–76.

King, R. D., Henery, R., Feng, C. and Sutherland, A. (1995). 'A comparative study of classification algorithms: Statistical, machine learning and neural networks'. *Machine Intelligence, 13*. K. Furukwa, D. Michie and S. Muggleton. Oxford: Oxford University Press.

Kittler, J., Hojjatoleslami, A. and Windeatt, T. (1997). 'Strategies for combining classifiers employing shared and distinct pattern representations'. *Pattern Recognition Letters* 18(11–13): 1373–77.

Kuncheva, L. I. (2002). 'Switching between selection and fusion in combining classifiers: An experiment'. IEEE Transactions on Systems, Man and Cybernetics – Part B. *Cybernetics* 32(2): 146–56.

Kvanli, A. H., Pavur, R. J. and Keeling, K. B. (2003). *Introduction to Business Statistics*, 6th edn. Thomson Learning.

Lee, E. T. (1980). *Statistical Methods for Survival Data Analysis*. Wordsworth.

Lewis, E. M. (1992). *An Introduction to Credit Scoring*, 2nd edn. San Rafael: Athena Press.

Linder, R., Geier, J. and Kölliker, M. (2004). 'Artificial neural networks, classification trees and regression: Which method for which customer base?'. *Journal of Database Marketing & Customer Strategy Management* 11(4): 344–56.

Little, R. J. A. and Rubin, D. B. (2002) *Statistical Analysis with Missing Data*, 2nd edn. New Jersey: John Wiley & Sons.

Mantel, S. J., Meredith, J. R., Shafer, S. and Sutton, M. (2007). *Project Management in Practice*, 3rd edn. New Jersey: Wiley.

Mathiason, N. and Insley, J. (2008). 'Anger at egg ban on prudent customers'. *The Observer*.

McNab, H. and Wynn, A. (2003). *Principles and Practice of Consumer Risk Management*, 2nd edn. Canterbury.

Menard, S. (2002). *Applied Logistic Regression Analysis*. Thousand Oaks, California: Sage.

Myers, J. H. and Forgy, E. W. (1963). 'The development of numerical credit evaluation systems'. *Journal of the American Statistical Association* **50**: 799–806.

Quinlan, J. R. (1992). *C4.5: Programs for Machine Learning*, 1st edn. San Mateo, CA., Morgan-Kaufman.

Reichert, A. K., Cho, C. C. and Wagner, G. M. (1983). 'An examination of the conceptual issues involved in developing credit scoring models'. *Journal of Business Economics and Statistics* **1**(2): 101–14.

Rosenblatt, F. (1958). 'The perceptron: A probabilistic model for information storage and organisation in the brain'. *Psychological Review* **65**.

Rosenberg, E. and Gleit, A. (1994). 'Quantitative methods in credit management: A survey'. *Operations Research* **42**(4): 589–613.

Rumelhart, D. E., Hinton, G. E. and Williams, R. J. (1986). 'Learning representations by back-propagating errors'. *Nature* **323**(6088).

Ruppert, D. and Carroll, R. J. (1980). 'Trimmed least squares estimation in the Linear Model'. *Journal of the American Statistical Association* **75**: 828–38.

Schapire, R. (1990). 'The strength of weak learnability'. *Journal of Machine Learning* **5**: 197–227.

Siddiqi, N. (2006). *Credit Risk Scorecards: Developing and Implementing Intelligent Credit Scoring*, 1st edn. New Jersey: John Wiley & Sons.

Thomas, L. C., Banasik, J. and Crook, J. N. (2001). 'Recalibrating scorecards'. *Journal of the Operational Research Society* **52**(9): 981–8.

Thomas, L. C., Edelman, D. B. and Crook, J. N. (2002). Credit *Scoring and Its Applications*, 1st edn. Philadelphia: Siam.

Verstraeten, G. and Van den Poel, D. (2005). 'The impact of sample bias on consumer credit scoring performance and profitability'. *Journal of the Operational Research Society* **56**(8).

Viaene, S., Derrig, R. A., Baesens, B. and Dedene, G. (2002). 'A comparison of state-of-the-art classification techniques for expert automobile insurance claim fraud detection'. *Journal of Risk and Insurance* **69**(3): 373–421.

Weiss, G. M. (2004). 'Mining with rarity: A unifying framework'. *ACM SIGKDD Explorations Newsletter* **6**(1): 7–19.

West, D. (2000). 'Neural network credit scoring models'. *Computers & Operations Research* **27**(11–12): 1131–52.

West, P. M., Brockett, P. L. and Golden, L. L. (1997). 'A comparative analysis of neural networks and statistical methods for predicting consumer choice'. *Marketing Science* **16**(4): 370–91.

Wonderlic, E. F. (1952). 'An analysis of factors in granting credit'. *Indiana University Bulletin* **50**: 163–76.

Yen, S. and Lee, Y. (2006). 'Cluster-based sampling approaches to imbalanced data distributions', in *Data Warehousing and Knowledge Discovery 4081/2006*. Springer.

Zahavi, J. and Levin, N. (1997). 'Applying neural computing to target marketing'. *Journal of Direct Marketing* **11**(1): 5–22.

Zhu, H., Beling, P. A. and Overstreet, G. (2001). 'A study in the combination of two consumer credit scores'. *Journal of the Operational Research Society* **52**(9): 974–80.

Index